T0323495

Conversations with William Maxwell

Literary Conversations Series
Peggy Whitman Prenshaw
General Editor

Conversations with William Maxwell

Edited by Barbara Burkhardt

University Press of Mississippi   Jackson

www.upress.state.ms.us

The University Press of Mississippi is a member of the Association
of American University Presses.

First printing 2012

∞

Library of Congress Cataloging-in-Publication Data
Maxwell, William, 1908–2000.
  Conversations with William Maxwell / edited by Barbara Burkhardt.
    p. cm. — (Literary conversations series)
  Includes bibliographical references and index.
  ISBN 978-1-61703-254-7 (cloth : alk. paper) — ISBN 978-1-61703-255-4 (ebook)
  1. Maxwell, William, 1908–2000—Interviews. 2. Authors, American—20th century—
Interviews. 3. Editors—United States—Interviews. I. Burkhardt, Barbara A. II. Title.
  PS3525.A9464Z46 2012
  813'.54—dc23
  [B]   2011032981

British Library Cataloging-in-Publication Data available

Books by William Maxwell

Novels
Bright Center of Heaven. New York: Harper and Brothers, 1934.
They Came Like Swallows. New York: Harper and Brothers, 1937.
The Folded Leaf. New York: Harper and Brothers, 1945.
Time Will Darken It. New York: Harper and Brothers, 1948.
The Chateau. New York: Alfred A. Knopf, 1961.
So Long, See You Tomorrow. New York: Alfred A. Knopf, 1980.

Short Story Collections
Stories (with Jean Stafford, John Cheever, and Daniel Fuchs). New York: Farrar, Straus and Cudahy, 1956.
Over by the River and Other Stories. New York: Alfred A. Knopf, 1977.
Billie Dyer and Other Stories. New York: Alfred A. Knopf, 1992.
All the Days and Nights: The Collected Stories. New York: Alfred A. Knopf, 1994.

Nonfiction
Ancestors: A Family History. New York: Alfred A. Knopf, 1971.
The Outermost Dream: Essays and Reviews. New York: Alfred A. Knopf, 1989.

Tales
The Old Man at the Railroad Crossing. New York: Alfred A. Knopf, 1966.

For Children
The Heavenly Tenants. New York: Harper and Brothers, 1946.
Mrs. Donald's Dog Bun and His Home Away from Home. New York: Alfred A. Knopf, 1995.

Letters
The Happiness of Getting It Down Right: Letters of Frank O'Connor and William Maxwell, ed. Michael Steinman. New York: Alfred A. Knopf, 1996.
The Element of Lavishness: Letters of Sylvia Townsend Warner and William Maxwell, ed. Michael Steinman. Washington, D.C.: Counterpoint, 2001.
What There Is To Say We Have Said: The Correspondence of Eudora Welty and William Maxwell, ed. Suzanne Marrs. New York: Houghton Mifflin Harcourt, 2011.

Contents

Introduction

In William Maxwell's later years, he often agreed to interviews with an unusual request: he preferred to answer questions on his typewriter. "All the thoughts are in the typewriter," he explained to Edward Hirsch. "The typewriter is my friend," he confided to John Blades of the *Chicago Tribune*, and, "I think better on the typewriter than I do just talking," he told me. Maxwell's old Smith Coronamatic seemed an extension of his creative mind. With his hands on the keyboard—hands that Blades likened to "tree roots photographed in fast motion"—he was at home in his writer's world, crafting words into sentences, arranging and rearranging them until they rested where they belonged in novels such as *They Came Like Swallows*, *The Folded Leaf*, and *So Long, See You Tomorrow*. During interviews, pages he pulled from the typewriter often read like his late published prose—the same bare, elegant style; the kindly, sensitive voice balanced with intellect and emotional steel. Indeed, such conversations with William Maxwell allowed a glimpse of the writer at work.

My interviews with Maxwell began in November 1991 in his apartment on East 86th Street in Manhattan. When my cab pulled up to his building for the first time, I stood for a moment looking up to the apartment windows and across to the park on the river's edge, the neighborhood that inspired "Over by the River," one of his finest stories. I remembered how he once wrote about gazing day after day at the writer Colette's windows at the Palais Royale in Paris. Now he was the one inside, and after a polite inquiry and nod from the doorman in his white, brass-buttoned uniform, I took the elevator to the eighth floor. In his cozy, spare study, Maxwell carefully considered each of my queries, rolled a sheet of paper into the clattering Coronamatic and composed for up to five minutes at a time. He paused occasionally, his lips moving slightly as he reread the words through tortoiseshell glasses. Once satisfied, he turned the typewriter stand around on its squeaky wheels to show me his response. The next summer, he met me at the Croton-Harmon railway station wearing a broad-brimmed straw hat and drove me to his country home in Yorktown Heights. There, he suspended a long extension cord through the back window and brought his typewriter outdoors, where we sat for two afternoons at a picnic table on the patio overlooking a rolling lawn, flower beds, and an art studio, where his wife, Emily, painted. Sitting by his side, reading his words as he typed them, I could ask follow-up questions immediately, which made for a smooth interchange, a true conversation.[1] Through the last decade of his life, our visits became more informal, over breakfast, lunch, or tea, all lovingly prepared by Mrs. Maxwell.

Maxwell's interview method had practical benefits: the typed record prevented misquotes and transcription errors and alleviated his concern that a tape recorder would not pick up his soft, muffled voice. He observed that Vladimir Nabokov, whose work he edited at the *New Yorker*, did not speak to interviewers, but rather answered questions submitted to him in writing. Maxwell's hybrid approach—with the interviewer present and speaking—assured accuracy, yet also allowed for a personal interchange. The visitor, freed from listening, had plenty of time to watch the author working and absorb the atmosphere among his photos and paintings and books, or play with his cat, Genji, to the clacking of keys.

Our interviews began when Maxwell was eighty-three, and as the years passed, I wondered with each trip to New York if it would be the last. I arrived with pages of questions numbered and categorized, but sometimes altered my plan, skipping ahead to what seemed most important in case this was my final chance to ask. Our exchanges appear here as they transpired— as Maxwell pulled his words from the Coronamatic—often covering one of his works in depth, then touching on his impressions and preferences in the way of other authors, politics, art, food, and cars. Over time, we often reflected on prior conversations, revisiting issues discussed months or years earlier for clarification and attention to nuance. My side of these interviews has been reconstructed as faithfully as possible: returning home from our first meeting with a long recording of keys clacking clearly established that our conversations could not be captured on audio cassette.

The pages Maxwell typed during our years of interviews remain a gift, which I have the pleasure to share in this volume. They are published here for the first time, grouped together and marked by date and location, and collected with the writer's other interviews and public remarks. Spanning five decades, these conversations and speeches reveal the writer in his own words: spoken aloud or through the typewriter; in his Manhattan apartment or in his country home in Westchester County; to other interviewers for print, radio, and television, as well as to those working independently or with small literary journals. Over the years, he spoke as a guest on college campuses, as a member and president of the American Academy of Arts and Letters, and as a recipient of literary awards. Readers will recognize the precise and sensitive way he treats his subjects on these occasions. Speaking before a crowd, his reflections on the artistic life, his Midwestern home, and literary friends and mentors retain the reserved poignancy of his fiction.

Early in his career, in the 1940s, Maxwell read excerpts from *They Came Like Swallows* (1937) on a New York radio station and perhaps sat for a brief interview. His novels *The Folded Leaf* and *Time Will Darken It* were listed among the year's best by the *New York Times* in 1945 and 1948, and, long-awaited, *The Chateau* appeared in 1961, followed by a collection of short stories and a nonfiction family history in the 1970s. In 1979, the impending publication of *So Long, See You Tomorrow* (1980), the author's first novel in nearly twenty years, inspired new interest in his work, and Robert Dahlin interviewed him in his 86th Street apartment (without the typewriter) for *Publishers Weekly*. Reviewed widely and admiringly, the book received the National Book Critics Circle Award, the American Book Award, and the William Dean Howells Medal of the American Academy of Arts and Letters. A flurry of interviews appeared in publications ranging from small-town newspapers in Maxwell's native Illinois to the *Village Voice* and *Paris Review*. Like many of its conversations with authors over the years, the *Paris Review* interview is particularly enlightening and thorough. George Plimpton and John Seabrook visited the author at his apartment in the fall of 1981 for a wide-ranging and convivial conversation about his writing habits, literary influences, fictional works, and years at the *New Yorker*. Geoffrey Stokes's *Village Voice* interview appears to have been the first in which Maxwell typed his responses. As Stokes describes, when he suggested that queries sent through the mail would not allow for personal interchange, the author invited him to the apartment to ask questions while he composed at the typewriter. Stokes's article championed Maxwell's work in the face of past neglect, claiming *Time Will Darken It* as one of the finest American novels between World War II and 1985, the year of their meeting.

Interviewers have vivid impressions of their time with Maxwell, whether they met him in person, on the phone, or by mail—and whether they enjoyed ongoing friendships or visited on one occasion. As the editor of *Tamaqua*, an Illinois literary journal, Bruce Morgan remembers how impressed he was with Maxwell's graciousness in agreeing to a lengthy interview—conducted through the mail and followed by my first visit in New York—and in giving permission to print excerpts from his abandoned novel *At the Pension Gaul-lard*, based on his travel to Martinique in the mid-1930s. Maxwell wrote a reflection on the previously unpublished work, which gives the interview a unique focus.

When Knopf published *All the Days and Nights*, Maxwell's collected stories, in December 1994, another outpouring of tributes ensued. He appeared on television with Charlie Rose and on National Public Radio with Linda Wertheimer, who took turns with him reading his fables aloud on *All Things Considered*. Wertheimer remembers,

> The bedtime stories that Mr. Maxwell and I read together won me on the page and then even more when he told me about inventing these little stories to tell at night, in bed, to help his wife get to sleep. They are tiny stories and don't necessarily end; they fall asleep also. Hearing him read was wonderful—he had a great voice for reading aloud. He was in New York and I was in Washington—but those little stories felt very intimate despite the distance.[2]

While interviews during this period often turned to his forty years at the *New Yorker*—covering his association with writers whose work he edited there, including Nabokov, Updike, Welty, Salinger, and Cheever—they also focused, as Wertheimer did, on his literary legacy, especially the stories in the collection, his last published book.

Edward Hirsch's essay in *A William Maxwell Portrait: Memories and Appreciations* (2004) describes his interview with the author in 1997. Commissioned by *Doubletake* magazine to write a piece on his friend, Hirsch put it off because he did not like the idea of treating all the novels one by one. He shared his dilemma with Maxwell, who offered a suggestion: his own life had been "dealt with" perhaps "too thoroughly." Why not focus an interview on old age and "what it is like to be aware that your days are numbered?" He invited Hirsch to have the interview on the day of his eighty-eighth birthday party. As Hirsch writes, "Maxwell not only became the subject of my piece; he also taught me how to conceptualize it." The author spoke with Hirsch in his Yorktown Heights home about age, memory, and the presence of the past, and then they adjourned to a birthday lunch in Emily Maxwell's art studio behind their home.[3]

Taken as a whole, the interviews reveal how Maxwell's ideas about his work evolved over time. For example, for many years he considered *The Folded Leaf* to be his personal favorite of the novels—it contained "the whole of his youth," he once told me, and his attempt at suicide during his college years. But by his eighty-eighth birthday he explained to Hirsch that he had come to recognize the perfection of *So Long, See You Tomorrow*, particularly its structure, which seamlessly melds the story of two young boys and a heartland murder in the 1920s, his Illinois youth with his Manhattan adulthood, and newspaper reporting with his memory and imagination. Readers may also note how the author occasionally remembers things differently in subsequent interviews, the effect perhaps of passing years and distance from events. Such instances remind us, though, of one of his central subjects: the gains in memory that come with age—the "opening up," he called it—and the corresponding losses. As he wrote in *So Long, See You Tomorrow*, "In talking about the past, we lie with every breath we draw."

On March 3, 1955, Maxwell took a train from New York to Northampton, Massachusetts, where he had been invited by Smith College to speak at a symposium, "The American Novel at Mid-century," with Alfred Kazin, Saul Bellow, and Brendan Gill of the *New Yorker.* On board, he penned notes for his finest speech[4], "The Writer as Illusionist," and this collection opens with the publication of this handwritten draft.

Maxwell arrived at Smith in time for Kazin's keynote address that evening and shared the stage with Bellow and Gill for a panel on novel-writing the next afternoon. He appreciated Bellow's opening remarks on "The Novelist and the Reader," particularly his adage, "a writer is a reader moved to emulation," which Maxwell quoted thirty and even forty years later in interviews with George Plimpton and Charlie Rose. Following Bellow, Maxwell paid homage to some of the writers *he* was moved to emulate—Stephen Crane, Willa Cather, Anton Chekhov—and offered thoughtful rumination on the storyteller's art. He also shared a maxim of his own: writers "are people who perform tricks." This image—magic and illusion as metaphor for fiction-writing—provided the framework for his talk with faculty, students, and visiting literati at Northampton and reappeared as an important element in his subsequent novels. For example, when he finished *The Chateau* several years later, he felt that threads of the story were left hanging, that fates and motivations of various characters remained unknown. In an attempt to resolve these mysteries, he added a brief epilogue in which an authorial figure speaks with a reader about the narrative "tricks" performed in the novel. This echo of the speech marks the beginning of a more experimental approach for Maxwell, his first move toward a seamless blend of story and method masterfully realized twenty years later in *So Long, See You Tomorrow*. Early in this final novel, the narrator suggests that the reader "must imagine a deck of cards spread out face down on a table, and then he must turn one over, only it is not the eight of hearts or the jack of diamonds but a perfectly ordinary quarter of an hour out of Cletus's past life." Through this illusion, the reader slips easily into a young boy's world, guided by a narrator who shares both his story and creative process.

Maxwell had long admired the personal essays of his friend and *New Yorker* colleague, E. B. White, but had not felt confident in his own attempts to create a first-person narrator. In talking to the Smith audience, he found a voice and persona that translated to print, for the speech has the sensibility and tone of the modest, reliable, and wise narrator who speaks directly to readers in his late works—works that brought new clarity and refinement to his themes and illuminated in quick strokes the fiction he had published over the previous fifty years. Sometime after his train ride, Maxwell added to his speech a long list of scenarios he might use to begin a story, a simulation of his thought process for writing fiction. Before launching into this, he made a small but significant request: he asked his audience to "give what I am now about to read to you only half of your attention." Here, readers will be reminded of the narrator in *So Long, See You Tomorrow* who asks us to "disregard" anything implausible in his story of Illinois farm families in the 1920s. Such candor created a new intimacy with his readers, an intimacy that originated in part with his appearance at Smith and then evolved through *The Chateau* and the nonfiction *Ancestors* (1971). Ultimately, the Maxwell narrator took his place as a character among others, a person in whom readers could place their trust.

When the speech was published the next year, the editor and essayist Clifton Fadiman called it "the finest short discussion of the art of the novelist to appear in English since Virginia Woolf's 'Mr. Bennett and Mrs. Brown,'" an especially appropriate association for Maxwell, who took Woolf as one of his earliest and most important literary influences. In the published version, reprinted in *A William Maxwell Portrait*, readers find the polished expression of Maxwell's views on his art; here, with the appearance of his draft, they find the artist's sketch, the first flow of ideas that came to him on that train, and from which he continued to work.[5]

With the benefit of hindsight, "The Writer as Illusionist" is helpful in understanding the development of Maxwell's fiction at the artistic midpoint of his career: after his major novels of the 1940s, *The Folded Leaf* and *Time Will Darken It*, and in the throes of writing *The Chateau*, which took his narrative in new directions. Smith marked the first time Maxwell shared his methods with an audience, which in turn led him to draw back the curtain for readers of his fiction: from this point, his artistic journey became a part of his stories, told in a voice modeled on his own.

After the formal speeches, a panel with Kazin, Bellow, Gill, and Maxwell assembled to close the Smith symposium. The student newspaper, the *Sophian*, described a "battle of the books," a "crossing of verbal swords," during the session, which pitted Kazin and Bellow against Gill and Maxwell on the issue of the modern novelist's use of self-conscious prose. Kazin proposed that an emerging focus on method rather than subject created a contrived and objectionable style in some contemporary novels. Bellow agreed, while Gill and Maxwell countered that writers were working in "individual" and innovative styles. Kazin and Bellow also joined forces in suggesting that fiction in the *New Yorker* adhered to a specific "formula," a notion disputed by Gill and Maxwell, colleagues at the magazine, who defended the "great variety" of work it published. As reported in the *Sophian*, the evening became a bit heated by literary standards, and Bellow, at least, remembered it that way. Fifteen years later, he wrote a letter accepting Maxwell's invitation to join the American Academy of Arts and Letters. He thanked Maxwell for the honor and added: "I remember our meeting at Smith. You were the one speaker in that symposium who did not misbehave. I admired, and envied, your conduct."[6]

Maxwell also spoke on two occasions at the University of Illinois at Urbana-Champaign, where he graduated in 1930 and taught as a doctoral candidate from 1931 to 1933 before leaving to pursue a career in writing. In 1963, he was invited by his dear friend, Charles Shattuck, an English professor and prominent Shakespearean scholar, to appear at the campus's Festival of Contemporary Arts. Maxwell chose autobiographical fiction as his subject, and although no known transcript of the speech exists, an article detailing the highlights appeared in the Lincoln *Courier*, his hometown newspaper. Included here, the piece offers the flavor of Maxwell's remarks about the nature of novelists who work with material from life. "To him, life is a play with himself both the leading actor and a substantial part of the audience," he told the students and faculty at Illinois, a perspective that would be fully realized in *So Long, See You Tomorrow*. Ten years later, he returned to his alma mater to receive an honorary doctorate. His brief remarks at the campus commencement celebrate his Illinois roots. These words, considered in tandem with those he spoke to the Academy in New York during the same year, offer a snapshot of the two worlds he embraced through his adult life, both of which were essential to him: the literary environ in Manhattan where he could pursue writing professionally and the central Illinois towns that comprised what he called his "imagination's home," the place on which his writing often depended.

In 1958, several years after the Smith engagement, Glenway Wescott wrote to Maxwell with news that he had won the Academy Award in Literature from the American Academy of Arts and Letters, which included a $1,500 prize in recognition of his "creative work."[7] As the presentation neared, the Academy asked the author to write a page describing his literary aims and working methods. He replied:

> I have only one aim and that is to induce a group of in varying degrees and usually in the end quite imaginary characters to take over, speak in their own voices, do what hell itself cannot stop them from doing, and humanly live through the consequences. My method is to sit down in the angle between a desk and a typewriter, at quarter of eight, four mornings a week, and get up when my head is too tired to be trustworthy or my three-year-old daughter [Kate] calls me to lunch. I have no plans, but I would be very grateful if, some time in the next two or three years, I could finish the not at all ambitious book I have been engaged on for the last nine [*The Chateau*]. As for how the Grant will be of assistance to me, a friend, the wife of a writer, once observed sadly that all writers are children and need to be told once a day that what they are writing and have published is good. I do not despise money, but if the Grant had been in the form of fifteen hundred white violets or fifteen hundred fireflies in a large bottle, it would have produced the same result—that is to say, it would have made me very happy, and for the moment at least, more confident and hopeful about my work.[8]

He received the award in the Academy auditorium during the group's May ceremonial and decades later recalled "how kind the expression on Malcolm Cowley's face was when he handed me a check. . . . And so, in giving awards, I tried to convey a similar warmth." The *New Yorker* writer Harold Brodkey and his wife were among the friends Maxwell invited that day, along with an important figure from his youth: Mildred Ormsby Green, a surrogate mother who supported his literary ambitions with affection and lodging on her Wisconsin farm, where he returned off and on for years and wrote his first novel in the 1930s.[9]

Five years later, he was elected to the 250-member Academy of the nation's leading writers, composers, artists, and architects and from 1969 to 1973 served as its president. As part of the Academy's activities, Maxwell addressed the group to bestow or receive awards and to pay memorial homage to fellow writers he had known as colleagues and friends. "I didn't have a carrying voice," Maxwell told me, "and the deafer members would call 'louder, louder,' and I would have to say, 'I can't speak any louder,' until another friend advised me to speak to the person in the room who was farthest away from me and after that I had no more trouble." This volume collects a selection of the comments and tributes Maxwell made in his gentle, non-carrying voice from 1969 through his acceptance of the Gold Medal for fiction, the Academy's highest honor, in 1995.

Maxwell delivered these talks in the Academy's Italian Renaissance headquarters on Audubon Terrace—a sanctuary of quiet grandeur sheltered from the bustle of Manhattan on a brick, tree-lined block of West 155th Street across from Trinity Cemetery at Broadway. During Maxwell's years of membership, writers such as Carl Sandburg, Katherine Anne Porter, Truman Capote, John Updike, John Cheever, Ralph Ellison, Robert Frost, Norman Mailer, Tennessee Williams, and Kurt Vonnegut mingled at Academy events with musicians and artists including Aaron Copland, Leonard Bernstein, Stephen Sondheim, Edward Hopper, Mark Rothko, I. M. Pei, and Louis Kahn. As Updike wrote in 1998, "Most, it seems safe to say, of the major American writers, artists, architects, and composers of the twentieth century have become members."[10] Such luminaries of the arts and letters comprised Maxwell's audience for the talks in this volume.

Before presenting the annual awards each May of his four-year presidency, Maxwell offered brief reflections on the creative life shared by the writers, musicians, and artists in attendance. At other times, Academy members gathered for dinner meetings with panel discussions. One of these, in November 1970, focused on ethics in biography and the use of private papers, featuring the biographer Leon Edel, the writer Glenway Wescott, and Maxwell. Presiding over the discussion, Maxwell said very little that evening, so the transcript is not included here, yet his sole contribution to the conversation offers a rare glimpse of the steely resolve beneath his reserved and gentle nature. From the floor, the abstract sculptor Louise Nevelson objected to the panel of writers' "general concern with the 'truth' as a matter of research and erudition rather than creative power." She asked, "What is truth? . . . . Truth we cannot define." For Maxwell, who preferred representational rather than abstract art, the nature of truth was neither relative nor negotiable. "You don't need a definition," he replied. "It is. It exists. You feel it. I will not have my sense of truth taken away. I believe it and there we are."[11] Wescott refocused the discussion: "This goes far beyond the issues of the evening. Nonrepresentational painting and sculpture avoid or evade what novelists and biographers mean by truth."

At another dinner meeting two years later, Maxwell paid tribute to the literary mentor of his young life, Zona Gale, the first writer he knew, who had returned from New York to her Wisconsin home, where Maxwell met her in the 1920s. A Pulitzer Prize winner for drama in 1922, she would have been a likely candidate for membership in the Academy had more women been invited to join at the time. Maxwell's homage, included in this volume, offers one of the few portraits of Gale, an author and activist who was celebrated in her lifetime, yet largely forgotten since the mid-twentieth century.

Maxwell first knew a number of the Academy's writers through the *New Yorker*, where for forty years he nurtured their fiction as he slowly but steadily published his own. As he once told me, "I get a good deal of pleasure out of contemplating other people's talent." Naturally, when one of his writers received an award, he spoke with particular authority and intimacy. This volume includes two of Maxwell's tributes from 1969: his introduction of Eudora Welty when she read "The Demonstrators" at an Academy dinner meeting and congratulatory remarks to Vladimir Nabokov when he received the Award of Merit for the novel. The latter, in Montreux at the time of the presentation, sent characteristically Nabokovian words to be read to the group in his absence: "I am terribly sorry not to be present in the handsome old flesh at this Ceremonial. I can never remember if time is six hours slow or fast in the New World, but anyway, so as to thwart error, I am being telepathically active in Switzerland at both 9:00AM and at 9:00PM on this 21st of May. A Nabokov-shaped shimmer of grateful elation should be visible just a foot or so to the anatomical right of Bill Maxwell's right shoulder."[12]

Maxwell's longest and most moving remarks came in the form of memorial tributes to writers he had known for decades, a selection of which appear in this volume: Robert Fitzgerald (1910–1985), poet, classics scholar, and renowned translator of the *Odyssey*, met Maxwell, a fellow Illinois native, as a student at Harvard. Maxwell enjoyed a close, lifelong friendship with Fitzgerald, whom he credits with turning him to fiction-writing in graduate school, and to whom he dedicated *So Long, See You Tomorrow*. And Francis Steegmuller (1906–1994), the famed biographer and translator of Flaubert's *Madame Bovary*, helped Maxwell with the French in his novel *The Chateau*. Steegmuller's widow, the writer Shirley Hazzard, requested that Maxwell offer the tribute to her late husband and five years later presented the Academy's memorial tribute to Maxwell after his death in July 2000.

In 1980, the Academy honored Maxwell with the William Dean Howells Medal, recognizing *So Long, See You Tomorrow* as the most distinguished work of American fiction published in the preceding five years. Appointed by I. M. Pei, then Chancellor of the Academy, Eudora Welty, John Cheever, and Ralph Ellison chose the novel from a list of works by major writers including John Barth, Saul Bellow, Norman Mailer, John Updike, and Joyce Carol Oates. Willa Cather, one of Maxwell's literary touchstones, was a past recipient along with William Faulkner, William Styron, Cheever, and Welty, who was asked to present the award.[13]

As was (and is) tradition, members and guests gathered for cocktails at noon in the Academy's South Gallery to view manuscripts and documents related to the winners, including the original manuscript of *So Long*, a letter to Maxwell from his *New Yorker* editor Roger Angell, and copies of "The Writer as Illusionist." Lunch followed under a tent on the terrace, where Maxwell and his wife had asked to sit with Robert Fitzgerald, who traveled to New York for the occasion. Afterwards, in the auditorium, members sat on the stage facing the audience for the Ceremonial. Welty, who had traveled from Jackson, Mississippi, rose to pay tribute to her friend:

> The most important facts in our experience, answerable or unanswerable, never go away. William Maxwell has written his best novel out of his comprehension of this. . . . In the writing, [the novel's] tension is finally strong and unremitting. . . . We are face to face with other people's mystery and with our own. There's nothing between us and the realization that without love and without death we should never have come into the presence of human mystery at all.[14]

Published here, Maxwell's acceptance was characteristically brief, yet reveals his sense of gentle bemusement and the important role of his literary friendships with both Welty and Louise Bogan, whom he acknowledged for her early assistance in his career.

In March 1995, Maxwell learned he had been selected for the Gold Medal for Fiction, the highest honor given by the Academy, conferred once every six years for an individual's entire work. His collected stories, *All the Days and Nights*, had recently appeared to acclaim, and the Gold Medal represented the first of a series of awards that followed, including the PEN/Malamud Award for Short Fiction and the National Book Critics Circle Award for lifetime achievement in publishing. He replied to the architect Kevin Roche, then Academy President:

> I read your letter standing in the foyer outside the door of our apartment and was simultaneously unable to believe what I was reading and caught up in a wave of happiness. I have two or three times in my life been the runner up for a major award and had come to believe that the runner up was my inevitable fate, and even a reasonable one.
>
> When I read over the names of the other writers who have had this award, it makes my head swim with pleasure that I should be among them.[15]

Once again, Maxwell followed in the path of Willa Cather, the fellow Midwestern writer for whom he felt particular affinity and admiration.

Maxwell also reported to Roche that on May 17, the day of the Ceremonial, he and Emily would be in Venice celebrating their fiftieth wedding anniversary. He regretted the conflict and offered to send a representative to read his remarks. A case of bronchitis, however, changed his plans. At the age of eighty-seven, unable to travel and still under the weather, he went to the Ceremonial and spoke to the group, a consolation for the missed anniversary trip. He asked Joseph Mitchell, who had nominated him, to read the citation:

> William Maxwell's principal theme, like James Joyce's, is the sadness that often exists at the heart of the family. The families that he has written about in his novels and short stories and fables range in time and place from eighty or so years ago in a frame house in a small city in central Illinois to the present—high up in an apartment house over by the river on the Upper East Side of New York City. Maxwell writes in a style that is quiet and plain and reflective and restrained. Nevertheless, in his pages one often reads with surprise descriptions and observations that seem truer and more revealing and more powerful and more memorable and more shocking than the deliberately shocking scenes and observations found in the pages of many of his contemporaries.
>
> He is as aware as any novelist who ever lived of what human beings are capable of, and he sometimes displays this knowledge with a kind of worldly resignation and sometimes with a kind of dry American humor and sometimes with a kind of joyousness—a joyousness in simply being alive and a participant and a witness. But the sadness is always there, or at least a hint of it. And a good example of this is the subtle and sweet and barely recognizable sadness in the title of one of his novels, *So Long, See You Tomorrow.*

After the event, Maxwell heard from his dear friend, John Updike, who had received the William Dean Howells Medal for *Rabbit at Rest* the same evening:

> But it was your speech that redeemed the day—totally marvelous, the way you stood there and, in a clarion though bronchially challenged voice, drew out of the ether one amazing sentence after another, put forth side by side like the shining pieces in a Tiffany lamp, winding up with that beautiful pairing of the vanished elms of Lincoln and your mother's death, which I took to be the event that alerted you to life's fragility. It was just grand speechifying, wonderfully modest, firm, and luminous, and I hope your health recovered its full timbre as an immediate byproduct.
>
> It was lovely to see you there, and to see Emily anywhere. . . . It was a good day for *New Yorker* contributors and Maxwell protégés. May you get to Venice momentarily. [16]

In 2000, William Maxwell and his wife, Emily, died within eight days of each other. Six years later, I was in New York for a pair of lectures and decided to walk by their apartment building on East 86th Street for one more look up at the windows and perhaps to say hello to the doorman who had always greeted me kindly on my visits. From across the street, I could see a different, younger doorman standing outside. I hesitated, then crossed over to speak to him. No, he had not heard of the Maxwells. He had started working there a year earlier, when the previous doorman retired.

I thought of Maxwell's disdain for what he called the plowing under of the past, to use his distinctly Midwestern image, and of the title of his fourth novel, *Time Will Darken It*, which alludes to the fading of a painting's bright hues with the passage of years. In one of our interviews, Maxwell said he would always choose the life of the preserver—"it has more resonance"— and in this spirit, he offered his work as a stay against the plowing under, against the fading brought on by time. I need not have worried that the new doorman did not know William Maxwell or that time had already begun to darken memories of his presence on the street where he lived for decades. The author had already saved the neighborhoods of Manhattan in his story, "Over by the River," just as he had preserved the Victorian homes of Lincoln, Illinois, on streets once canopied by majestic elms. In the following conversations with William Maxwell—in the New York apartment, in his country home, on the telephone, at the American Academy—we find other kinds of stories worth preserving: stories of writing and literary friendship, of reconsiderations, new recognitions, and gratitude for his full, artistic life. May this volume, in its modest scope, celebrate and share another facet of his literary legacy and help illuminate the writing he left us.

Acknowledgments

It is a privilege to continue focusing my work on the literary life of William Maxwell. My first thanks go to Debbie Watts for her extensive assistance in preparing this volume for publication and for twenty-five years of friendship. Special thanks to Mr. Maxwell's daughters, Kate Maxwell and Brookie Maxwell, along with his literary executor, Michael Steinman, who read the typescript and provided valuable suggestions. Kathy Kienholz, beloved former archivist for the American Academy of Arts and Letters, New York City, was her usual ebullient and supportive self, making possible the inclusion of Maxwell's talks at the Academy. She provided insight and information for the introduction, which she kindly read in draft form. Thanks to Scott Richardson, convivial friend, for his expert design of the website and many other kindnesses. I again benefitted from the sound editorial advice of Michael Putzel, good friend and Maxwell's godson. I am grateful for the University Scholar Award and sabbatical from the University of Illinois Springfield, both of which helped me to complete this project; for assistance from the Rare Book and Manuscript Library at the University of Illinois Urbana/Champaign, especially that provided by Gene Rinkel and Valerie Hotchkiss; for friends from the Washington Biography Group, especially Jamie Morris, Kristie Miller, Robin Rausch, and Amy Schapiro; and for years of hospitality, good care, and feeding from friends at the Sofitel Lafayette Square, Washington, D.C. Many thanks to Peggy Ryan, Ryan Roberts, Jacqueline Jackson, John and Jackie Stuemke, and Norma and Jack Burkhardt. Finally, and most of all, I thank my husband, Craig.

BB

Notes

1. A more detailed account of our meetings appears in *William Maxwell: A Literary Life,* University of Illinois Press (2005).

2. Linda Wertheimer to Barbara Burkhardt, March 20, 2009.

3. Charles Baxter, Michael Collier, Edward Hirsch, ed. *A William Maxwell Portrait: Memories and Appreciations.* W. W. Norton and Company, 2004, p. 194–99.

4. Alec Wilkinson, *My Mentor: A Young Writer's Friendship with William Maxwell.* Mariner Books, 2003, p. 78.

5. As far as anyone knows, Maxwell's exact words to his audience that night were neither recorded nor transcribed, but a report in the Smith College newspaper, the *Sophian,* makes clear that he added material to his draft before delivering the speech, including the opening, stage-setting image: a Chinese painting of a spring festival on the riverbank, where entertainers—including storytellers—practice their crafts. The published version of the speech referenced by Hadiman, and which appears in *A William Maxwell Portrait,* includes all the essential material from his handwritten notes as well as the additional material described by student journalists in attendance.

6. Saul Bellow to William Maxwell, March 14, 1970. With permission of the American Academy of Arts and Letters. Today's American Academy of Arts and Letters, an organization of 250 members, was originally founded as the National Institute of Arts and Letters in 1898. In 1904, the American Academy of Arts and Letters was founded as an inner body of the Institute. Its membership was limited to fifty persons, selected from the Institute membership for special distinction. In 1976, the Institute and the Academy merged into one institution with a single Board of Directors, committee structure, and budget, called the American Academy and Institute of Arts and Letters. The Academy continued to function as an inner body of the Institute, and its membership remained fixed at fifty. In 1993, the Academy and Institute merged into the American Academy of Arts and Letters forming a single body of 250 members. Maxwell was elected to the Institute in 1963 and served as its president from 1969 to 1973. In 1993, when the Institute and Academy unified, all Institute members, including Maxwell, became Academicians. For simplicity's sake, in the introduction, I refer to both groups as the "Academy." Many thanks to Katharine Kienholz, archivist of the American Academy, for providing this explanation.

7. Glenway Wescott to William Maxwell, March 10, 1958.

8. William Maxwell to Matthew Johnson, April 16, 1958. With permission of the American Academy of Arts and Letters.

9. William Maxwell to Felicia Geffen; April 17, 1958. With permission of the American Academy of Arts and Letters.

10. John Updike, Foreword to *A Century of Arts and Letters,* John Updike, editor, Columbia University Press, 1998.

11. *Proceedings of the American Academy of Arts and Letters and the National Institute of Arts and Letters.* Second series, No. 21. New York: American Academy of Arts and Letters, 1971.

12. "Presentation to Vladimir Nabokov of the Award of Merit Medal for the Novel by William Maxwell of the Institute at the Ceremonial, May 21, 1969." *Proceedings of the American Academy of Arts and Letters and the National Institute of Arts and Letters.* Second Series, No. 20. New York: American Academy of Arts and Letters, 1970, p. 23.

13. Records at the American Academy of Arts and Letters indicate that Ralph Ellison was unable to attend the committee meeting; as a result, the vote was taken by Welty and Cheever.

14. "Presentation to William Maxwell of the Howells Medal for Fiction, by Eudora Welty at the Ceremonial, May 21, 1980." *Proceedings of the American Academy of Arts and Letters and the National Institute of Arts and Letters.* Second Series, No. 31. New York: American Academy of Arts and Letters, 1981, p. 24.

15. William Maxwell to Kevin Roche, March 23, 1995. With permission of the American Academy of Arts and Letters.

16. John Updike to William Maxwell, May 19, 1995. Courtesy of the Rare Book and Manuscript Library of the University of Illinois at Urbana–Champaign.

Chronology

1908   William Keepers Maxwell, Jr., born in Lincoln, Illinois, on August 16, second child of Eva Blossom (Blinn) and William Keepers Maxwell, an agent for Hanover Fire Insurance Company. He joins older brother, Edward, known all his life as "Hap," who was then three years old, in a home on Eighth Street. Maxwell is known as "Billie" throughout his childhood.

1910   The Maxwells move to a larger home on Ninth Street in Lincoln, diagonally across from the Blinns, his maternal grandparents. Here, the future writer finds his hallowed ground, the place that becomes so much a part of him that its mere mention still moves him at the end of his ninety-one years. The world in this house holds the heart of his childhood and later of his fictional universe. In his mind, it is forever associated with his mother: "I didn't distinguish between the house and her," he wrote in *Ancestors* in 1971. "When I was separated from it permanently, the sense of deprivation was of the kind that exiles know."

1914   Enters a private preschool in downtown Lincoln, escorted there everyday by Grace McGrath, who later becomes his stepmother.

1918   Maxwell's father reads about the worldwide influenza pandemic in the *Chicago Tribune*. In the fall, the devastating disease comes to Lincoln, located on the railway line between St. Louis and Chicago. During World War I, troops regularly travel this line, many of whom contract the disease. On Christmas Eve, William, Sr., boards the train with his wife so that she can deliver their third child at Brokaw Hospital in Bloomington, Illinois, a larger town thirty miles away. Maxwell and his older brother are left in the care of their Aunt Maybel, their father's sister. On Christmas Day, young Billie and Hap come down with the flu.

1919   Maxwell's younger brother, (Robert) Blinn, is born on New Year's Day. Two days later, his mother dies at age thirty-seven from double pneumonia, a common complication of the flu. His father, weak with flu himself, returns to Lincoln the next day with his new baby and his wife's remains. As Maxwell later wrote, after his mother's death "the shine went out of everything." This tragic loss becomes the centerpiece of much of Maxwell's work.

1921   Maxwell's father marries Grace McGrath at her sister's home in Lincoln on October 5 and sells the beloved family home on Ninth Street. The family moves to a rented house on Eighth Street while a new house is being built for them on Park Place, a fashionable street developing at the edge of the cornfields on the town's north side. Nearly sixty years later, the Park Place home assumes importance in his final novel, *So Long, See You Tomorrow.*

1922   In September, Maxwell begins freshman year at Lincoln High School, where he is elected class president and publishes in the school's journal a story about a French aristocrat who hides in a grandfather clock during the Revolution.

1923   Maxwell's father accepts a promotion to vice president in the Chicago office of the Hanover Fire Insurance Company and moves in the spring to an apartment in Rogers Park on the city's north side. Young Billie stays behind in Lincoln to finish his freshman year at Lincoln High School, then joins his family when school dismisses for the summer—driven there by Grace's amiable brothers. Younger brother Blinn remains in Lincoln to be raised by his Aunt Maybel and Uncle Paul—a circumstance Maxwell's father later regrets. In the fall, Maxwell enters Senn High School, many times the size of Lincoln High, where he publishes in the *Forum* literary journal and receives guidance in reading and art by exceptional teachers. Meets friends Susan Deuel and Jack Scully.

1925   Spends summer at Bonnie Oaks, a farm near Portage, Wisconsin, which is run as an informal artist's colony. Here he meets Zona Gale, the Pulitzer–Prize winning writer who becomes his first literary mentor and also develops lifelong friendships with the Green family, owners of the farm.

1926   Graduates from Senn High School. After his best friend, Jack Scully, contracts pleurisy, Maxwell accompanies him to the University of Illinois in Urbana-Champaign to help him register for the fall semester. His brother, Hap, also a student in Urbana, arranges for him to stay in his fraternity house. Maxwell decides to enroll himself, changing his plans to attend the School of the Art Institute of Chicago.

1928   During Maxwell's sophomore year at Illinois, his best friend, Jack, begins an intimate relationship with Margaret Guild, a fellow student Maxwell was courting. Distraught, Maxwell attempts to end his life by cutting his throat and wrists. While he is recovering in the hospital, his trusted friend, Susan Deuel, invites him to the Kappa Alpha Theta spring dance. Decades later, Maxwell writes her, recalling how he had worn a turtleneck and "had a wonderful time, and danced my head off."

1930   Graduates from the University of Illinois with highest honors and in the fall enters Harvard University on a scholarship.

1931   In his words, a "block" on the German language prevents him from attaining his Ph.D. at Harvard—his scholarship is not renewed, and he is unable to pay for the tuition himself. He receives his master's degree from Harvard and returns to the University of Illinois, where he takes courses toward his Ph.D. and teaches for two years.

1933   Leaves the University of Illinois to pursue a writing career in New York. Unable to find a job, he returns to Bonnie Oaks where he writes his first novel, *Bright Center of Heaven*, on the third floor of the farm's converted water tower. With his manuscript complete, he sails from New York City to Martinique in December, where he stays nearly a month. He returns to the United States when he learns that Harper and Brothers is considering publication of his novel.

1934   First novel, *Bright Center of Heaven*, is published in September by Harper and Brothers.

1935   In the summer, Maxwell takes up residence at the MacDowell Colony in Peterborough, New Hampshire, where he works on his second novel. He continues writing in Urbana, Illinois, and Bonnie Oaks, Wisconsin.

1936   With his second novel accepted by Harper and Brothers, Maxwell is hired by Katharine White to work at the *New Yorker* in the art department. He soon moves to fiction editing and for forty years edits the work of writers including John Cheever, John Updike, Eudora Welty, J. D. Salinger, Vladimir Nabokov, John O'Hara, and Mary McCarthy.

1937   *They Came Like Swallows*, Maxwell's second novel, is published to good reviews and becomes "Book of the Month Club" main selection. Maxwell wins Friends of American Writers Award.

1938   Meets Louise Bogan, who would become an important literary mentor as he wrote *The Folded Leaf.*

1940   Meets Eudora Welty, whose work he edits at the *New Yorker* and who becomes a lifelong friend.

1944   Begins psychoanalysis with Theodor Reik, a Freud protégé who emigrated from Vienna and sees many artists and writers as patients.

1945   *The Folded Leaf* is published on April 4. Maxwell marries Emily Gilman Noyes on May 17 at First Presbyterian Church, New York City.

1946   *The Heavenly Tenants*, a fantasy for children, is published.

1948   Harper publishes *Time Will Darken It* while the Maxwells are on an extended trip to France, Italy, and Austria. Upon their return to New York, Maxwell begins writing novel about their experiences in France, which is published thirteen years later as *The Chateau.*

1954   The Maxwell's first daughter, Katharine Farrington (Kate), is born on December 19.

1955   Delivers speech, "The Writer as Illusionist," as part of a symposium, "The Novel at Mid-Century," at Smith College on March 4. Other participants included Alfred Kazin, Brendan Gill, and Saul Bellow. Ralph Ellison is in attendance.

1956   The Maxwell's second daughter, Emily Brooke (Brookie) is born on October 15. *Stories*, a short fiction collection with works by Maxwell, Jean Stafford, John Cheever, and Daniel Fuchs, is published by Farrar, Straus, and Cudahy. Maxwell contributes his stories "The Trojan Women," "What Every Boy Should Know," and "The French Scarecrow."

1958   Receives $1,500 grant from National Institute of Arts and Letters.

1961   *The Chateau* published by Alfred A. Knopf, Maxwell's new publisher, in March.

1963   Elected to membership in the National Academy of Arts and Letters.

1966   *The Old Man at the Railroad Crossing and Other Tales* is published by Knopf in February.

1969   Elected president of the American Academy of Arts and Letters. He serves in this position until 1972.

1971   *Ancestors*, a family history, published in June by Knopf.

1976   Retires from the *New Yorker* after forty years of editorial service. Continues to publish stories and reviews in the magazine until 1999.

1977   *Over by the River and Other Stories* published in September by Knopf.

1979   *So Long, See You Tomorrow* first appears in two installments in the *New Yorker* on October 1 and 8.

1980   *So Long, See You Tomorrow* is published by Knopf in April to excellent reviews. Maxwell receives the William Dean Howells Medal of the American Academy of Arts and Letters for the novel on May 21 in New York. Presented to him by Eudora Welty, the award is given to the most outstanding novel published by an American in the previous five years.

1983   *Letters: Sylvia Townsend Warner*, edited by Maxwell, is published by Viking Press.

1989   *The Outermost Dream: Essays and Reviews* published by Knopf in April.

1992   *Billie Dyer and Other Stories* published by Knopf.

1995   *All the Days and Nights: The Collected Stories* published in January by Knopf. Maxwell receives the Gold Medal for Fiction from the American Academy of Arts and Letters on May 17 in New York and the National Book Critics Circle Award for Lifetime Achievement in Publishing. In a reading and ceremony at the Shakespeare Folger Library in Washington, D.C., he receives the PEN/Malamud Award for short fiction on December 8 with the writer Stuart Dybek.

2000   Emily Maxwell dies on July 23 of ovarian cancer. Maxwell follows her in death on July 31 at age ninety-one, about two weeks before his ninety-second birthday. A memorial service is held for both Maxwells at St. John the Divine, New York City in September. His brother, Blinn, travels from California to speak at the ceremony. Afterwards ice cream is served outside and there are pony rides for children.

Conversations with William Maxwell

Handwritten Notes for "The Writer as Illusionist"

William Maxwell/1955

From the Archives at Smith College. Reprinted by permission of Smith College and the Estate of William Maxwell.

So far as I can see, there is no legitimate sleight-of-hand involved in pursuing the arts of music and painting. There is in writing—in all writing, but particularly in narrative writing. The person who wrote, "It was said that a new person had appeared on the sea-front—a lady with a dog . . ." was, quite simply, practicing magic. Disbelieve in either the lady or the dog if you can. Or for that matter, the sea-front. The music lover in the concert hall may be carried out of himself by what he hears, but it isn't part of the arrangement that he should be. He can simply and agreeably follow the score. Or think about his own affairs. He cannot read and do this, for more than a few seconds. The reader, skeptical, experienced, busy, is asked to put aside his own real concerns and follow what happens to people who don't exist; to be present at a scene that is only words on a printed page; to be amused, or moved or instructed, just as he would in real life, only the life is on the page in front of him; no dog or cat has ever been able to figure this out, and I'm not sure that I can. But if, as Mr. T. S. Eliot says, humankind cannot bear very much reality, then perhaps reading is a kind of device we have arrived at for seeing, in the abstract, in printed symbols, that degree of reality, of the truth about ourselves, that we can endure, with the willing assistance of the writer, who is a kind of charlatan, and needn't be taken too seriously. The writer has everything in common with the Vaudeville magician, including, sometimes, physical appearance, but there is one essential point of difference. The writer must be taken in by his own tricks. Having practiced more or less incessantly for five, ten, fifteen, or twenty years, knowing that the trunk has a false bottom and the opera hat a false top, with a white dove in a cage ready to be handed to him from the wings, and his clothing full of unusual, deep pockets containing odd playing cards, and colored scarves that are and are not knotted together and of course the American flag, he must begin by pleasing himself. His mouth must be the first mouth that drops open in surprise, in wonder, as (presto-change-o!) this character's heartache is dragged squirming from his inside coat pocket, and that character's future has become his past while he was not looking.

Though a writer has to have an idea, he is not really the richer for it until the idea has him. At which point, magic begins to be involved. He may complain that his characters have gotten out of hand, that they are doing and saying things he doesn't intend them to. Pay no attention to these complaints. They are insincere. All they mean is that he is sitting pretty. Nothing more is required of him than that he stand to one side, observing, admiring, commenting if he likes, but not interfering in what happens. If he does interfere, some of the heat goes out of the sun. And if he fails to give the performance his undivided attention—if he lets himself be distracted from the imaginary happenings by some happening in the real world—the jig is up. The characters have their feelings hurt, won't talk, won't act, won't do anything. They may even without a word turn and go away forever, without leaving a farewell note or an address at which they can at some time be reached. Though the writer may entertain paranoiac suspicions about critics and book reviewers, about his publisher, and even about the reading public, the truth is that he has no enemy but interruption.

But while he stands back, listening, admiring, deeply attentive to the action, he will probably hold one thing back. There will probably be, somewhere at the back of his mind, a useful, corrective vision, something simple and easy to remember, that represents the task as a whole. He will see the material of his story as a pond into which a stone is tossed, sending out a circular ripple. And then a second stone is tossed into the same pond, sending out another ripple that is inside the first and ultimately overtakes it. And then a third stone, a fourth stone, and so on.

Or he will see himself, in his mind's eye, crossing a long, level plain, chapter after chapter, toward the mountains on the horizon. If there were no mountains, there would be no novel; but they are still a long long way away—those scenes of excitement, of the utmost drama, so strange, so sad, that will write themselves; and meanwhile, all the knowledge, all the skill, all the imaginative dexterity at his command will be needed to cover this day's march on perfectly level ground.

As a result of too long, too intense, too solitary concentration, the novelist sometimes begins to act queerly. During the genesis of his book, particularly, he talks to himself in the street, smiles knowingly at animals and birds, offers Adam the apple, for Eve, and with a half involuntary movement of his arm imitates the writhing of the snake that nobody else as yet knows about.

He spends the greater part of the days of his real creation in his bathrobe and slippers, unshaven, his hair uncombed, drinking quarts of water to clear his brain and hardly distinguishable from an inmate in an asylum. Like many such unfortunate people, he has delusions of grandeur. With the cherubim row on row among the constellations, the seraphim in their more privileged seats in The Primum Mobile—waiting, ready, willing to be astonished, to be taken in—the novelist, in his bathrobe, with his cuffs rolled back to show there is no possibility of a deception being practiced, says *let there be*—(after who knows how much practice beforehand). *Let there be*—(and is just as delighted as the angels and the reader and everybody else when there actually is) *Light*!

Not always, of course. It doesn't always work. Sometimes the audience yawns or snickers. But say that it does work . . . Then there is light, the greater light to rule the daytime of the novel and the lesser light to rule the night scenes, breakfast and dinner, one day, and the gathering together of the characters to make a lively scene, grass, trees, apple trees in bloom, adequate provision for sea monsters if they turn up in a figure of speech, birds, cattle, and creeping things, and finally and especially man; male and female, Anna and Vronsky, Emma and Mr. Knightly.

Literary prestidigitation is tiring and requires lots of sleep. When the novelist is in bed with the light off, he does not sleep; he tosses. He turns the light on long enough to write down four or five words that may or may not mean something to him in the morning. And when he is at last asleep he is bound to dream. He may even dream that he had a dream in which the whole meaning of what he is trying to do in the novel is brilliantly revealed to him. Just so the dog asleep on the hearthrug dreams. You can see by the faint jerking movement of his four legs that he is after a rabbit. The novelist's rabbit is the truth—about life, about human character, about himself and therefore, by extension, it is to be hoped, about other people as well. He is committed to the belief that this is all knowable, can be described and recorded by a person sufficiently dedicated to describing and recording, can be caught in a net of narration. In this he is encouraged by the example of other writers—Turgenev, say, with his particular trick of spreading out his arms and taking off, like a great bird, leaving the earth and soaring high above the final scenes; or D. H. Lawrence, with his marvelous ability to make two people who are only words on a printed page reach out—actually reach out and touch one another; or Virginia Woolf, with her love of fireworks; or E. M. Forster, with his fastidious preference for what many nice people wish were not so.

But what, ultimately, was accomplished by them or can he hope to accomplish? Not life—not the real thing, but only a clever facsimile that is called literature. To achieve this counterfeit, he has, more or less, to renounce his birthright to reality, even though nobody has a better sense of what it is—how beautiful, how various, of its rewards and satisfactions. If you ask him why the successful manipulation and projection of illusions is everything to him, you will probably get any number of answers, none of them straightforward. You might better ask a sailor why he chooses to spend his time at sea.

An Image of an Image: Maxwell Topic: Autobiographical Novelist

Bob Adams/1963

From *Lincoln Courier* (Illinois), 13 March 1963. Reprinted by permission of *Lincoln Courier*.

William Maxwell, novelist and fiction editor of the *New Yorker*, painted a wry but warm portrait of the autobiographical novelist here Tuesday night.

A former teacher of English at the University of Illinois, Maxwell spoke to an audience of over a hundred persons in the U. of I. Law Building auditorium as part of the University's spring Festival of Contemporary Arts.

Throughout his half-hour talk, Maxwell coupled candor with dry wit to present a sympathetic but penetrating mosaic of a central figure in today's literature: the novelist who writes about himself.

"The autobiographical novelist was born an egoist," he began. "To him, life is a play with himself both the leading actor and a substantial part of the audience.

"The finer shades of his interest are always for what is going on in his own mind."

At Odds with Society

Besides being an egoist, he's also a bit odd: "Whatever standard of human behavior is applied," Maxwell said, "all writers are abnormal and peculiar. The autobiographical writer is always a little out of step with his environment."

The autobiographical writer, he said, is one who'd never go anywhere without having something wrong: "He would have forgotten to change his shirt, or he'd need a haircut"—or wear brown shoes with a black suit.

The editor-author gave a brisk run through the greater writers of the past to prove his point. "Whitman told whoppers. . . Dostoevsky was a compulsive gambler. . . Henry James couldn't ask the way to the corner drug store so that anyone could understand him."

But he noted a possible reason for the "queerness": "Perhaps the brown shoes are a protest. . . . The truth is that the autobiographical writer is nearly always subversive."

And, he observed, "In the solitude of the soul, everybody's queer."

More Than Just Recording

From these qualities, Maxwell said, may spring the force which marks the novelist as more than simply a recorder of case histories.

"He has an inner photographic plate that is highly sensitive to sights and sounds. He also has an unusually retentive memory."

If it's traditional for the novelist to "hold a mirror up to life," Maxwell said, then the autobiographical writer "holds a mirror up to the mirror. And the mirrors do not exclude the rest of life, but take more in than ever before."

Citing passages from contemporary novels, Maxwell showed how the sensitive writer can take day-to-day objects—a crumpled newspaper, a telephone line—and mold them into art by way of his own experience.

"He is an explorer going through a country that's never going to be well mapped," Maxwell said. "The reader has the choice of reading it, or going through it himself."

Remarks Delivered at American Academy of Arts and Letters

William Maxwell/1969

From *Proceedings of the American Academy of Arts and Letters and the National Institute of Arts and Letters*. Second Series, No. 20. New York, 1970. Publication No. 262. Printed with permission of the American Academy of Arts and Letters, New York City. Delivered May 21, 1969.

There are two things that an artist commonly needs to be assured about—that his work is good, and that it is wanted. No amount of self-confidence can do the trick. The reassurance must come from the outside. But a commercial success is no guarantee that his work is good, and a grant from a foundation is not evidence that it is in any general way wanted. The Academy-Institute awards this year are in the amount of $81,500. They are unique in that they are given to artists by artists, to composers by composers, to writers by writers. It is an inside job. And what is superfluous or not in some way good doesn't stand a chance. The recipients can, therefore, take heart and go on working.

Tribute to Vladimir Nabokov, Recipient of the Award of Merit, American Academy of Arts and Letters

William Maxwell/1969

From *Proceedings of the American Academy of Arts and Letters and the National Institute of Arts and Letters*. Second Series, No. 20. New York, 1970. Publication No. 262. [pp. 23–24] Printed with permission of the American Academy of Arts and Letters, New York City. Delivered May 21, 1969.

The Award of Merit consists of a medal and one thousand dollars, given in rotation for Painting, Sculpture, the Novel, Poetry, and Drama. It cannot be conferred on a member of the Institute. It has been given to these five novelists only—to the author of *Appointment in Samarra*, to the author of *Point Counter Point*, to the author of *The Sun Also Rises*, to the author of *Death in Venice*, and to the author of *Sister Carrie*. It is being given this year to Vladimir Nabokov, born in St. Petersburg in 1899.

Mr. Nabokov is the phoenix we had no reason to expect. He is one more in the line of great Russian storytellers, and, strangely, he is our own. We got him through accident; history displaced him. Personal deprivation made him a great literary artist. We are forever indebted to him for a divine comedy about the faculty of communication between the hand and the head, and for a grand tragedy in which a blind man is undone in a game of hide-and-seek with his tittering tormentors. Nabokov's characters are deceiving and self-deceiving human beings in whom we recognize, profoundly, ourselves. His plots are chess games, in which the chessmen try to make up their own rules and, naturally, they fail at it. Their failure is transmuted into art. His account of a heartless middle-aged man's sexual pursuit of an even more heartless pre-adolescent girl turns out in the end to be, by a feat of presti-digitation, heartbreaking. No living novelist is better at sensory description, or has written more movingly of the longing of the living to be reunited with the dead. He is the vaudeville magician par excellence, astonishing us again and again by producing out of the air, in front of our eyes, life untampered with. He is also a poet dealing in prose fiction with the shifting, fictitious nature of reality, with the artifice that we call Time, with the aurora borealis of memory. There is no discoverable limit to the range of his talent. And sadness is his very home.

Introduction of Eudora Welty for Her Reading of "The Demonstrators" at the American Academy of Arts and Letters

William Maxwell/1969

From *Proceedings of the American Academy of Arts and Letters and the National Institute of Arts and Letters*. Second Series, No. 20. New York, 1970, 53. Reprinted by permission of the American Academy of Arts and Letters, New York City. "The Demonstrators" was published in 1966 by the *New Yorker* magazine. Welty gave her reading at the Academy on November 13, 1969.

Being one of us, Eudora Welty doesn't need to be introduced to the people in this room. I have never ceased to be astonished by her work, but there was one moment when the astonishment went far deeper than ever before, and I have never forgotten it. It was in a story that was based on but not exactly about the murder of Medgar Evers in Mississippi. The murderer was not a pleasant man, and no person of Liberal sympathies could fail to be horrified by all he stood for. Nevertheless, in the final paragraph, Miss Welty ended up inside the killer strumming his guitar. You can only do this if you are in a state of Grace.

Remarks Delivered at American Academy of Arts and Letters

William Maxwell/1970

From *Proceedings of the American Academy of Arts and Letters and the National Institute of Arts and Letters*. Second Series, No. 21. New York, 1971, 11. Reprinted by permission of the American Academy of Arts and Letters, New York City.

As president, Maxwell made these brief comments before presenting awards at the annual ceremonial of the American Academy of Arts and Letters in New York City on May 26, 1970.

I have an ineradicable memory of standing on this platform ten years ago, for the first time. When I left my seat I was expecting merely to be handed an envelope with a check in it, for which I was, in fact, most grateful. But I also got something I was not expecting. For as the envelope was put into my hand, I saw that Malcolm Cowley was looking not at me but directly into my eyes, in full recognition of who I was and all that had brought me here. And I was startled and so moved that for an instant I totally forgot that I was supposed to leave the platform and go back to my seat.

What is singular about the grants of the Academy and the Institute is that they represent a kind of awareness that is neither commercial nor institutional—a recognition given to artists by artists, to writers by writers, to composers by composers. No outside influence can be brought to bear on it. Only the accomplishment can bring it about.

The three grant committees, in art, literature, and music, working sometimes in easy agreement and sometimes in profound and total disagreement but in any case working like the devil, have in the end arrived at these seventeen men and women whom it is our delight to honor today, and to each of whom we are extending, with these grants, our love—for his beautiful work, for his courageous and patient and hard-driving life as an artist, and for his incorruptible self.

Remarks Delivered at the American Academy of Arts and Letters

William Maxwell/1971

From *Proceedings of the American Academy of Arts and Letters and the National Institute of Arts and Letters*. Second Series, No. 21. New York, 1971. Publication No. 269. Printed with permission of the American Academy of Arts and Letters, New York City.

Every work of art, in its making, requires privacy of a kind that most resembles the self-absorption of the mad. And the artist is tormented by frivolous questions that cannot be answered—such as *Will I ever hear it performed?* And *Will my gallery disown me?* And *What will Edmund Wilson think of it?* He needs praise more than most people do, more than is strictly reasonable, childishly. And because of his seclusion gets it only intermittently, when some kind person bothers to tell him that he was talked about. But always at the back of his mind is an ultimate moment of exposure, publication, or performance which will lead—to what, is the question. To a kind of general appreciation of what he has tried to do and what he has actually done. To a kind of rough justice, is another way of putting it. At the moment, and perhaps at every moment, this kind of justice is in short supply. The imitative and the flimsy and the flawed quite often pass for what they are not. Who can be counted on to know, to recognize a solid accomplishment when the moment of exposure comes, is another artist. No matter how deeply immured in his own privacy he is, he nevertheless knows, he sniffs out of the very air that something good has happened. He cannot not know, because his own work in progress will in some degree be altered.

It is the peculiar virtue of the Academy-Institute awards that they represent the awareness and judgment of the fellow practitioner. On a material plane, they add up to $85,000—twenty-two awards of three thousand dollars each and a few more of varying amounts. The brief citations I am about to read have been written either by or with the assistance of the awards committees in art, literature, and music.

Tribute to Zona Gale at the American Academy of Arts and Letters

William Maxwell/1972

From *Proceedings of the American Academy of Arts and Letters and the National Institute of Arts and Letters*. Second Series, No. 23. New York, 1973, 61. Reprinted by permission of the American Academy of Arts and Letters, New York City.

This tribute was delivered at a dinner meeting of the Academy entitled "Crucial Encounters" on November 15, 1972. Several distinguished members were asked to speak about "an occurrence in the life of an artist, composer, musician . . . of such a character that thereafter the work, the attitude towards the cosmos, was changed." Maxwell's words on Zona Gale were later published in the *Yale Review* 76 (1987): 221.

I have a theory that behind every artist there is another artist; that there is a perpetual passing on of talent. I was sixteen years old when I first met Zona Gale, in the early summer of 1925. Her name is remembered by older people, but I don't know if anybody reads her. She was sufficiently famous then. Her play *Miss Lula Bett* had won the Pulitzer Prize, and if you picked up a magazine there was a very good chance you'd find a story of hers in it.

I had a job working on a farm ten miles outside of Portage, Wisconsin. I went to Portage by train, from Chicago, and was met at the station by a young woman in her twenties, the daughter of Mrs. Green, who owned the farm. They were not ordinary people—that is to say, they were not farmers, and when I came to read *The Cherry Orchard* many years later I found people who were somewhat like them. The young woman had a box of strawberries that she wanted to leave for Miss Gale's father, and so we stopped at her house by the Fox River. While she talked to the old man, who sat in a chair, with a shawl over his knees, Miss Gale talked to me. I remember her showing me a Hiroshige print of some men walking in the rain, and a parchment lampshade with cutouts and explaining that they were of mystical significance. She also—and it is the one thing that always makes an adolescent's head swim—treated me as an intellectual equal. There was thirty-four years' difference in our ages, and I was by no means her intellectual equal. I had just finished my junior year in high school.

The next day, while I was pulling weeds in the vegetable garden, I heard the telephone ring. A few minutes later, Mrs. Green came out on the porch of the farmhouse and called to me. "That was Miss Gale. She wants me to come to dinner on Wednesday, and bring the little Maxwell." It was one of the best days of my life.

My visits to Zona Gale fell into a pattern. Some member of the Green family would let me off at her house and then go on about the family shopping. I came to talk and we talked. Her voice was both sad and humorous at the same time. Suddenly the car would be waiting at the curb, and it would be time for me to go. I had been immeasurably enriched, in ways I didn't even try to understand. I said goodby on the front steps and at that moment a curtain came down over my mind and I could not to save my life have told anybody what happened inside that house or even what we talked about. In later years I used to wonder uneasily if what we talked about was me, but I don't think this was so.

It was understood that I would make something of my life, but meanwhile it was life—the secret nature of all the things that were something more than they appeared to be—that's what she talked to me about. She showed me letters from writers—a note from Elinor Wylie, a letter from AE, etc. These were talismans.

I remember her telling me once that she had stayed up all night hoping to hear that there had been a stay of the execution of Sacco and Vanzetti. I was brought up in a Republican household and had heard their names, but knew nothing about the trial and was a little surprised that she cared so much about them. I went back to that farm, on and off, for the next twelve years. When I was there I went to see her. And when I was away at school I wrote to her, and she answered my letters, never predictably. A letter would come down out of the sky, like a snowflake. Once she wrote from Japan, to say that she had been the guest of honor at a dinner party and after dinner, for entertainment of the guests, five hundred fireflies were released in the garden. When I was at college at Urbana, Illinois, she came there to lecture and she had a supper party for my friends in the upstairs dining room of a Chinese restaurant. My friends took her simply as a visitation. Which is what she was. I don't know which of the nine orders of angels she belonged to—was she a power, a dominion, a principality, an archangel? All I know is that when I was with her I had her undivided angelic attention. When I wrote a novel I took it to her, not to find out if it was any good but to find out whether it was a novel. But she had had trouble sleeping, and had stayed up all night reading it, and at four o'clock had gone downstairs to her study, looking for the last chapter. Oh no, I said, that is the last chapter. That's all there is. She didn't argue with me, but when I read the book twenty years later I suddenly saw it had not ended properly. I even saw the chapter she had gone downstairs looking for at four o'clock in the morning.

Later on, I wrote a three-act play, and when I finished it I got a book of plays out of the library and compared mine with those in the book, and I saw that it wasn't nearly long enough. So I made it long enough. She read the play as she had read the novel, and this time, sitting in a window seat of her study, she put her finger on every line that I had added and said they must come out. She said nothing against the play, but when I woke up the next morning I was aware of something missing, and it was her praise. As an editor I have often wished I knew how she managed that trick. So I put the manuscript in a drawer and never looked at it again.

I saw her in Portage and I saw her away from Portage. When I was a graduate student at Harvard she took me to dinner in a restaurant and carried me off afterward to an informal meeting where she spoke to a group of young people about writing. What I remember is that an over-serious young man stood up and said, after she had finished speaking—he meant no offense: he was speaking as one writer to another—"Miss Gale, when you read something that you have written are you ever ashamed of it?" And she smiled mischievously and said, "Not as often as I should be."

In the early 1930s I came to New York and was living in the railroad men's YMCA on 49th Street, looking for a job during a period when there weren't any, and I got a telegram from her, which read, "Meet me at six o'clock this evening and wear your tux." The telegram arrived at two o'clock. It didn't say where I was to meet her, and neither did I have my tuxedo with me in the railroad men's YMCA. But at six o'clock I was there, at the Gotham Hotel, at the right place, and in a tuxedo, and we went to dinner at Brock Pemberton's and then on to the second night of Eugene O'Neill's *Ah Wilderness*.

When I got a full-time job in the art department at the *New Yorker*, to my surprise she was distressed. "But you won't have any time to write," she said. She was as correct about that as she was about the play. Within four years I had stopped writing entirely.

I do not understand why Zona Gale's books are not read today. Some of them are very good indeed. And what she was concerned about is what young people now—the young—are concerned about: an order of existence that is not grounded in materialism. Perhaps it is because she was gentle and vague and not sufficiently didactic. She suggested spiritual possibilities, rather than laying down rules. In her concern that life should be proved to be something more than people believe it to be, for example, she believed that the machine would somehow make possible a spiritual breakthrough; she was—or so it seems to me—about some things credulous. In Portage there was a quack named Dr. Lohr, who had a machine, a chair—I know it is incredible, but I am not making this up—and you were strapped into it, in a sort of barber's apron, and then lights flashed on the machine indicating kidney stones, or gall bladder, or heart trouble or whatever. She not only went to him, she sent other unfortunate people to him. I don't know whether the machine diagnosed double pneumonia in December of 1938, but anyway that's what she had and when she was moved to a hospital in Chicago, it was much too late.

At her funeral three Indian women stood outside the church during the service. I have no idea how many people enjoyed her undivided attention. I would think hundreds.

Only once in those thirteen years did she ever talk openly about herself. We were sitting in the garden, with the leaves coming down around us. It was after the death, in childbirth, of a writer named Marjorie Latimer, whom she had loved very much, and with a kind of amazement I realized that I was being taken into her confidence, and treated as a grownup, and as a friend. It was the only time I ever came close to knowing her. Though I called her by her first name, I never hugged or kissed her. We never even shook hands. The contact was merely entirely between my eyes and her eyes, which drew me on, into the world of powers, dominions, principalities, and archangels, into a life that is something more than we believed it to be.

Remarks on Receiving Honorary Doctorate, University of Illinois at Urbana-Champaign

William Maxwell/1973

From the Archives, University of Illinois at Urbana-Champaign. Reprinted by permission of the University of Illinois.

W. H. Auden once remarked that nobody ever wrote a novel without giving himself away. What the novelist gives away, among other secrets, is his attachment to a particular place. Though I have lived in New York City for nearly forty years, when I sit down at the typewriter and begin to write, it is nearly always about Illinois.

I have no choice, really. Other places do not have the same hold on my imagination.

I am very moved by the high honor the University has bestowed on me—how could I not be, when what it amounts to, in the logic of emotions, is that the place where I belong has laid formal claim to me.

CA Interviews the Author

Jean W. Ross/1979

From *Contemporary Authors*, vol. 93–96, 347–48. Detroit: Gale, 1980. Reprinted by permission.

William Maxwell was interviewed by phone at his home in New York City on April 13, 1979.

CA: How did you become a part of the *New Yorker* staff in 1936?

MAXWELL: I had one book published, and my publisher gave me three letters—one to the *New Republic*, one to *Time*, and one to the *New Yorker*. I was unsuited for the *New Republic* because I was politically uninformed. I don't know if I was unsuited to *Time* as well; I got to the *New Yorker* before I got to *Time*, and they hired me, and that was that. There was a vacancy in the art department, and I found myself sitting in at the weekly art meeting, and on the following day I would tell the artists whether or not their work had been bought, and any changes in their drawings that the meeting wanted. Technically, I guess I was an assistant to Rea Irvin, the art director, who lived in the country and only came to town for the art meeting, but the *New Yorker* has no masthead, and I never asked what I was.

CA: You have primarily been fiction editor for the *New Yorker*?

MAXWELL: I was a fiction editor—one of, usually, six or seven; I was never the head of the fiction department. I retired from the *New Yorker* three years ago, after roughly forty years. Most of the time, I worked only two or three days a week so that I would have the rest of the week for writing.

CA: As fiction editor, you must have had to deal with a great many manuscripts from unknown or unpublished writers. How did you manage it?

MAXWELL: The usual way: I would read them quickly for signs of talent. When there were such signs I would put the manuscript aside and read it again later, carefully. One of the best of all the *New Yorker*'s fiction writers turned up for the first time in that pile, but she was discovered by Mildred Wood, not by me.

CA: Brendan Gill has said there has never been a conscious *New Yorker* style. Do you agree?

MAXWELL: I do, definitely. *New Yorker* editors tend to cut out unnecessary words and to punctuate according to the house rules, and most often the prose advances sentence by sentence in its effects, rather than by paragraphs in which any given sentence may not carry that much weight. The result is a certain density that may appear to be a "style." But when you consider the fiction writers who have appeared frequently in the magazine, for example, John Updike, John Cheever, John O'Hara, Vladimir Nabokov, Mary McCarthy, Mavis Gallant, Sylvia Townsend Warner, Shirley Hazzard, Eudora Welty, J. D. Salinger, Frank O'Connor, Maeve Brennan, and Larry Woiwode—it is immediately apparent that there is no style common to all of them.

CA: Gill has also commented on the amount of work you did behind the scenes to turn out good finished stories from manuscripts. Was there a lot to be done?

MAXWELL: Some manuscripts arrive in a virtually perfect state; others require a certain amount of cutting and clarifying—in short, editing.

CA: What writers have you been instrumental in developing?

MAXWELL: I'd rather not answer that question. I'm not sure I know, anyway. If a writer continues to grow in stature, it is because he has put everything he has into his work, and not because an outsider has been steering him in the right direction. Most writers could do with a little appreciation, though. An editor can offer that.

CA: How was your association with O'Hara?

MAXWELL: Agreeable. He was a fine writer, and my dealings with him were always very pleasant.

CA: What about Cheever?

MAXWELL: What about him? He's a marvel, isn't he?

CA: Behind the scenes, has the magazine undergone many changes?

MAXWELL: American fiction has undergone so many changes and these have been reflected in the magazine as changes in length, in subject matter, in technique, in language. Essentially, with fiction at least, a magazine has no choice but to go the way its most talented contributors are going. Anything else would probably be highly destructive.

CA: Were you writing in your undergraduate days at the University of Illinois?

MAXWELL: I was writing poetry.

CA: What influenced you to become a writer?

MAXWELL: Well, I suppose I always had my nose in a book, from an early age. I also met certain people—the Wisconsin novelist and playwright Zona Gale, and the poet Robert Fitzgerald, who was a Harvard undergraduate when I went there for an M.A.—who set fires blazing in my mind. I was lucky in my teachers. Lucky generally.

CA: Do you still write poetry?

MAXWELL: No, I gave up poetry. I realized I wasn't a poet. All the true poets I have ever known agreed that it is given to them in that it comes from a source outside themselves. Prose is, on the contrary, something you work at until it achieves the effects you want it to achieve.

CA: You've written many stories—"fables"—in fairy-tale form.

MAXWELL: I've also published a volume of stories that are not in this form, but the ones you are referring to are half-fable, half-fairy tale.

CA: Does your fondness for this genre go back to childhood reading?

MAXWELL: It probably does.

CA: In the *New York Review of Books*, the person reviewing *The Old Man at the Railroad Crossing* (1966), discusses the combination of this form with your concern for contemporary issues and calls the result "something midway between the Brothers Grimm and Kafka, with perhaps a touch of Zen." Do you like this description?

MAXWELL: Well, at least it places me in good company.

CA: Much of your writing—the novels especially—shows a great pride in your Midwestern heritage, unlike the satire in some of the earlier Midwestern writers. Would you comment on that?

MAXWELL: I grew up in the Midwest; I think and speak as a Midwesterner. I've lived in New York City most of my adult life, and I like it here, but I still think of myself as a Midwesterner.

CA: Are the experiences of living in New York City heightened by contact with your Midwestern background?

MAXWELL: No. I'm afraid I've tried to create a small-town life in the middle of a great city.

CA: Do you see any trends in fiction today?

MAXWELL: I don't think about it. I just enjoy reading.

CA: Unlike the *New Yorker*, many good magazines haven't been able to stay in business. What do you attribute this to?

MAXWELL: Postal rates have gone up tremendously over the years. The very thing the government should subsidize is instead being penalized out of existence. It's lamentable.

CA: What do you think is the future of magazines?

MAXWELL: Oh, I'm no good at predicting the future. Some people can do it, unusually thoughtful people, perhaps, but I'm not one of them.

PW Interviews William Maxwell

Robert Dahlin/1979

From *Publishers Weekly*, 10 December 1979, 8–9. Reprinted by permission.

"As I get older," says the novelist, "I stick more and more to what happened. It's not shallow. You can count on it having some meaning."

Properly attired in jacket and tie, William Maxwell guides the way through a sprawling apartment on New York's Upper East Side where the seventy-one-year-old writer lives with his wife of thirty-four years. He reaches a small undistinguished room at the back, his office.

"Do you prefer sitting at a desk, or would you rather that chair?" he asks pointing to a wooden-armed easy chair. Knowing that Knopf's imminent publication of *So Long, See You Tomorrow* prompts this interview, he says, "There's a lapboard at the side, if you want it."

Turning the straight chair at the desk to face his guest, he sits, crosses his arms and waits expectantly for the conversation to begin. When Maxwell responds to a question about his writing and his career at the *New Yorker*, he speaks affably in an earnest, quiet voice.

Maxwell worked first in the magazine's art department, then in fiction under Katharine White. "I quit art when they taught me to edit," he says. Actually, Maxwell concedes, he learned editing by doing it. "Wolcott Gibbs gave me a story to edit, and I didn't really know what to do, so I just cut out what I didn't like."

Some people smile from the mouth, others with the eyes. Maxwell's smile brings a rush of gleeful light to his entire face.

"An editor," Maxwell explains after the smile subsides, "is someone who understands what a person is after, who can help by taking out the dead parts." He thinks back over the years, and says, "I've had a passionate pleasure in other people's work." An exclamation with a decided emphasis on the emotive adjective.

26

After Katharine White left the magazine, Maxwell became one of seven fiction specialists at the *New Yorker*. "It was a peaceable kingdom working under Mr. Shawn," he says. (William Shawn has been editor of the magazine since 1952.) "All of us had our own authors, and we all consulted with one another. There was great freedom. You can imagine how pleasant that was."

Maxwell retired three years ago after a forty-year editing career at the *New Yorker*.

About himself, he says, "I'm a slow writer." In fact, *So Long, See You Tomorrow* is his first novel in eighteen years. Engaged in smoothing the wrinkles in others' short fiction, he wrote only short fiction himself during that time, save for *Ancestors*, a factual, book-length account of his forebears.

"I revise, revise, and revise so much, that by the time I've finished, I'm fairly secure in what I've done," he says. "When it came time to go through the novel for the last time, when all the material was there, it was a matter of sticking to the tone, taking out what was pokey and slow. Doing that is rapture."

Maxwell finds the next step in the publication process less pleasant. "I have a terror of copyeditors," he says. "I know they are working toward clarity, but a mistake can be made in the tone. The only real difficulty with this one is that I was not only using language from a particular part of the country, but also using the language of the 1920s."

As in his earlier fiction, Maxwell returns to the Illinois of his youth in *So Long, See You Tomorrow*. That long-ago Midwest, where the family is paramount, is a setting to which he is drawn.

Crossing his legs and gazing at the wall, Maxwell muses, "I think it's an unconscious choice of scene. Writers don't really choose their material. I've lived in New York since 1936, and I've written an ocean of short stories about New York, but I would never feel at ease with it in a novel. New York is so big, I wouldn't know how to come at it. In general, there is something about the Midwest, something that claims my imagination."

He considers his words before continuing. "And that time is safe. It's safe in my memory. I was treated well there. I was surrounded by people who loved me, and I suppose that is reflected in the book. I'm sure if I still lived there, I would write about the Midwest differently."

So Long, See You Tomorrow, which was written after Maxwell left the *New Yorker*, is told mostly by an older man recalling the world of his adolescence and some of the grim events that occurred then: a neighbor's adulterous affair and the murder that ensued. The son of the murderer is, in a manner of speaking, snubbed by the narrator when he unexpectedly encounters him a few years later in a Chicago school. The narrator lacks the maturity to do otherwise. In that thoughtless and unintentionally cruel act is the ache that gave rise to the novel.

In the book, Maxwell writes: "This memoir—if that's the right name for it—is a roundabout futile way of making amends."

During the conversation, he says, "I didn't realize I was going to write this, but one day I remembered that meeting in the school corridor, and I winced. Literally winced. I said to myself, 'There is something here that has to be looked into.'"

The look produced the soon-to-be-published novel, a slim 135 pages in length.

"It's so mysterious," he acknowledges. "I knew that it would be so many pages long, even though I didn't know just what the material would be. Oh, I did write a full-length novel, one much longer, but most of it went into the wastebasket. I cut and cut and cut until it moved like a rocking horse." Maxwell holds up his hand and tilts it back and forth. "A steady pace with no dull spots, nothing unnecessary."

The man shifts slightly in his chair. "I work terribly hard, so that the work doesn't show, but so that the book is a pleasure to read." He confides: "The sentences in this book were in ten places until they settled down where they are now. It's closer to the method of the lyric poet, although I'm not a poet. I work with very small things at a time and try over and over to find the proper frame for them."

A rueful smile this time: "The reader doesn't need that much work spent on him."

Maxwell doesn't harp on how much of the novel is fiction and how much not, but not all of it is based on actuality. "When I was writing about the farm," he says, "I didn't know all of that. I hadn't lived on a farm." (The adulterous couple share adjoining acres.) "I had to fall back on the storyteller that exists in all writers. He knows everything about everybody," Maxwell laughs, pleased. "He led me through."

Somewhat embarrassed by what he fears might be interpreted as a step into high-flown observation, he says, "The storyteller exists outside society. He's in the business of putting himself in other people's shoes. He must have some kind of Platonic idea of what life could or should be. The writer, of course, doesn't describe that. That remains a shadow, but there is a larger matter of reconciliation between that shadow and reality."

Pausing once more, Maxwell comments, "It occurs to me, perhaps it's essentially a maternal thing to want to make life acceptable. You know how a mother comforts a child who's come up against the world. Perhaps my writing is the ghost of my mother working through me."

In the book, Maxwell suggests: "Too many conflicting emotional interests are involved for life ever to be wholly acceptable, and possibly it is the work of the storyteller to rearrange things so that they conform to this end. In any case, in talking about the past, we lie with every breath we draw."

Today he says, "As I get older, I stick more and more to what happened. It's not shallow. You can count on it having some meaning. Events spring from causes and reach conclusions. It's life I'm trying to get at. I think plot, as such, doesn't exist in my mind. If I've accomplished a plot at all, I'm surprised. I didn't mean to. But life does deliver plot from time to time, when it feels like it."

The interview, which has long since become easy conversation, draws to an end, to the participants' expressed regret.

Maxwell walks us from the office, then stops in the living room and plucks what appears to be a piece of paper from the mantel. It's a proof of the dust jacket for *So Long, See You Tomorrow*. As the family is ballast in the past, it anchors the writer to the present. The artwork on the jacket, a youth poised with arms outstretched on an unfinished roof top, is by Brookie Maxwell, one of his two daughters.

Remarks on Receiving the William Dean Howells Medal, American Academy of Arts and Letters

William Maxwell/1980

From *Proceedings of the American Academy of Arts and Letters and the National Institute of Arts and Letters*. Second Series, No. 31. New York, 1980. Publication No. 336. [pp. 24–25] Printed with permission of the American Academy of Arts and Letters, New York City. Delivered at the Academy May 21, 1980.

Miss Welty has just slipped me an empty box. The catch was broken and she thought it would probably fall on the floor—the medal, that is—and it's been in my pocket since ten minutes after three. When Miss Welty got the Howells Medal, a stranger came up to her afterwards and asked to see it and Miss Welty obliged and the stranger promptly dropped the medal on the floor, and it cost $50.00 to have the damage repaired. There is no empty box I could prize as highly as this one, because of what it stands for and because of those writers who have had it before me.

I believe that it behooves the living, for our own sake, to keep the memory of the dead alive and vivid, and so I would remind you now of Louise Bogan, of her ravishing formal poetry and her literary criticism, so free from intellectual display and so on target. Because of her encouragement at a critical period of my life I stopped being a full-time editor and went back to writing novels and I therefore have her to thank for the fact that I am standing where I am this minute.

In a talk that she gave at New York University in the nineteen-sixties, there is a precise and moving description of the creative process. Actually, she is speaking of poets but it applies equally to every artist who, after many years of effort and apprenticeship, has at last come into his own talent. The passage concludes:

> . . . a poet can never be certain, after writing one poem, that he will ever be able to write another. Training and experience can never be completely counted on; the "breath," the "inspiration," may be gone forever. All one can do is try to remain "open" and hope to remain sincere. Openness and sincerity will protect the poet from . . . small emotion with which poetry should not, and cannot, deal, as well as from imitations of himself or others. The intervals between poems, as poets have testified down the ages, is a lonely time, but then, if the poet is lucky and in a state of grace, a new emotion forms, and a new poem begins, and all is, for the moment, well.

Novelist Preserves Youth

Gordon McKerral/1981

From *Decatur Herald and Review* (Illinois) 28 February 1981, F9. Reprinted by permission of *Decatur Herald and Review*.

"W. H. Auden once remarked that nobody ever wrote a novel without giving himself away. What the novelist gives away, among other secrets, is his attachment to a particular place," notes William K. Maxwell.

"Though I have lived in New York City for nearly forty years, when I sit down at a typewriter and begin to write, it is nearly always about Illinois."

Maxwell spoke those words at a reception for honorary degree recipients at the University of Illinois in 1973.

In 1980—after an eighteen-year hiatus—Maxwell's sixth novel, *So Long, See You Tomorrow*, was published by Alfred A. Knopf.

This 135-page quasi-autobiographical blend of fact and fiction fortifies Maxwell's 1973 statement: It's about Illinois.

"Maybe I can clarify what I meant back then," Maxwell says today. "When my imagination begins to function, it's on my life in Illinois. I left Lincoln when I was fifteen. This capsulized my youth. The way I remember Lincoln and growing up there never changed."

Maxwell was born in Lincoln in 1908. When he was fourteen, his family moved to Chicago. He returned to Central Illinois to attend the U of I, graduating in 1930.

After a year at Harvard Graduate School, he went back to Urbana and taught freshman composition. Then he turned to writing professionally.

His first novel, *Bright Center of Heaven*, was published in 1934. And in 1936 he took up a forty-year career as editor, first in the art and then in the fiction department for the *New Yorker* magazine.

He now spends most of his time writing at his home in New York.

At the center of the short novel *So Long, See You Tomorrow* is a murder that occurred in Lincoln in the early 1920s. The details were taken from the newspaper files of the Illinois State Historical Library.

Framing the story of the murder is one of two thirteen-year-old boys—Maxwell, from a middle class family and raised in town, and another, a farm boy—who become friends in the schoolyard. The two boys play together for a week or so, ending each day expecting to meet again the next day. But the murder disposes of any tomorrows they might have had together.

The novel was nominated by the National Book Critics Circle for the most distinguished novel of 1980. It was awarded the William Dean Howells Medal given by the American Academy of Arts and Letters once in five years for the most distinguished work of American fiction published during that time.

The praise given it might reflect the author's torment while writing it.

"It was hell," he says. The novel was a blend of fact and fiction—each of those specifically identified throughout the book—and the difficulty arose "because there was no model for me to use."

"It isn't common to mix reporting with a piece of fiction. I had facts about the murder, I knew how it affected me and the people I met—but I couldn't judge the feelings of other people involved, and that's where the fiction enters."

Maxwell agrees that Midwest themes are more realistic than most regional writing. But even within that realism he sees definition.

"Some realism is sordid and harsh, and some is very emotional. In my novels I deal with the emotional type. I don't go looking for the seamy side of growing up in Central Illinois because I didn't experience that. I write about what I experienced. One of the most important reasons for my writing novels is to preserve the past."

The Folded Leaf, a Maxwell novel published in 1945, dealt with a young man's experiences while attending a Midwest university (i.e. the U of I), and more recently he published *Ancestors,* an autobiographical account of his boyhood experiences in Lincoln.

Throughout his career Maxwell also has been a prolific short story writer. His stories have been printed in the annual O. Henry and Best American Short Stories collections, and in Martha Foley's *200 Years of Great American Short Stories.*

These stories also mirror Maxwell's appreciation for his Midwestern roots.

In the July 1980 issue of *Vogue* magazine, columnist Cathleen Medwick discussed Maxwell's obvious regional style. About his latest novel she said: "Maxwell's characters for the most part keep silent about their pain, and it is that American prairie silence that fills the book."

Another quality of Maxwell's style is its bareness.

Critics have described it with the words "uncluttered," "uncomplicated" and "direct." In her *Vogue* article, Ms. Medwick corralled them all: "When Maxwell tells you something, you know it's because he had to."

This style does not stem from the setting of his regional works. "There is plenty of landscape and style in Central Illinois," he says. "The visual nature of an area and sense of place are a very important part of my writing."

Writers who influenced Maxwell when he was growing up were poets: "The poetry of the age—T. S. Eliot," he says. Some of the writers who give him most pleasure now are Virginia Woolf, E. M. Forster, and Colette, and in poetry William Meredith.

Maxwell says he doesn't get back to Central Illinois very often. "What usually brings a person back home at my age is funerals."

His physical separation hasn't diluted an emotional and imaginative mixture that connects him to this area.

His feelings might best be summed up in concluding remarks at the honorary degree reception in Urbana back in 1973. He said the degree signified "that the place where I belong had laid formal claim to me."

William Maxwell: The Art of Fiction

George Plimpton and John Seabrook/1981

From the *Paris Review*, IXXI (July, 1982), 106–39. Reprinted in *Writers at Work: The Paris Review Interviews, Seventh Series*, Ed. George Plimpton. Copyright 1986 by the *Paris Review*, Inc. Reprinted by permission.

William Maxwell was interviewed in his East Side New York apartment. He wore a tie and blazer for the occasion. A tall, spare man, he sat on the edge of a low sofa, his knees nearly touching his chin. Twice he rose and went to the walnut bookcase, once for Virginia Woolf's *Between the Acts*, and then for Eliot's *Four Quartets*, which he studied patiently for the lines he needed. At the end of the living room, two large windows looked out on the street, eight floors below, where one could see the morning traffic, but not hear it. The spacious room was furnished austerely—two vases of flowers stood on the mantel, a piano occupied one corner. The décor did not suggest Maxwell's profession. The rapture with which he recited Eliot did.

One of his colleagues at the *New Yorker*, Brendan Gill, has supplied the following report on his friend:

"In this interview William Maxwell at one juncture urges that the subject under discussion veer away from the *New Yorker*, on the grounds that the magazine has been almost done to death, in one book or another. No doubt a book that I once wrote is one of the death-dealing volumes that Maxwell has in mind, but no matter—let me offer a brief quotation from my *Here at The New Yorker* (a title suggested, by the way, by the editor of the magazine, William Shawn; I would never have dared to propose it on my own):

One day in my office I was showing Maxwell a Roman coin that I had pur-chased at Gimbels. With thousands of similar coins, it had been buried in the sands of Egypt by Ptolemy's army paymaster, in order to keep it from falling into the hands of the rapidly approaching Caesar. Maxwell jiggled the coin in his palm. "The odds," he said, "are on objects."

True enough, but since Maxwell made the remark well over thirty years ago and since he and I are both in rude health and are evidently convinced that we have outwitted the need ever to die, we may be said to be doing not so badly, either as objects or subjects. And though Maxwell will enter history as a distinguished American author of the middle years of the twentieth century, he will also enter it in the reminiscences of many of his fellow authors as an exceptionally sympathetic and adroit editor. When I first met him, forty-five years ago, he was serving as Katharine White's assistant, but he looked so young and so readily abashable that I mistook him for an office-boy. I was right about his being young; I was wrong about his being abashable. He has a gentle voice to match his seemingly gentle heart, and yet I was to discover that on some level of his being he is as tough as nails. Maxwell said once of Shawn that he combines the best features of Napoleon and Saint Francis of Assisi; it is often the case when one makes such a comment about an associate that it will prove, at bottom, autobiographical. Unlike Shawn, Maxwell has been a joiner of organizations and has been happy in the acceptance of honors from the hands of his peers; at the same time, he is a loner. If he is a clubman, he is a clubman who eats and drinks by himself. Dr. Johnson would have stared askance at him, not in the least to Maxwell's dismay.

Over the years, how much Maxwell taught me about the art that I was trying to master and that was forever turning out to be more difficult than I had expected! How reluctant he was to reject a piece until every means of salvaging it had been explored! For a long time, Maxwell and I occupied adjoining offices in the squalid rabbit-warren of the *New Yorker*; now and again in those days I would hear the faint, mouse-in-the-wainscot rustle of a note being slipped under my door. Opening the note, I would encounter five or six hastily typed words from Maxwell, in praise of something I had written. Snobbish as it is sure to sound, at the *New Yorker* we write not so much for readers out in the world as for one another, and it has always been for Shawn and Maxwell and Mitchell and Hamburger and the rest of my colleagues that I have written; on the occasions when a note from Maxwell appeared under my door, I felt ten feet tall and befuddled with joy."

Interviewers: *So Long, See You Tomorrow* comes nineteen years after your previous novel. Why this gap?

Maxwell: Nothing but being an editor probably, and working on other people's work. Which interested me very much. I had marvelous writers to work with. Quite a lot of me was satisfied just to be working with what they wrote. Besides, I write terribly slowly. The story "Over by the River" was started when the children were small and my older daughter was twenty when I finished it—it took over ten years. Undoubtedly if I knew exactly what I was doing, things would go faster, but if I saw the whole unwritten novel stretching out before me, chapter by chapter, like a landscape, I know I would put it aside in favor of something more uncertain—material that had a natural form that it was up to me to discover. So I never work from an outline. In 1948 we came home from France and I walked into the house, sat down at the typewriter with my hat still on my head, and wrote a page, a sort of rough statement of the book I meant to write, which I then thumbtacked to a shelf and didn't look at again until it was finished. To my surprise everything I had managed to do in the novel was on that page. But in general the thing creeps along slowly, like a mole in the dark.

With *So Long, See You Tomorrow* I felt that in this century the first-person narrator has to be a character and not just a narrative device. So I used myself as the "I" and the result was two stories, my own and Cletus Smith's, and I knew they had to be structurally combined, but how? One day I was in our house in Westchester County, and I was sitting on the side of the bed putting my shoes on, half stupefied after a nap and thinking, If I sit on the edge of the bed I will ruin the mattress, when my attention was caught by a book. I opened it and read part of a long letter from Giacometti to Matisse describing how he came to do a certain piece of sculpture—*Palace at 4 A.M.*—it's in the Museum of Modern Art—and I said, "There's my novel!" It was as simple as that. But I didn't know until that moment whether the book would work out or not.

Interviewers: Much of your work seems to some extent autobiographical. Is autobiography just the raw material for fiction, or does it have a place in a novel or a story as a finished product?
Maxwell: True autobiography is very different from anything I've ever written. Edmund Gosse's *Father and Son* has a candor which comes from the intention of the writer to hand over his life. If the writer is really candid then it's good autobiography, and if he's not, then it's nothing at all. I don't feel that my stories, though they may appear to be autobiographical, represent an intention to hand over the whole of my life. They are fragments in which I

am a character along with all the others. They're written from a considerable distance. I never feel exposed by them in any way.

As I get older I put more trust in what happened, which has a profound meaning if you can get at it. But what you invent is important, too. Flaubert said that whatever you invent is true, even though you may not understand what the truth of it is.

When I reread *The Folded Leaf*, the parts I invented seem so real to me that I have quite a lot of trouble convincing myself they never actually happened.

Interviewers: How do you apply that to character? What is the process involved in making a real person into a fictional one?

Maxwell: In *The Folded Leaf*, the man who owned the antique shop bore a considerable resemblance to John Mosher, who was the movie critic at the *New Yorker*. He was a terribly amusing man whom I was very fond of. Nothing that John ever said is in that book, but I felt a certain security at the beginning in the identification. Then I forgot about Mosher entirely, because the person in the book sprang to life. I knew what he would do in a given situation, and what he would say . . . that sudden confidence that makes the characters suddenly belong to you, and not just be borrowed from real life. Then you reach a further point where the character doesn't belong to you any longer, because he's taken off; there's nothing you can do but put down what he does and says. That's the best of all.

Interviewers: Virginia Woolf was an influence in your early work, wasn't she?

Maxwell: Oh, yes. She's there. Everybody's there. My first novel, *Bright Center of Heaven*, is a compendium of all the writers I loved and admired. In a symposium at Smith College, Saul Bellow said something that describes it to perfection. He said, "A writer is a reader who is moved to emulation." What I wrote when I was very young had some of the characteristic qualities of every writer I had any feeling for. It takes a while before that admiration sinks back and becomes unconscious. The writers stay with you for the rest of your life. But at least they don't intrude and become visible to the reader.

Interviewers: Well, all young writers have to come to terms with their literary fathers and mothers.

Maxwell: And think what *To the Lighthouse* meant to me, how close Mrs. Ramsay is to my own idea of my mother . . . both of them gone, both leaving the family unable to navigate very well. It couldn't have failed to have a profound effect on me.

Interviewers: What exactly is the force that makes you a writer?

Maxwell: Your question reminds me of something. I was having lunch with Pete Lemay, who was the publicity director at Knopf and is now a playwright, and he said that he had known Willa Cather when he was a young man. I asked what she was like and he told me at some length. It wasn't what I had assumed and because I was surprised I said, "Whatever made her a writer, do you suppose?" and he said, "Why, what makes anyone a writer—deprivation, of course." And then he begged my pardon. But I do think it's deprivation that makes people writers, if they have it in them to be a writer. With *Ancestors* I thought I was writing an account of my Campbellite forebears and the deprivation didn't even show up in the first draft, but the high point of the book emotionally turned out to be the two chapters dealing with our family life before and after my mother's death in the Spanish flu epidemic of 1918. I had written about this before, in *They Came Like Swallows* and again in *The Folded Leaf*, where it is fictionalized out of recognition, but there was always something untold, something I remembered from that time. I meant *So Long, See You Tomorrow* to be the story of somebody else's tragedy but the narrative weight is evenly distributed between the rifle shot on the first page and my mother's absence. Now I have nothing more to say about the death of my mother, I think, forever. But it was a motivating force in four books. If my mother turns up again I will be astonished. I may even tell her to go away. But I do not think it will be necessary.

Interviewers: But to what extent can writing recover what you lose in life?

Maxwell: If you get it all down there's a serenity that is marvelous. I don't mean just getting the facts down, but the degree of imagination you bring to it. Autobiography is simply the facts, but imagination is the landscape in which the facts take place, and the way that everything moves. When I went to France the first time I promptly fell in love with it. I was forty years old. My wife had been there as a child, and we were always looking for two things she remembered but didn't know where they were—a church at the end of a streetcar line and a chateau with a green lawn in front of it. We came home after four months because our money ran out. I couldn't bear not to be there, and so I began to write a novel about it. And for ten years I lived perfectly happily in France, remembering every town we passed through, every street we were ever on, everything that ever happened, including the weather. Of course, I was faced with the extremely difficult problem of how all this self-indulgence could be made into a novel.

Interviewers: Do you have an ideal reader in mind when you write? I've heard it said that a writer writes for himself and strangers.
Maxwell: I think I write for myself, and I'm astonished that strangers are moved by it. I know that nobody else's praise or approval is enough for me to say, "All right, I don't have to worry about it any more" . . . I have to be satisfied myself that there is nothing more I can do to make it better.

Interviewers: But you must imagine readers.
Maxwell: Oh yes, of course. While I'm writing I think I would like so-and-so to read this; but so-and-so changes from time to time, according to what I'm writing.

Interviewers: Will you talk about something while you're working on it?
Maxwell: Oh, no, that would be a serious mistake.

Interviewers: Why?
Maxwell: Because more often than not the writer who talks about something he's working on talks it right out of existence.

Interviewers: Let's go back to what you were saying about re-creating experiences in your fiction. What about writing that comes entirely from the imagination?
Maxwell: I would love to be able to do that. Just open the door and invite everybody in.

Interviewers: Have you ever tried?
Maxwell: I've tried in shorter things, in those tales that are neither fables nor fairy tales. I just hang over the typewriter waiting to see what is going to happen. It begins with the very first sentence. I don't will the sentence to come; I wait, as actively passive as I can possibly be. For some reason the phrase "Once upon a time" seems to be essential. Then, if I am sufficiently trusting, the rest of the story follows, and the last sentence is straight from the first. I also did it, to a considerable extent, in *Time Will Darken It*.

Interviewers: But would you suggest that would-be writers wait for something to drop into their heads? Isn't this a refutation of the theory that writing is ninety percent perspiration and ten percent inspiration?

Maxwell: If they just sat and waited, maybe nothing would happen. Maybe they'd fall asleep. I think they should read—to learn how it is done—writing, I mean—and in the hope that what they read will in some way make their own experience available to them.

Interviewers: Do your best sentences come from on high, or are they the product of much working and reworking?

Maxwell: There's something in the *Four Quartets* about language that doesn't disintegrate. That's what I try to do—write sentences that won't be like sand castles. I've gotten to the point where I seem to recognize a good sentence when I've written it on the typewriter. Often it's surrounded by junk. So I'm extremely careful. If a good sentence occurs in an otherwise boring paragraph, I cut it out, rubber-cement it to a sheet of typewriter paper, and put it in a folder. It's just like catching a fish in a creek. I pull out a sentence and slip a line through the gills and put it on a chain and am very careful not to mislay it. Sometimes I try that sentence in ten different places until finally it finds the place where it will stay—where the surrounding sentences attach themselves to it and it becomes part of them. In the end what I write is almost entirely made up of those sentences, which is why what I write now is so short. They come one by one, and sometimes in dubious company. Those sentences that are really valuable are mysterious—perhaps they come from another place, the way lyric poetry comes from another place. They come from some kind of unconscious foreknowledge of what you are going to do. Because when you find the place where a sentence finally belongs it is utterly final in a way you had no way of knowing: it depends on a thing you hadn't written. When I wrote those fables and sat with my head over the typewriter waiting patiently, empty as a bucket that somebody's turned upside down, I was waiting for a story to come from what you could call my unconscious. Or it could be from the general unconscious. Often before poets write a poem they begin to hear the cadences of it, and then they begin to hear humming in their ears, and there are other strange manifestations, and then finally words. The last is the words.

Interviewers: Are story writing and novel writing two vastly different enterprises?

Maxwell: When I'm writing a novel, there's a sense that I have something more important by the tail; the reason for writing the novel is often that I don't know exactly what I do have. Sometimes I'm sustained by a metaphor or an image. In *The Folded Leaf,* I knew that the suicide attempt was the climactic part of the novel but I didn't know how I was going to get there; the image that sustained me throughout the whole of the writing was that of walking across a very flat landscape toward the mountains; when I got to the mountains the necessary scenes would occur. In *They Came Like Swallows,* I felt the book had to be like a stone cast into a pond. And a second stone, and a third—with the ripples moving outward from inside the first ones but never overtaking them.

Interviewers: How do you know when it's time to write another novel? Is it some sort of instinctual act, like the impulse that impels birds to migrate?

Maxwell: I expect to live forever, and therefore I never get worried about what I ought to be writing, or about anything undone. In the case of *So Long, See You Tomorrow*, I was sitting at my desk, and something made me think of that boy I had failed to speak to, and thinking of him I winced. I saw myself wincing and I thought, "That's very odd indeed that after all these years you should have a response so acute; maybe that's worth investigating." And so that's what I set out to do.

Interviewers: You wrote somewhere that *So Long, See You Tomorrow* was a futile way of making amends. Was it really futile? Can't fiction make amends for real life?

Maxwell: Forgiveness is in the hands of the injured, not the injurer. I don't know. Would you forgive me?

Interviewers: I would, sure.

Maxwell: Well that's comforting.

Interviewers: You said that your mother's death made you a novelist. When did you first start writing?

Maxwell: I sometimes think that children, without knowing it, are projected into the unlived lives of their parents. My mother's sister told me that when my mother was twelve years old she used to go up into the attic and "write on her novel." So perhaps I am a projection of my mother's unlived literary life. When I first began to write I was a freshman in a small-town high school. I wrote a story about an aristocrat during the French Revolution who hid in a clock. If there were any French aristocrats in central Illinois in my boyhood I didn't know them. But at least we had a grandfather's clock in the front hall. Then we moved to Chicago and I wrote a little for the high school magazine. In college I began to write poetry. I'm not a poet, though. I've never written anything that comes from the place poetry comes from.

Interviewers: Is it a different place?

Maxwell: When I was at Harvard I got to know Robert Fitzgerald, and I used to show my poems to him. In spite of the fact that I was older than he was—I was a graduate student and he was a sophomore—I had enormous respect for him. He was better educated than I was, and intransigent, and he despised anything that wasn't first rate. One day he looked at my poem and then he looked at me, rather in the way you look at children who present a problem, and he said, "Why don't you write prose?" I was so happy that he thought I could write anything that I just turned to and wrote prose—as if he'd given me permission to try. The prose took the form of fiction because I do like stories and don't have a very firm grasp on ideas.

Interviewers: How long was it after you began to write prose that you became sure you would be a writer?

Maxwell: Oh, it began in pure pleasure. I left Harvard and went back to Urbana, and was rooming in the house of a woman who was teaching at the University of Illinois. A professor at Yale, a friend of hers, was doing a series of biographical essays; he sent her a two-volume life of Thomas Coke of Holkham—Coke introduced in Parliament the bill to recognize the American colonies, and was also an important agriculturist—and asked her to do a forty-page condensation that he could work from, and she split the job with me. She wanted to save me from becoming an English professor. I was then twenty-three. She let me have all the big scenes and she concentrated on the agriculture, which she said interested her. It did not interest me. The book was full of interesting people—for example, Lady Mary Coke, who was Coke of Holkham's aunt. She dressed her footmen in pea-green and silver livery and suffered from the delusion that the Empress Maria Teresa was trying to take her servants away from her. When she was depressed she would fish for goldfish in the ornamental pond in front of her house. And in her old age she slept in a dresser drawer. Anyway, I had so much pleasure in working with this material that I began to write my first novel, *Bright Center of*

Heaven, because I didn't want the pleasure to end. Writing fiction was, and still is, pure pleasure. Oh, I ran out of steam from time to time. After I got to the *New Yorker*, particularly when I was working five days a week and seeing both artists and writers, I wrote less and less and almost stopped writing altogether. But then I quit the *New Yorker* in order to write. It was a genuine parting; I left fully intending never to return. But something always brought me back. I never came back five days a week, though. If I hadn't worked at the *New Yorker* there might have been more books, but I'm not sure if they would have been as good. Writing part-time forced me to write slowly, and I think I was more careful. I write much more slowly now than I used to.

Interviewers: Why? What does age do to a writer?

Maxwell: I think it makes you more serious. It makes you more aware of other people's lives. You see more from the inside: the troubles, the sorrow, and the unfairness. And then when you accept the idea that life is good, no matter how unlucky you are, you get a firmer insight into it.

Interviewers: What about your schedule: When do you work?

Maxwell: Well, I don't want to be uncooperative, but are you sure you want to ask that?

Interviewers: It *is* sort of a boring question.

Maxwell: If you have any reason in the world for wanting to know, I'll tell you. . . I like to work in my bathrobe and pajamas, after breakfast, until I suddenly perceive, from what's on the page in the typewriter, that I've lost my judgment. And then I stop. It's usually about twelve-thirty. But I hate getting dressed. The cleaning woman, who may not approve of it, though she's never said, my family, the elevator men, the delivery boy from Gristede's—all of them are used to seeing me in this unkempt condition. What it means to me is probably symbolic—you can have me after I've got my trousers on, but not before. When I retired from the *New Yorker* they offered me an office, which was very generous of them because they're shy on space, but I thought, "What would I do with an office at the *New Yorker*? I would have to put my trousers on and ride the subway downtown to my typewriter. No good."

Interviewers: Maybe once you got there you could strip down.

Maxwell: I don't think it would work. It isn't the same as going straight from the breakfast table.

Interviewers: Do you find certain environments more conducive to good work than others?

Maxwell: I'm just as able to work on Cape Cod as here in New York or in Westchester. I prefer small messy rooms that don't look out on anything interesting. I wrote the last two sections of *They Came Like Swallows* beside a window looking out on a tin roof. It was perfect. The roof was so boring it instantly drove me back to my typewriter.

Interviewers: Do you isolate yourself totally when you're working?

Maxwell: I don't mind interruptions, unless there are terribly many of them. When the children were small, they came and sat on my lap and punched the keys as I did, but they soon lost interest. My younger daughter told me recently that when she was a child she thought the typewriter was a toy that I went into my room and closed the door and played with. Once when I was typing with great concentration she touched one of the releases, and the carriage shot out from under me. I roared at her, and she went and knelt like an Arab under the dining room table, with her face against the floor, and would not accept the apology that I, also kneeling like an Arab, with my face next to hers, sincerely offered. In general I don't mind domestic sounds. I find them reassuring.

Interviewers: Do you keep a notebook?

Maxwell: No, I never have. I like the insecurity and the danger of not keeping a notebook. I've tried writing notes down on file cards, but I find I never look at them again.

Interviewers: Do you think there's such a thing as writer's block?

Maxwell: There's such a thing as loss of confidence.

Interviewers: Have you ever experienced it?

Maxwell: I've come close. There was a period after I left the *New Yorker* for the first time, when I thought I knew enough about writing stories to be able to make a living by it, but it turned out that every idea I had for a story was in some way too close to home. The stories I did write weren't bought. I began to feel that my hands were tied. I guess, though, I have always believed that if the material interested me enough to want to write about it, then it was all right; it wouldn't go away and so I should just keep working on it. Updike said once, riding in a taxi—he was talking about the reviewers, who had been scolding him for not writing what they thought he ought to be writing—"All I have to go on," he said, "is something I caught a glimpse of out of the corner of my eye." That seemed a very nice way of describing the way material comes to you. That glimpse, it's all you have. I don't think a writer's block is anything more than a loss of confidence. It certainly isn't a loss of talent.

Interviewers: Do you find it gets easier or hard to write as you get older?
Maxwell: I think it's easier when you are young. My first novel was written [at Bonnie Oaks]. Very Chekhovian, that farm was. I wrote in a room that had been converted from a water tank next to the windmill. Some of the characters were derived from people living on the farm at the time, so it was a handy place to be. I would come for lunch and they would make remarks I had put in their mouths that morning. Which wasn't really mysterious, because if you are conscious of character—in the other sense of the word—you can't help being struck by how consistent people are in everything they do and say. I finished the book in four months, with the help of Virginia Woolf, W. B. Yeats, Elinor Wylie, and a girl on the farm who was also writing a novel. When somebody said something good we would look at each other and one of us would say, "I spit on that," meaning, "keep your hands off of it."

The farm was ten miles out of Portage, where Zona Gale* lived. Nobody reads her now or knows who she was, even, but they did then. I had known her since I was sixteen years old. She was a kind of fairy godmother to me. I took my manuscript to her. I wanted to know if I had written a novel or not. When she gave it back to me she said that she had been unable to sleep and had read until four in the morning, and then gone downstairs to her study looking for the last chapter. I was too thickheaded to understand what she was trying to tell me, and said, "No, that's all there is." Twenty years after it was published I reread the book and saw the chapter she went downstairs looking for. The next novel was more difficult, and the novel after that was even more painful. By pain I don't mean the agony of writing, I mean the uncertainty of not knowing what you're going to do or how you're going to do it. It was awfully slow. One book took ten years, one four, and my last, though not very long, took two years.

Interviewers: When you write a novel, do you try to stick to the chronological narrative as you're writing, or do you jump around?

---

*She was a Wisconsin novelist and playwright—her *Miss Lulu Bett* won the Pulitzer Prize.

Maxwell: I don't really depart from the "and then. . . and then" of the storyteller, but if I am lucky I know what the last sentence is going to be. And sometimes I realize that a rounded-out scene early in the novel has shut the door too soon on something. So I take part of that scene away, and use it later on in the book. It is the death of a novel to write chapters that are really short stories.

Interviewers: Do you have a favorite novel?
Maxwell: I think *The Folded Leaf.* It may be for personal reasons—the whole of my youth is in it. Also, when I was working on it, in my mind's eye I kept seeing the manuscript burning in the fireplace; I was so sure nobody would be interested in it.

Interviewers: You taught for two years. Did you care much for that?
Maxwell: I liked it. I taught freshman composition. It was lovely when you found students who responded to things you were enthusiastic about. Teaching them to punctuate properly and to analyze the periodic sentences in Matthew Arnold's "Gregarious and Slavish Instincts in Animals" was something else again. But that wasn't what drove me away from teaching. What drove me away was a silly novel by Robert Nathan called *One More Spring*, about some people who went to live in a toolshed in Central Park. The gist of the book was that life is to be lived, and well, it is, of course. Anyway, that book made me restless with my prospects. I saw myself being promoted from assistant to associate to full professor, and then to professor emeritus, and finally being carried out in a wooden box. This was 1933, and only an idiot would have thrown up a job at that point. But I did anyway. And I floundered for several years.

Interviewers: Do you think the writing of fiction can be taught?
Maxwell: I expect you can be taught to write a clean, decent sentence.

Interviewers: After teaching you started editing. How did you first come to work at the *New Yorker*?
Maxwell: Do we have to go into the *New Yorker*? There have been all those books. The subject has been done to death, almost.

Interviewers: Maybe we could talk about it just a little.
Maxwell: I needed a job in order to stay in New York. Eugene Saxton at *Harper's* wrote to Katharine White about me, and she astonished him by

replying that there were not many openings at the *New Yorker* at that time, but that she would talk to me. This was 1936—the Depression—and nobody had heard of an opening anywhere in years. In the course of my interview with Mrs. White she asked me what salary I would require. Some knowledgeable acquaintance had told me I must ask for thirty-five dollars a week or I wouldn't be respected; so I swallowed hard and said, "Thirty-five dollars." Mrs. White smiled and said, "I expect you could live on less." I could have lived nicely on fifteen. A few days later I got a telegram from her asking me to report for work on the following Monday at the salary agreed upon— thirty-five dollars a week.

In those days—it is no longer true—fiction, humor, and art were handled by the same editors. The artists brought their work in on Tuesday and it was looked at by the Art Meeting on Wednesday afternoon. At the Art Meeting were Harold Ross, Mrs. White, Rea Irvin, Wolcott Gibbs (until he gave up his place), Mrs. White's secretary, who took notes of the proceedings, and an office boy named Wilbur, whose mind was on basketball. The editors sat on one side of a big table, with knitting needles. The covers and drawings were placed on a stand by Wilbur; Ross would lean forward and touch the parts of the drawing that were unsatisfactory with the end of his needle. I too had a knitting needle, which I did not use for quite some time. Occasionally Mrs. White would say that the picture might be saved if it had a better caption, and it would be returned to the artist or sent to E. B. White, who was a whiz at this. Ross would lean forward and peer at a drawing with his lower lip sticking out and say, "You can't tell who's talking." Or he would say, "Bird Rock"—a remark that mystified me until I learned that many years before this the *New Yorker* had published a drawing of a seagull standing on a rock and a man saying to another man, "They call it 'Bird Rock.'" It had become a generic term for an undesirable form of humor. A great deal of what was put before the Art Meeting was extremely unfunny. Gibbs was repelled by the whole idea of grown men using their minds in this way and seldom said anything. Rea Irvin smoked a cigar and was interested only when a drawing by Gluyas Williams appeared on the stand.

On Thursday the artists returned to find out what had happened at the Art Meeting. Someone had to convey this information to them. Gibbs felt he had been doing it long enough, and so I was taken on. It was called "seeing artists." The first time they paraded in one after another I was struck by the fact that they all looked like the people in their drawings. George Price looked like the man who floated up near the ceiling of that disreputable apartment week after week; Otto Soglow looked like his Little King. Cotton was kind and fatherly. Alajalov wore yellow kid gloves. Some artists were too important to be entrusted to me. Peter Arno and Helen Hokinson were seen by Mrs. White. I noticed that they didn't look like the characters they drew.

Interviewers: Then from the Art Meeting you graduated on to the editorial board?

Maxwell: Yes. Only it wasn't called that. I sat in a big room where the secretaries were; there wasn't even an office for me. But it was a wonderful place to be, because I was right beside the door of Katharine White's office. She moved with majestic deliberation, and between the time she got up from her desk and the time she put her foot on the catch that released her door so that it would swing shut I learned a lot about the workings of the magazine. I remember when Gibbs's parody profile of Henry Luce was going to the printer. Time-Life was in an uproar about it; there was a continuous procession of people in and out of Mrs. White's office. I sat taking in snatches of the excitement.

When the door was closed I sat and worried about how long it would take them to decide it was not worthwhile to go on paying me thirty-five dollars a week. On Mondays and Fridays I had nothing whatever to do but stare at a Thurber drawing above my desk—until Mrs. White suggested that I get the scrapbooks from the office library and read them. She also gave me a pile of rejected manuscripts and asked me to write letters to go with those that showed any promise. After she had gone over my letters she called me into her office and said, "Mr. Maxwell, have you ever taught school?" It was a fact that I had kept from her in our interview: instinct told me that it was not something you were supposed to have done. Anyway, from her I learned that it is not the work of an editor to teach writers how to write.

One day Wolcott Gibbs asked me if I'd like to try some editing. He handed me a manuscript and walked away, without explaining what he meant by editing. I didn't think much of the story, so I cut and changed things around and made it the way I thought it ought to be. To my surprise Gibbs sent it to the printer that way. And I thought, "So that's editing." The next time he gave me a piece to edit I fell on my face. I straightened out something that was mildly funny only if it wasn't too clear what was going on. Gibbs was kind, and said that my editing revealed that there wasn't very much there, but I got the point. In time I came to feel that real editing means changing as little as possible. Various editors and proofreaders would put their oar in, and sometimes I had to change hats and protect the writer from his own agreeableness, or fear, or whatever it was that made him say yes when he ought to have said no. What you hope is that if the writer reads the story ten years after it is published he will not be aware that anybody has ever touched it. But it takes many years of experience—and love—to be able to do that.

Interviewers: Why was this drawing by Thurber in front of you?
Maxwell: It was drawn right on the wall. A self-portrait. His drawings were everywhere, all over the office. There was one drawing on the nineteenth floor by the watercooler of a man walking along happy-as-anything and around the corner a woman is waiting for him with a baseball bat, ready to swing. One night some fool painter came in and painted over every last one of them. It was a tragedy. Brendan Gill talks about how difficult Thurber was. On the other hand, there's that story of the maid at the Hotel Algonquin who was straightening up his room and found, written in shaving soap on the bathroom mirror, the words "Thurber is a bastard." For that you can forgive quite a lot. Of course, what it comes down to in the end is that an artist is loved for his work, not his sweet disposition.

Interviewers: What was the chemistry of working with Harold Ross? Why was it so exciting?
Maxwell: It had to do with his personality. And being taken into his confidence. People don't often strike me as being larger than life-size, but he did. He was not the unintelligent oaf he has sometimes been portrayed as being. He was clearly in command of the magazine. And he saw things through a prism of humor. I remember his telling me with amusement that his mother used to touch her hair here and there with her hand before she answered the telephone. Also, he was so decent. And, up to a point, much too trusting. It was like having a terribly funny father. He had a personal relationship with everybody in the office, including Wilbur, the office boy. Once, during a period when I had left the magazine to write a novel, I met him on 43rd Street at about one o'clock, and he said, "Maxwell, what are you doing in town?" and I said, "I came in to go to the theater." It didn't occur to me to explain that my ticket was for the evening performance. He went on to the office and told somebody, "I met Maxwell on his way to a matinee. I don't understand it. I thought only women went to matinees." He was genuinely disturbed, and didn't know whether he was under a misapprehension about matinees or about me. What he cared most about, I think, were writers—about bringing them along. So long as they didn't try to proselytize in the *New Yorker*, it didn't matter to him what their political opinions were; it was their talent that interested him. I also think he thought that people with talent didn't in

general know enough to come in out of the rain, and he was trying to hold an umbrella over them.

Interviewers: It must have bothered him terribly when those feuds began—as with O'Hara, for instance.

Maxwell: Before the feud with O'Hara, Ross worried that O'Hara would manage to get some sexual innuendo into the magazine that the editors had failed to recognize. As he once or twice did. O'Hara as a person amused Ross. Perhaps because they were all young together. O'Hara thought up the idea (based on need) that if he turned in a story and it wasn't accepted he should be paid five hundred dollars anyway. The trouble was, O'Hara could write a story a day without half trying. So instead of the five hundred, Ross went out and bought a large, inexpensive watch and had it engraved, "To John O'Hara from the *New Yorker*." I don't know how the joke went over.

Interviewers: There's a story in Brendan Gill's book about your going out to O'Hara's house to read three manuscripts he had, and your getting terribly nervous when you disliked the first two. You liked the last. Which was the one you liked?

Maxwell: "Imagine Kissing Pete." I think it is one of the best things he ever wrote. The falling-out with the *New Yorker* was over the way two of O'Hara's early novels had been reviewed in the magazine. Fadiman's review of—*Butterfield 8*, I think it was—appeared under the heading, "Disappointment in O'Hara," and the pun rankled. O'Hara was not of a forgiving disposition, and the feud lasted for years. I had no part in it whatever. It all went on over my head. Finally O'Hara sent word through St. Clair McKelway that he had finished three novelettes which the *New Yorker* could see if they would send an editor out to his house in Quogue to read them. I went. I must have been out of my mind. I mean, what if none of them had been right for the magazine? Fortunately, one was. At one point I had three wonderful writers all named John: John O'Hara, John Cheever, and John Updike.

Interviewers: Could you talk a little about editing those three? How does somebody deal with a writer as distinguished? O'Hara, to start with. He was so touchy, wasn't he?

Maxwell: Not about editing. During the first period that I edited his work I barely knew him. I inherited him from Gibbs, who had given up editing entirely to take over the theater page from Robert Benchley. I was young and inexperienced as an editor, but fortunately O'Hara had a respect for

New Yorker editing. When his stories were collected in a book, he always followed the edited version. What I worked on was mostly the "Pal Joey" series. I knew nothing whatever about Broadway argot, and sometimes now in the middle of the night I groan, thinking about what I may have done to them, especially in the way of cutting. In later years O'Hara would occasionally say no to a suggested change. In one story the words "George Carlin said" turned up every time George Carlin opened his mouth. I suggested in the margin of the galleys that it had somewhat the appearance of a mannerism, and would he consider using "he said" here and there in the story. He wrote me a long, rather preachy letter on style. *His* style.

Updike is an extreme perfectionist. His manuscripts are always cleanly written, and he usually makes a great many interesting changes on the galleys. When the page proofs were ready I would mail him a set and we would talk sometimes for an hour or two on the phone. . . mostly about whether this or that new change—his change, not mine—was for the better, or might possibly do some damage to the surrounding sentences. It was an education in how to refine language to the point where it almost becomes something else. The pure practiced effectiveness and verve of an Olympic athlete is what it often reminded me of.

Interviewers: And Cheever?
Maxwell: I don't know what service I provided for Cheever except to be delighted with his work. He brought me "The Country Husband" when I was sick in bed with bronchitis. I remember the rapture of reading it.

Interviewers: Did you show your own manuscripts to any of these three?
Maxwell: No, but I did to other *New Yorker* writers. Frank O'Connor came out to our house in the country for the day, with his wife and baby, and in the course of the conversation he extracted from me the information that I had been working for eight years on a novel I was in despair over. "Let me see it," he said, and I was appalled. I was not in the habit of mixing my two lives. At that time the manuscript of what turned out to be *The Chateau* filled a good-sized grocery carton. I hadn't been able to make up my mind whether it should have an omniscient author or a first-person narrator, whether it should be told from the point of view of the French or the Americans traveling in France. I was afraid it wasn't a novel at all but a travel diary. I told O'Connor that the manuscript was in such a shape that it was unreadable, but he assured me that he could read anything. He had been sufficiently trusting to let me see the rough draft of section after section of

An Only Child, and I didn't feel like saying that it was one thing for me to see his unfinished work and another for him to see mine. He went off with the grocery carton in the backseat of the car, and read through the whole mess. Then he wrote me a wonderful letter in which he said he didn't understand what I was up to. There seemed to be two novels—which he then proceeded to discuss, in detail, as separate works. My relief was immense, because it is a lot easier to make two novels into one than it is to make one out of nothing whatever. So I went ahead and finished the book.

I showed the next-to-final draft of *The Chateau* to Francis Steegmuller, who straightened out my wobbly French in places where corrections were called for.

Before that, at a time when I had almost stopped writing entirely, I showed what I thought was a short story to Louise Bogan, and she said it was a novel, so I kept on writing about those two characters. I sent her what I wrote, chapter by chapter, through four versions, and she never said enough is enough. From time to time I got a penny postcard from her with "v. good" or something like that on it. Once she objected to a physical description, on the ground that the writing wasn't very fresh, so I sweated over it. And another time, when I was stuck, I had a postcard from her saying, "Get that boy up off the bed on the sleeping porch." When I finished the novel she found me a title for it, from Tennyson's *The Lotos-Eaters*:

> Lo! In the middle of the wood
> The Folded Leaf is woo'd from out the bud
> With winds upon the branch. . .

I also, at times, showed my work to Harold Brodkey. I knew his first wife when she was a little girl, and shortly after they were married she brought him to our house and we became friends. During part of the time I was writing *The Folded Leaf* I was in analysis with Theodor Reik, who thought the book ought to have a positive ending. And Edward Aswell at *Harper's* thought the story would be strengthened if I combined some of the minor characters. I was so tired and so unconfident about the book that I took their word for it. Later I was sorry. And when it came out ten years later in the Vintage Press I put it back pretty much the way it was in the first place. While I was making the corrections Harold brought me a marked copy of the book. Mostly the things he objected to were ideas I had absorbed from Reik rather than arrived at from my own experience, and I either cut or rewrote those sentences. When I was working on *Ancestors* he got so interested in the structure that I showed the manuscript to him chapter by chapter, as I had with Louise Bogan. We had a running argument: what I cared about in fiction was emotion, and though he was not indifferent to emotion he thought—I hope I am quoting him correctly—that ideas mattered as much or more. They aren't, of course, mutually exclusive. But as a result of our argufying I became aware of the extra dimension that abstract thinking brings to fiction.

Now that I think of it I have always shown whatever I was working on to somebody—most often my wife, whose opinions tend to be detached and trustworthy. When I was writing *Time Will Darken It* I found that the book was proceeding by set conversations, rather like a play. A had a conversation in the backseat of the carriage with B, and as a result B had it out with C, and when C met D on the stairs she said—you get the idea. When I started a new chapter I asked myself who hadn't talked to whom lately. It's not a bad method. Anyway, when I finished a chapter I would read it to my wife, sitting outside on the grass in the sunshine, and it was like sharing news from home.

Interviewers: So you think writers are apt to be good judges of other writers' work?

Maxwell: Well Updike certainly seems to be a good judge. O'Hara was very good in his letters.

Interviewers: No professional jealousies? O'Hara, who was so competitive about his writing: if he thought for a minute you were on his level . . .

Maxwell: I don't think he thought for a minute that I was on his level, so that was no problem. No, I don't think writers are necessarily competitive. There was a period when I thought they weren't at all. Lately they have seemed more so. In any case, I felt it was important, as an editor, to play down as much as possible the fact that I also wrote. I wanted the writers I worked with to feel that nothing was more important to me than their work. And for the three days a week that I was at my desk at the *New Yorker*, nothing was.

Interviewers: Ever since the days of O'Hara, something has endured—a *New Yorker* story. Do you agree? Is there such a thing?

Maxwell: The usual answer from the magazine is no; they point out the range and variety of the fiction writers who have been published in the *New Yorker*. From Nancy Hale to Vladimir Nabokov is a very wide sweep. Irwin Shaw when he was a young man said once that in the typical *New Yorker* story everything occurs at one place in one time, and all the dialogue is beside the point. It was not, at the time, a wholly inaccurate description. That is to say, there were lots of stories like that. Something that *is* characteristic of the writers who appear in the *New Yorker* is that the sentence is the unit by which the story advances, not the paragraph, and the individual sentence therefore carries a great deal of weight and tends to be carefully constructed, with no loose ends. And style becomes very important. Gibbs said in a memo he wrote on the theory and practice of *New Yorker* editing— "If a writer has style, leave it."

Interviewers: That memo would be an extremely interesting document to have.
Maxwell: Gibbs was a wonderfully fast and expert editor. In those days *New Yorker* stories were short—twelve pages was a very long story. And he edited by cutting entire paragraphs. In some mysterious way they were not missed afterward. I never learned how to do this: instead I operated on the principle of never taking out anything I liked. After Gibbs left, the fiction began to get long, perhaps because he was not there to cut it. Or maybe it was just that the subject that could be dealt with in twelve pages had been exhausted and writers were forced to take in more territory.

Interviewers: How did editing the work of others affect your own work?
Maxwell: I expect it affected the quality of it, made it better. It could hardly hurt anybody to have to pay close attention, word by word, and sentence by sentence, to the work of writers such as those I mostly dealt with.

Interviewers: There was no chance of losing your own voice amidst theirs?
Maxwell: Well, you could just as easily *find* your voice amidst theirs. The essays of E. B. White are a great help if you are trying to use the pronoun "I" in a way that is natural and unself-conscious.

Interviewers: Could you take time off to write your novels?
Maxwell: No, not as a rule. Mostly I went on working at the office two or three days a week. It took much longer to write a novel that way, but did allow me to pick up where I had left off with a fresh view of things. Ross heard that I had been working on a novel for four years and came into my office to talk to me about it. He knew that what I was working on—it was *The Folded Leaf*—was of no conceivable use to the *New Yorker*, but he didn't like the idea of a writer having to spend such a long time over something. The

upshot of the conversation was that he sent me home for six months on full pay so I could finish my novel. When it was published and got good reviews, he was pleased. He felt he had a stake in the enterprise.

Interviewers: What a lovely story.

Maxwell: Well, he was a lovely man, and it doesn't come out in the books at all. I really loved him. And two more different people than Ross and me you could hardly conceive of. There was a story, perhaps legendary, that Mrs. White so enraged him by something she said that he picked up a telephone and threw it at her. But he never even raised his voice at me.

Interviewers: Did things change when William Shawn took over as editor-in-chief?

Maxwell: How could they not change? Gently and slowly changes have occurred. If nothing changed then the whole thing would come to an Egyptian end. Do you like Egyptian sculpture?

Interviewers: Yes. Cats.

Maxwell: My wife loves it dearly. But when we went down the Nile I was troubled by the fact that the motifs were unchanging for two thousand years—the king of Egypt holding his enemies by the hair, in temple after temple. That's what would happen if the *New Yorker* never changed—that dead quality would creep in.

Interviewers: Do you have any advice for writers trying to get published in the *New Yorker*?

Maxwell: I don't think anybody can write decent fiction and at the same time try to match the requirements of a magazine—maybe, but I don't think so. You do what your heart cries out to do. In my own case, I'm often in doubt about something I've written—and I think, well, if I like it, perhaps someone else will like it, too. That's the final criterion—whether or not the writer likes what he has written.

Interviewers: As an editor, in deciding whether or not to read a story, how much weight do you place on the first sentence?

Maxwell: A great deal. And if there is nothing promising by the end of the first page there isn't likely to be in what follows. I love first sentences, anyway. When you get to the last sentence of a novel you often find that it was implicit in the first sentence, only you didn't know what it was.

Interviewers: What are some of your favorite first lines? Do you collect them?

Maxwell: No, but offhand I think of "None of them knew the color of the sky," which is *The Open Boat* and "All the sisters lay dreaming of horses," which is "National Velvet." And the wonderful first line of *Pride and Prejudice.* "It is a truth universally acknowledged, that a single man in possession of a good fortune must be in want of a wife."

Interviewers: Do you spend a lot of time on your own first sentences? *So Long, See You Tomorrow* begins, "The gravel pit was about a mile east of town and the size of a small lake and so deep that boys under sixteen were forbidden by their parents to swim in it."

Maxwell: Originally the first sentence was, "Very few families escape disasters of one kind or another." When the *New Yorker* bought it, the editors were troubled by the fact that for the first twenty pages it read like reminiscence. A good many readers don't enjoy that sort of thing, and over the years the *New Yorker* had been blamed for publishing too much of it. Actually, if writers don't put down what they remember, all sorts of beautiful and moving experiences simply go down the drain forever. In any case, the *New Yorker* was afraid that readers, seeing also that it was very long, would stop reading before they discovered that it was really about a murder. So I moved things around a bit at the beginning.

Interviewers: That didn't bother you, to start at a different place?

Maxwell: I could see that they had a point. Of course there was a certain amount of straining at the seams—any writer would feel it—but I got past that. The effect on me was as if I were shaving and some hand came and took the razor from me and did this part of my face.

Interviewers: It's nice to be shaved sometimes.

Maxwell: And it's nice to have someone genuinely care about your work, to the point that they can do for you what you have failed to see needed doing. In my experience at the *New Yorker*, the best writers were very good-tempered about suggested changes. I can only remember one instance when the editing process broke down and the writer took back his story. Between the time that we had accepted it and the time we prepared the galleys, another story came in and was rejected, and I suspect that his anger over the galleys was really anger about the rejection. That was the only time. It's almost axiomatic—the more talented the writer, the easier he is to work with, if the editor is both sensitive and sensible.

Interviewers: Are you in the habit of writing every day?
Maxwell: Yes. Seven days a week. An insane life, but what happiness! It's really self-indulgence. I resent any social invitation that keeps me up after ten-thirty, so that I'm not bright as a dollar the next morning.

Interviewers: What if you hadn't been a writer at all?
Maxwell: I can't imagine, I really can't imagine. I would have been so deprived of everything I love if I hadn't been a writer. It would have been awful, awful.

GLR Interview: William Maxwell

Gerald C. Nemanic/1982

From *Great Lakes Review*, 9–10 (Fall 1983-Spring 1984): 1–15. Reprinted by permission.

William Maxwell was born in 1908 at Lincoln, a small town in central Illinois. His mother died in the Spanish influenza epidemic of 1918; four years thereafter Maxwell's father, who had since remarried, moved his family to the North Side of Chicago.

Maxwell attended Senn High School, and during one summer worked on a farm [Bonnie Oaks] near Portage, Wisconsin, which became a second home. There he made the acquaintance of the novelist and playwright Zona Gale. After high school, Maxwell obtained a bachelor's degree from the University of Illinois, then an M.A. in English at Harvard in 1931.

Maxwell's first novel, *Bright Center of Heaven*, was published by Harper in 1934. Two years later he joined the staff of the *New Yorker*, where he worked at first in the art department and then, under the direction of Katharine S. White, began to read and edit fiction. Over a span of forty years, until his retirement from the magazine in 1976, Maxwell worked with many distinguished writers, including John O'Hara, John Cheever, Vladimir Nabokov, Mary McCarthy, Oliver LaFarge, John Updike, Eudora Welty, Wright Morris, and Larry Woiwode.

Meanwhile, Maxwell continued to publish his own novels. *They Came Like Swallows* (1937, Harper) won the Friends of American Writers Award. *The Folded Leaf* (1945, Harper) mirrored the lives of two adolescent boys growing up together in Chicago and at the University of Illinois. This was followed by two more novels, *Time Will Darken It* (1948, Harper) and *The Chateau* (1961, Knopf), three collections of stories (one of them [*Stories*] with John Cheever, Daniel Fuchs, and Jean Stafford) and a children's book. Maxwell published an extensively researched history of his family and their commitment to the Disciples of Christ, *Ancestors* (1971, Knopf).

From *Bright Center of Heaven* through his most recent novel, *So Long, See You Tomorrow* (1980, Knopf), Maxwell has continued to create settings and characters drawn from his memories of a Midwestern youth. *So Long, See You Tomorrow* retells the story of his mother's death, his father's remarriage, and the family move to Chicago; woven into this autobiographical narrative is the tale of another young boy, Cletus Smith, whose father murdered his wife's lover and then killed himself. Maxwell based this portion of the narrative on an actual murder and suicide, the details of which he found in the files of the Lincoln *Evening Courier* of the 1920s.

A number of Maxwell's fictions reflect his experience of life in New York (see especially *Over by the River and Other Stories* (1977, Knopf) and his travels through France notably *The Chateau* and several of his stories). An address delivered at a literary symposium at Smith College, *The Writer as Illusionist*, was privately printed in 1955.

Since his retirement from the *New Yorker*, Maxwell has continued to live on New York's Upper East Side with his wife, the former Emily Gilman Noyes. The Maxwells were married in 1945. They have two grown daughters.

The interview was conducted by Gerald Nemanic at the Maxwell apartment on November 29, 1982.

Gerald Nemanic. Reading your fiction set in Central Illinois—a place you left at the age of fourteen and return to imaginatively so often—I'm reminded of Goethe's remark that "Beginnings are always delightful. The threshold is the place of pause." Apparently you agree.
William Maxwell. If you rush on without reflection you don't take advantage of what you might have found there. Is that what he means?

GN. I thought he meant that the beginnings of stories are always the most delightful part.
WM. They are the part I enjoy most. I could begin a new story every morning. What keeps me from beginning a new story every morning is the realization that there has to be also an ending, that the ending has to have a point, and if I haven't thought my way through to this I will sail right off into space.

GN. Your most recent novel, *So Long, See You Tomorrow*, seems so carefully crafted that I imagine it went through many drafts. Did you feel that the first one was in some way more—to use Goethe's word—"delightful," or more alive?

WM. My first drafts are always inadequate. They are a kind of armature to which I add and add as I work out the form and meaning of the novel. I once got quite far into a work without knowing what it was about or why I was writing it. It began with an evening party, and the details flowed with absolute confidence through six or eight chapters. Then I had a dream that revealed to me where I was, in fact, going. My father could barely read music but he could play by ear almost any instrument that he got his hands on. When I was about nine or ten, he tried to put on an operetta, with local talent, and the rehearsals were held in our living room. My mother was present but not part of it. Perhaps she didn't have a good enough voice, but also she was a large woman—they didn't understand about calories in those days—and that alone would have kept her from appearing on stage. My father sat at the upright piano and directed the singers. Nothing came of it, mostly because the cast, and particularly the tenor, was slack about showing up for rehearsals. My father called one last meeting, to discuss whether they should abandon the project, and the only person who showed up was a pretty young woman with dark hair and blue eyes. Two and one half years after my mother's death, my father married her. I rather think I picked something out of the air—not that he had fallen in love with her but that there was an attraction of some sort. Children cannot approach adult situations rationally because there is too much they are not told, and so they get the facts by some other means, and don't always know what they know.

GN. You mentioned a dream.

WM. The dream was close enough to what I was writing for me to grasp the fact that the husband in the novel represented my father and the wife my mother and the inadvertent troublemaker was the young woman who came to that last rehearsal. And that it was because of what I had felt, long ago, sitting on the sofa beside my mother, that I had chosen to write about a triangular relationship that I knew instinctively would sustain me through the writing of the book, even though I had no idea how it would work out.

GN. If you are working in the dark like that, can you feel responsible for what you choose to write about?

WM. I feel ultimately responsible, in that I know I am not going to allow myself to publish a bad book.

GN. *So Long* struck me as a tragic story. One of the most revealing passages occurs where the narrator, whose mother had recently died, talks about how happy his father is during the period when he is engaged to the woman who eventually becomes the narrator's stepmother. The passage reads: "I'm old enough to be that man's father, and he's been dead for nearly twenty years, and yet it troubles me that he was happy. Why? In some way his happiness was, at that time, and forever after it would seem, a threat to me. It was not the kind of happiness that children are included in, but why should that trouble me now? I do not even begin to understand it." In the parallel story of the tenant farm families, Fern Smith is in love with Lloyd Wilson, and ecstatically happy, but her happiness is not acceptable to those around her, because she is a married woman and he has a wife. What I'm getting at is: does the Smith/Wilson situation relate in any way to the fact that you couldn't accept your own father's happiness?

WM. No, I don't think so. I am not a moralistic person. I like people to be happy and I go to considerable lengths to make them happy if it is in my power. But passionate love can be destructive—like making a large hole in the roof and letting in the wind and the rain. Everything that children depend on can be wiped out by the emotional behavior of adults, which the children are in no position to comprehend. All that they understand is disaster, standing in the ruins. Or they are uprooted, which is equally disastrous. It is the effect on children of passions they cannot share that I was concerned with.

GN. In an address you gave at Smith College, "The Writer as Illusionist," you said that the fiction writer is an entertainer of the trickster/magician sort. You go on to say that the only difference is: the writer must be taken in by his own illusions—fool himself, as it were.

WM. The vaudeville magician is just a hard-working man, not too different from a plumber, I think.

GN. Your comment about the writer as illusionist reminded me of an artist like Thomas Mann, who so often thought of himself as a sort of confidence man. He even signed letters to his family simply "Z" for "Zaubérer" and his children called him "The Magician." Apparently he liked the idea that he was bamboozling people.

WM. Also his secret sexual fantasies may have made him feel allied with confidence men and crooks and people who were not what they appeared to be.

GN. Is it necessary for a writer to stand back a little from his work and think of himself as a manipulator?

WM. Especially in autobiographical fiction as distinct from reminiscence, which is simply remembering for the pleasure of remembering. In autobiographical fiction the writer tends to think of himself as a character in a story—a character he has a thorough, detailed knowledge of, but, on the other hand, no more sympathy or protectiveness for than he has for the others.

GN. So that sometimes, having created a character that is a projection of himself, the writer finds that he can sit in judgment on himself.

WM. Or even, since he has become a character in a story, that he can expose his private self with impunity. In "Over by the River" a man looks at himself in the bathroom mirror as he is shaving and thinks, *If people knew how little I cared about them they wouldn't have anything to do with me.* It is just a passing thought and not really true. I knew, as I wrote it, that some readers would interpret this to mean that I and not the man in the story felt that way. And they in fact did.

GN. Speaking of Mann, when I started reading *The Folded Leaf* I was immediately reminded of *Tonio Kroger*.

WM. It is like that, isn't it? The two types, the brown-eyed and the blue-eyed.

GN. The graceful boy and the boy who is always "falling down at the dance." And then there's the girl, later on in both stories, creating a triangle. It's interesting that in both *The Folded Leaf* and *So Long, See You Tomorrow* there's a triangular relationship. In *So Long* you have the two men who love each other and then the woman as a third element who comes between them and is destructive. And the suicide in *So Long* parallels the attempted suicide in *The Folded Leaf.* You never thought of that parallel?

WM. No. I didn't think of it because all the facts in *So Long* came out of the Lincoln *Evening Courier.* Of course what made me choose that story to write about? I chose it because of something that actually happened, the incident in the school corridor where the "I" character meets a boy he knew in another place and out of an uncertainty as to how to behave, because the other boy's father committed a murder, fails to speak to him. What should I have done when I met the boy I never expected to see again? Was there a right way to have acted?

GN. A right way? I guess you could have gone running after him and said, "I'm sorry I didn't speak to you. I was taken by surprise." But then we wouldn't have had this novel. I found it rather hard to believe, as I was reading the book, that later on in your life you were plagued by this incident, which is so much the kind of thing that happens, and that most people regret for a short while and then dismiss from their minds forever.

WM. "Plagued" is too strong a word. From time to time I would suddenly remember what happened, but the recollection would not be accompanied by such a feeling of remorse that I would go and put my forehead on the mantelpiece, or anything like that. It would just be a painful thought.

GN. Did it get worse as you got older?

WM. No, it was always the same. Finally, I was made aware of the implications of it by—you know how you *feel* the expression that is on your face? When you smile, you can feel the smile? When you wince, you feel it. I worked backward from the physical expression to the feeling itself. And I thought, *After all this time that I should still care—how very odd.*

GN. I also found it hard to imagine that you didn't ever see him again. I would think that even if you didn't want to look for him, you would, in spite of yourself, be looking for that face.

WM. Senn was a big high school. It had three thousand students. And of course we're talking about something that happened fifty years ago. But I've dredged my memory as well as I know how, and I cannot find a visual recollection of a second encounter.

GN. You were living at that time with your dad. You don't remember going home and saying, "Hey guess who I saw at school?"

WM. I went to him if there was something I didn't understand, or if I was frightened, but not about this sort of thing. I think I just felt fatalistic about it. It had happened, and I wished I had behaved differently. But in any case I was not going to tell anybody that his father was a murderer. Having been chased home from school a lot when I was a little boy, my feelings tend to be with the outsider and the underdog. It has always been terribly easy for me to put myself in somebody else's shoes. And sometimes it amounts to an inability to get myself out of those shoes once I have stepped into them. With Cletus Smith, what was difficult was not him but his background. My father owned a couple of farms, and I sometimes went there with him and saw the tenant farmers' children. But I was shy and they were shy and so we didn't run off and play together. When I was writing *So Long* I spent a solid year trying to imagine what it was like to be one of those farm children. I even wrote to friends who have grown up on a farm and tried to learn from them what it was like. I thought about this so much that I finally said to myself, I guess I really *do* know, just from thinking about them, what their life was like. And I stopped worrying about it and wrote. It would have been just as difficult for Cletus to imagine what went on in our house.

GN. What about your teen-age years in Chicago? The places you describe in *The Folded Leaf* are around Devon Avenue and Sheridan Road on the North Side.

WM. I went to Nicholas Senn High School. Recently somebody sent me a newspaper article about it, with photographs that horrified me. The neighborhood has gone to hell, and the students are into drugs, and the corridors covered with graffiti. It was once a great school, with excellent facilities and marvelous teachers and an *esprit de corps*, in the student body—if a teacher was called from the room during class, one of the students would step up to her desk and the class would continue until she returned. It was a stroke of fortune—it changed my life when my father was promoted to a job in Chicago and I found myself in this huge school. The standards were so high that my first year at the University of Illinois seemed to me a come-down.

GN. Yet I got the feeling, mainly from *The Folded Leaf*—if it is at all autobiographical—that your life at this time was essentially sad.

WM. There is a difference between straight autobiography and autobiographical fiction. Fiction was to have a tone that is consistent with the events of the novel, and the events of this novel were heading toward heartbreak and suicide. In the beginning, before I knew anyone in Chicago, I *was* lonely, but after a while I enjoyed my school life very much. If I had dwelt on that it would have thrown the tone of the novel off completely. In the first draft I described my family life just as it was—my father and stepmother, her homesickness for Lincoln, their friends and parties and all, I thought, *You really can't do that to them. They have a right to their privacy, and you can't treat them like characters you made up.* I could have written about them flatteringly, but it wouldn't have been useful to the novel to do that. So I made Lymie Peters's father a seedy sporting character. After the book was published, a man in Lincoln said to me, "Why did you make your father like that?" So much for invention. When I read *The Folded Leaf* now, I have a very hard time distinguishing what is invented and what actually happened.

The high school part is fairly accurate, but the college part is half true and half imaginary. For example, the dormitory. There was no antique shop on the first floor and the character of the antique dealer is based on one of my colleagues at the *New Yorker*.

GN. Many writers first began thinking of a literary career during high school or college. Was that true for you? Did anybody influence you in that direction?

WM. In my freshman year in college my composition teacher, Paul Landis, read my first theme as an example of how not to write. It was a sobering experience. Then he turned around and was kindness itself. He became my mentor, told me what English classes to take, got me into the poetry society, read Homer in Greek with me, had me to Sunday breakfast week after week for the next four years, and kept me from doing silly things, without ever being possessive or dictatorial. As I grew older, my taste deviated from his. I don't think my books gave him much if any pleasure, but that doesn't mean I don't owe him a debt of gratitude. The first writer I came in contact with was Zona Gale. Oh God, what a lovely creature she was! And so kind to me. She was best known for a feminist novel, *Miss Lulu Bett*, which she dramatized. The play won the Pulitzer Prize and made her famous. Her early work was charming but sentimental—stories about a place called Friendship Village. Then, under the influence of Sinclair Lewis, she became a sharp and sometimes satirical realist. Her last work inclined more and more toward mysticism.

The summer I was seventeen I worked on a farm ten miles out of Portage, Wisconsin, where she lived. I met her through the family I was working for. At that time she lived in a big square frame house overlooking the Fox River and was perhaps in her early fifties. She had a soft, humorous, beautiful voice and heavy-lidded eyes. When I was talking to her I felt I was conversing with a celestial being, in a world of light. The farm became my second home. They fed and sheltered me when I had no money and no place else to go. It was understood, without my having to speak of it, that I would go to see Miss Gale. Since I didn't drive a car, one of the girls drove me there and hung around town for a couple of hours until it was time to pick me up. I would go to Miss Gale's house, and we would talk. And then the car would be waiting, and I would say goodbye at the door. The first time I went there I wrote down everything she said, but after that I couldn't. A curtain came down over my mind as she said goodbye. I have sometimes wondered if she was responsible for this.

It has also occurred to me, belatedly, that the thing between us was love. But what kind of love? Nothing sexual, in any case. I never touched her. She was so much a person of essences that in a sense there was nothing corporal there to touch. On the other hand, people did touch her. When I saw Mrs. Green, the woman who owned the farm, throw her arms around Miss Gale and kiss her, I was shocked. It seemed so insensitive. After she was no longer there, I thought about her, and about our meetings, and wondered what I was to her. I have no way of knowing. If I had asked her, at the time, she would probably have turned the question into another question. Or perhaps she would have answered it simply and truthfully, but not in a way that I could have anticipated. I remember once when I went to see her she told me she had stayed up all night the night before, hoping to hear that the execution of Sacco and Vanzetti had been stayed. I had been brought up in a Republican household, and assumed, without giving the matter any thought, that of course they were guilty.

She wrote on the fly-leaf of several of the books she gave me, "Life is something more than we believe it to be." In many ways she anticipated the ideas that came in with the Sixties, and it is odd that her work is so neglected. She was wonderful to me. She was just simply marvelous. I heard from her at intervals. Once I had a letter from her from Japan, saying that at a party in her honor they had released five hundred fire flies in the garden by way of entertainment for the guests. The last time I went to see her in Portage—by then I was in my twenties and she had married and was living in a different house—we sat in a small walled garden, with the leaves coming down around us like the last act of *Cyrano de Bergerac.* And suddenly I realized with astonishment that we were not talking about what she thought would be of interest to me but of something that was of deep emotional concern to her. She had a number of literary protégés and one of them was a young novelist who was brought up in Portage. I knew her only to speak to. At some point she turned against Zona and wrote a novel in which Zona figured as an evil, scheming, possessive woman. I had read the book and found nothing in the character that was recognizable to me. Occasionally, people who owe a great deal to someone will, in self-defense, because they can't bear the weight of indebtedness, in their minds turn that person into a monster. Zona never appeared to hold it against her or even admitted that the novel contained anything one might be offended by. And it was that that Zona talked about, with the leaves coming down around us. I was deeply stirred to realize we were not talking about the Tibetan *Book of the Dead* but something much closer to home—a woman who had been very dear to her and was now dead. I had grown up sufficiently that I could be treated not as a protégé but as a friend.

When I came to New York in 1936 and got a job on the editorial staff of the *New Yorker*, Zona was distressed. She didn't think it was a good idea for me to be there. She didn't like the *New Yorker* particularly, and she thought I would stop writing, as indeed I did after three or four years. I was too much caught up in editorial work, and the ideas for stories stopped coming. When *They Came Like Swallows* was chosen by the Book-of-the-Month Club, she wrote something about me for the news sheet that went out to subscribers. She also said, "Is there anybody in New York you would like to meet?" and I said "Willa Cather." At this period of her life Willa Cather was a recluse, and I had asked for the one person in New York that Zona couldn't take me to. I did meet Sherwood Anderson. She took me to the second night of Eugene O'Neill's *Ah, Wilderness*, and he was sitting in the row ahead of us. He turned around and spoke to her, and she introduced me. I'm glad I saw him.

GN. Do you appear in any of her work?

WM. There is a play she did eleven revisions of, and that was never produced. One of the characters has the name I was called when I was young, and was, I couldn't help thinking, modeled on me. Or rather, on what she thought of me as being. She said once that I was a harmonious being, and later, when I was a graduate student at Harvard, I repeated this remark to my friend Robert Fitzgerald, who said sardonically, "Well, be careful crossing the street."

GN. Were there other people who were important in giving you impetus to write?

WM. Robert Fitzgerald, among others. At the time I first knew him I wrote poetry, which I used to take to him, and he would criticize it patiently. He was younger than I, and was already being published. I knew that he was the genuine article, and that I had a long way to go. One day he looked at me queerly and said, "Why don't you write prose?" I respected him so much that I went and did it.

Louise Bogan noticed my stories in the *New Yorker*, and in the late 1930s we became friends. I showed her a story about some high school boys in a swimming pool, and she said that I must keep on with it. It turned out to be *The Folded Leaf*. Over a period of several years I mailed four complete drafts to her, a chapter at a time, and she read all of it. Occasionally I would get a postcard from her saying, "V. good. Keep on." Only once did she criticize a passage as being insufficiently worked over. When the book was finished, she found me a title. Her uncompromisingly serious attitude toward literature helped keep *me* serious, as well.

And there was Harold Ross, the first editor of the *New Yorker.* There have been so many things about him—about what an oaf and buffoon he was. He was neither. He was a highly intelligent and gifted man. And like nobody else who has ever lived. He happened to hear that I had been working on a novel for several years, and he came into my office one day to ask how it was getting on. The upshot of our conversation was that he sent me home for six months on full pay, and the novel got done.

GN. Larry Woiwode, whose work you've edited for the *New Yorker*, has recently published an article praising both *So Long* and your editorial work with him. Not many people have had such extensive experience both as a fiction writer and fiction editor as you've had. Did you have an editorial mentor?

WM. Katharine White taught me the fundamentals of being an editor, but I also learned a great deal more from her galleys and correspondence. She had a maternal concern for the welfare of the writers she dealt with—their emotional life, their financial difficulties, their literary efforts. If after many years I brought something to editing that was my own, it was that I loved to understand what writers were doing—I meant to say *"learned* to understand" but the way it came out is more accurate. If they were unconfident, or working partly in the dark, I could see what they were trying to do, and say, "Yes, it's all right. It's a wonderful idea, and it's going to work." Or just live through the uncertainty with them.

GN. Have you worked with an editor on your own fiction?

WM. I have shown what I was working on to other writers, and most of all, to my wife. But I have never shown a book to a publisher before it was finished. I wanted to be sure that I was satisfied that it was the best I could do before I exposed myself to criticism. Edward Aswell at Harper's made some suggestions about tightening up the structure of *The Folded Leaf* which I followed, but ten years later, when the book was reprinted in the Vintage edition, I put almost everything back the way I originally had it. Aswell's suggestions were neither necessary nor really helpful.

GN. What should an inexperienced writer do who feels the need of editorial guidance?

WM. Go to the bookcase. From reading, you learn how the good or the great writer does it. I've had experience, particularly when I was younger, of reading a novel and simultaneously writing a different novel in my head. The book I was reading released parts of my experience that I hadn't thought of or didn't know were there.

GN. I have the feeling, reading E. B. White, that either you were great friends or that you were strongly influenced by him.

WM. When I went to work at the *New Yorker* I was twenty-eight and White and Wolcott Gibbs and St. Clair McKelway and Ross and Mrs. White were roughly ten years older. I thought they were immensely sophisticated. But what I think it really was was that they had lived in New York for some time, and I was fresh out of the Middle West. White is not a wildly gregarious man, and so far as I know nobody has ever roped him into making a public appearance. Not even when he received the National Medal of Literature. If he was given the Nobel Prize, I have a feeling he'd find some excuse to keep from going to Stockholm. I think he offers the best living example of how to use the first person singular. I didn't ever sit down and study him, but reading him you cannot not be aware—if you are a writer—of the care he takes to present himself as an unpretentious human being. It is perhaps the way all the great familiar essayists' present themselves. Anyway, I was quite far along in my literary career before I dared to use "I" as the narrator of a story, and *So Long* is the only novel in which I have done it. It is so tricky. In the first place, it tends to make you garrulous, and in the second encourages irrelevancies and explanations that are tedious.

GN. I'd like to get back for a moment to your Midwestern experience. In *Ancestors*, your family biography, there is a telling comment on the people of Lincoln. You say that in the days of your childhood "men and women alike appeared to accept with equanimity the circumstances of their lives in a way that no one seems able to do now anywhere. I believe in Winesburg, Ohio, but I also believe in what I remember." What do you mean by this?

WM. Well, for one thing, the characters in *Winesburg, Ohio* are not very happy. And they are so cut off from one another. Do you remember Anderson's story "Hands"? There was an English teacher in Lincoln High School, a sandy-haired man, thin and intellectual, who had a way of putting his hands on the boys' shoulders just as Anderson describes Wing Biddlebaum doing. The Lincoln teacher had one friend, a woman teacher, but what was waiting for him at home was solitude. There must have been other Anderson characters that I was not aware of. I left Lincoln when I was an adolescent and never lived there again, and so I don't have an adult's perception of the place. For example, I don't know the part money played in the lives of people there. Or envy. Or desire. Men came home from work and watered the lawn or raked leaves into a pile and had supper and went to bed. Their calm behavior may have concealed all sorts of horrors and lusts, but they weren't visible to me. I had a one-tube radio set that was made by an older boy who lived down the street from me, but people in general didn't have radios and didn't seem dependent on outside entertainment. The farthest away that anybody talked about was Chicago, and only a handful of people ever went there. They went downtown. That was charge enough for them. I don't know whether I write about the "real" Lincoln and I don't care; I write about a place that I possess in my imagination. Also, of course, I led a ludicrously sheltered life.

GN. Well, "sheltered," my goodness. No one whose mother died when he was ten can have led a sheltered life. Perhaps what we are talking about is merely a difference of personality between you and Anderson.
WM. The tragic sense that Anderson brought to bear on the citizens of Winesburg, Ohio, no ten-year-old boy is likely to possess. He can experience tragedy, but he doesn't have the ability to generalize, to see the tragic thread that runs through the whole of human life.

GN. One of the things that struck me about *So Long* was that you have captured an elemental tragic feeling. When Lloyd is so consumed by love that he literally doesn't know what he's doing, and the cows turn their heads and look at him, sensing something wrong, it seemed to me to hark back to classical literature—to Virgil, say, where all nature is involved in people's lives. That's so hard, because if you fail, what a fall you are going to take.
WM. It's also true that, so far as their emotional life is concerned, people and animals are not as different as we pretend.

GN. But if it isn't handled just right, you've crossed the line into sentimentality.
WM. With material of this kind, the same thing is true every time you put a sentence down on paper. I always know. There's an angel who rings a bell at that point.

GN. Rereading *The Folding Leaf*, I felt that it was a good book but not anywhere near as good as *So Long*.

WM: I don't either. It was the best I could do at the time. And it was awfully hard to do. I said to myself, *This isn't the age of Booth Tarkington. Who is going to care about two adolescent boys?* I felt that the only way it would work was to enlarge the background and take in as much of the world around them as the book would stand.

GN. In *So Long* you must have felt surer about it all—about the material and your ability to handle it.

WM. As I grew older I came to believe that everything that happens is of profound significance, and if you are sufficiently aware of what that is you don't have to invent very much. Actually, *So Long* is more than half invented. It's just a different kind of invention. I don't monkey around with things that actually happened; they're straight out of the newspaper files. I only invented what it was like to be those people. And whenever I was inventing, I was at some pains to inform the reader of this. I also knew that in all probability the reader wouldn't keep fact and fiction straight in his mind and that the story would end up as being either a kind of fiction or a kind of fact. As for the autobiographical part—the death of my mother and its emotional reverberations—it was a story I had told before, but I don't think I'd ever managed to tell it quite so simply and truthfully. The mother isn't *there* at all—she's only an absence.

GN. Conrad said, in the preface to *The Nigger of the Narcissus*, "My task as a novelist is, above all, to make you *see.*" Yet only the best writers can pare down the story to its essentials, to make you "see" what's there instead of worrying about how to persuade you of something or try to figure out what it is you want from him.

WM. How could the novelist know what the reader might want? I'm not talking about writing for a mass audience, you understand.

GN. But you apparently felt, when you were writing *The Folded Leaf*, that you did have to think about that. You asked yourself, *Who will want to read this story?*

WM. Not who would want to read it but who would take it seriously. I knew it was serious to me, but would it seem that way to anyone else? I used to look at the fireplace and think, *that's where this novel belongs.*

GN. One of my students is from Lincoln. She went home recently and nosed around the library and talked to acquaintances. Later, she said to me, "The people down there are pretty reticent about Maxwell. They don't seem to want to say much, and they seem a bit uncomfortable. The fact that he wrote about actual people. And exposed them."

WM. The exposure, such as it was, occurred long ago in the evening paper. But of course these people hadn't read it. Probably some of it is a feeling about what should or should not be written about in a book. Popular romances are all right, but actual people and their passions is something else again. It is a feeling about art, too, as something alien to them. I wouldn't expect a small town to accept an artist of any kind whatever. Even if he happened to be born there. He simply is not one of them and never was, from the beginning. People—there aren't many left—who knew me when I lived there are very kind when I go home and I don't think they are much disturbed by my books, but you're talking about people who have never laid eyes on me.

GN. One can imagine why Sinclair Lewis or Sherwood Anderson or any number of Midwestern writers who had been isolated by the narrow attitudes of the small town people they had had to live with should feel the need to sit in judgment on them. But you depict Lincoln so lovingly. It's hard to understand why anyone should object to that.

WM. People bring their prejudices to a book and don't always read what is printed on the page. In any case, I don't want to change anything in Lincoln, or anybody. I don't even want them to vote Democratic. I like it when other people vote Democratic, but they can vote any way they please.

GN. Have you ever thought of going back there to live?

WM. I used to think of it sometimes, in daydreams. It's not something I could sensibly do to my wife, who doesn't have that sort of background. But I still identify myself with Lincoln, and am happy to be identified with it. I've never been able to understand the "identity" crisis. I've always known who I was, partly because, when I was a child, there was no form of protective coloration that would have helped in the slightest. It was born in on me, you might say, who I was. When I took my wife to Lincoln for the first time a friend of the family said to her, "He's a nice boy but queer. Very queer." Being different from other people has the corresponding advantage of there being no doubt in your mind that you *are somebody*—even if it's a unique kind of person. But then everything in a very small town supports this idea. I've never wanted not to have come from Lincoln. I've lived most of my adult life in New York City, and I loved the *New Yorker*, and for forty years I shaved with pleasure because I was going to work. Not too many people can say that, but all the same I wanted to have something which didn't belong to the *New Yorker*. And that was my own writing. In a way it was almost dishonest—the way people hide something in their pocket. The fact that I came from a small town a thousand miles to the west somehow made that private world easier to protect.

GN. In *Ancestors* you mention the fact that you like your name—William Maxwell—because when you were a child it was so often spoken with affection.

WM. I really don't want to be anyone else but me. It isn't that I think I'm flawless or don't wish I had qualities I don't have, but I was somehow made to feel, I guess, that I was the child my mother loved and therefore I don't want to be anybody else's child or any other person but the person I am. As a child I was surrounded by affectionate people—aunts, a wonderful uncle who was a doctor, my mother's friends, and so on. On that same first trip to Lincoln with my wife we paid a call on the elderly couple who lived next door to us during my childhood. He was eighty-five and bedridden, and his wife had had a bed set up in his study to make it easier for her to take care of him. It was a room I knew by heart. He made me sit on the edge of his bed and held my hand and began to tell me about the day I was born. Then he told me about his own growing up in Scotland. He was the most wonderful storyteller I have ever known. He worshipped my older brother, and as a child I thought if he loved my brother that much he couldn't also love me. But now I realize that he had in fact loved me, as all children are loved, for what they are.

GN. And yet you say that you led too sheltered a life. As if you disapproved of the comfortableness engendered by all that affection.

WM. What did the malicious fairy godmother say—"My child, I wish you a little misfortune"? Complacency is the enemy. I know of no good complacent writers.

GN. From things you have written it appears that your father was a blunt man. I certainly don't find you blunt, but on the other hand I find in your writing someone who wants to be clear and say what he thinks. Do you think there is a connection there, somehow?

WM. There certainly is a connection between any child and his parents. My father had no patience with any form of circuitiveness. He also didn't have a great deal of imagination. He was a business man. And I wasn't an easy child for him to bring up. He tried to bring me up for what he thought was the world, and I was headed for what I hoped would be a different world from his. He used to tell me that I had to learn to play bridge or I'd never be asked anywhere. As it turned out, never in the whole of my adult life has anybody ever asked me to play bridge. Or if they did I had no trouble wiggling out of it.

GN. Do you think that in the final analysis your father felt you'd made a success of your life?

WM. He used to say that all three of his sons had made a success of their lives. My two brothers are lawyers and live in California. I know that my father was happy when I appeared to be doing well at the *New Yorker.* But in 1940 I threw up my job in order to stay home and write—I quit on two different occasions and then, since I am a slow writer and we needed to eat—I went back. In 1940 I was making as much as my father did as an insurance executive, and when I was growing up I was so dreamy and impractical that he was haunted by the fear that he was going to have to support me. So, naturally, he was shocked and dismayed that I should walk away from such a good thing. But he never reproached me for it, and I would never have known how really upset he was if somebody hadn't told me. That he felt being a writer was a fit occupation for a man I am not sure. He did not distinguish between popular novels and literature. To him, novels were something that women read. So I don't really know the answer to your question.

Tribute to Robert Fitzgerald (1910–1985) at American Academy of Arts and Letters

William Maxwell/1985

From *Proceedings of the American Academy of Arts and Letters and the National Institute of Arts and Letters*. Second Series, No. 36. New York, 1985. Publication No. 367. [pp.73–76]. Reprinted by permission of the American Academy of Arts and Letters, New York City. Delivered at the Academy, Dinner Meeting, April 2, 1985.

Robert Fitzgerald said, "Poetry is at least an elegance and at most a revelation."

When I made his acquaintance he was a sophomore at Harvard and I was a graduate student. We were both from the Middle West—from two small towns that were separated by only thirty minutes of corn and wheat field. The fact that we found ourselves in a, so to speak, alien land, among people whose vowel sounds were really diphthongs and whose assumptions were often ludicrous, strengthened the connection. His room was on the top floor of Hollis Hall, on the same landing as the room that Thoreau had had roughly a hundred years before. A quarter of a century later, John Updike occupied the room. And, unless a pleasant custom has been discontinued by the College, if you go there you will find all three names on a plaque at the head of the stairs. On the left as you walked in, there was a small piano, and on the right-hand wall a framed print of the Hokusai wave, which had not yet become a cliché. Many years later, monitoring a Princeton seminar on Baudelaire, Robert was reminded of how in that room he read *Les Fleurs du Mal* for the first time, and of the sound the book made when he let it fall to the floor beside his bed at three o'clock of a cold winter night. The poems that he wrote while he was in Harvard are full of night images, night fears, darkness, and cold. In conversation he had a careful way of expressing any thought, as if the words were being passed on for accuracy and truthfulness before he allowed his tongue to utter them. This gave him a magisterial air that, though he was only twenty-two, sat quite securely on his shoulders. His nostrils flared disdainfully when he spoke of writing or writers that he considered second-rate. Just when you expected him to seize the jawbone of an ass and start laying about him, he would break into laughter. At himself. I loved him for his poetic gift, for his intransigence, for the fact that he looked the way a poet ought to look, and because he could play Mozart's Piano Sonata Number 11 in A Major.

Among the experiences common to his childhood and mine was the knowledge of what it is like to have a funeral wreath fastened to the front door. His mother died when he was three, and his younger brother when he was seven. He had, as he later expressed it, "a very good, direct sense of what it meant to die; it meant not to be there at all anymore." His father fell and injured his hip, and tuberculosis of the bone set in. For a while he was able to get around on crutches, and even to practice law, but from Robert's eighth year on, his father was confined to his bed in an upstairs room of Robert's grandmother's house in Springfield, Illinois. Before Robert started off to school in the morning he would open the door of his father's room, put down the window, pull up the shades, and turn on the radiator. Then, having wakened his father, he would empty out and rinse the urinal. On Saturday and Sunday mornings he would bring a basin of warm water from the bathroom and hold a mirror in front of his father's face while he shaved. In the evening he stood beside the bed with scissors, adhesive tape, and cotton, while his father changed the dressing on his wound. And then his father would make a place on the blanket for cards or the checkerboard. Once he took his fountain pen and wrote the Greek alphabet. Though bedridden, he was a better and more tender father than most. He died while Robert was away at boarding school. All this weight of early sorrow and deprivation stoically endured I felt in him. And in his poems as well:

[*Maxwell reads from Fitzgerald's poem "First Movement."*]

Robert began to write verse in high school—a great deal of it. When he graduated, his father, thinking that seventeen was a little young for entering college, sent him to Choate for a year. There he had Dudley Fitts as a teacher. Fitts encouraged him to learn Greek, read "The Wasteland" to him, and in one way and another changed his life.

He spent his junior year at Trinity College, Cambridge, where he attended lectures of the philosopher G. E. Moore and a seminar given by an obscure young Austrian named Wittgenstein. Of other disciplines than poetry he was most drawn to philosophy. General thought was to him simply another language, like Latin and Greek, to be mastered and used in describing the nature of experience. As an elderly man he observed, "Everything runs on as process without pause. We ourselves, who temporarily weight the chairs we sit in, cannot arrest our continual vanishing."

When he returned to Harvard for his senior year he took the lead in a production of *Philoctetes* of Sophocles, in Greek. Elliot Carter wrote the music for the choruses. Robert had to memorize seven hundred lines of Greek and I wonder if the experience didn't make him forever homesick for the ancient world.

His family meant him to practice law, as his father and two of his uncles had done. Robert was of two minds about this, and decided finally that if he could afford a legal education he could afford the alternative of devoting several years to writing—only to discover that he couldn't afford either one; his small inheritance had been wiped out in the failing stock market.

He went to work for the *New York Herald-Tribune* as a cub reporter, and was so obviously a fish out of water that the benign city editor transferred him to the job of assistant to the business editor, where he was no less out of his element, but at least he did not have to meet a daily deadline. After eighteen months he resigned in order to spend the summer at MacDowell Colony, putting together his first book of poems and collaborating with Fitts on a translation of *Alcestis* of Euripides. Their translation has an emotional simplicity that is almost Middlewestern. On the morning of the day that Alcestis gives herself up to death so that her husband can remain alive, she prays to the Hearth-goddess:

[*Maxwell reads from Fitts and Fitzgerald's* The Alcestis of Euripides]
I was at the Colony, too, that summer, and carried away, down through the years, a memory of the sound of his footsteps—of his highly focused being—mounting the outside stairs to his room, which was above mine.

He was hired by *Time* magazine to write stories about business. The managing editor said to him, "I want you to make the Business department sing." In due time he was promoted to Art. He was partly color-blind and had to take his wife with him when he looked at pictures, to correct his impression of the colors. His columns showed no trace of the homogenous prose characteristic of the surrounding pages, which means that the editors kept their hands off his copy. He had enough leftover energy to translate, with Fitts, the *Antigone* of Sophocles. Into it they poured their own poetic talent, producing an excitement you won't find in Gilbert Murray.

In the fall of 1940, wanting a longer stretch of free time before he was caught up in what he knew was coming, Robert got a year's leave of absence, and spent it in Santa Fe, writing poetry and translating *Oedipus at Colonnus*. Then he went back to *Time* and covered Books, with James Agee. In 1943 he joined the Navy as a lieutenant j.g. While he was stationed in Guam he had three books in his footlocker: the Oxford text of the works of Virgil, the *Vulgate New Testament*, and a Latin dictionary. Rather than spend evening after evening drinking at the Officers' Club, he "went through Virgil from stem to stern."

When the War was over, he wrote one book review a week for *Time*, to keep the wolf from the door, and translated *Oedipus Rex* with Fitts. Robert translated one of the odes seven times and was not satisfied. The eighth attempt was made during a stay in Rome, and, the spirit of the place supporting his endeavors, he got the lines to unfurl with the true Sophoclean grandeur:

[*Maxwell reads from* Oedipus Rex of Sophocles, *translated
by Fitts and Fitzgerald.*]

And so on. A marvel. How long he spent on something was never a consideration. In a letter to me he wrote: "What I would keep is our criterion of style. In behavior and in writing it looks as though you achieve it, you don't fall into it. This does not seem insupportable. It keeps things clear. I would also like to keep a sense of mystery, of the Unknown."

He was offered a part-time teaching job at Sarah Lawrence College, and this led to other teaching appointments, all of them temporary until Harvard claimed him for the Boylston Professorship of Rhetoric and Oratory. The house in Ridgefield, Connecticut, where he and his second wife were living in the early 1950s saw the arrival of one child after another in quick succession. A Guggenheim grant and a publisher's advance made it possible for them to live in Italy, where there were plenty of young women who were willing to change diapers and keep an eye on the infants with a tendency to wander off into harm's way. Robert sat down and copied the whole of the *Odyssey* into large ledger-like notebooks, with a blank line between every two written words, and then he began to reshape the Greek hexameters into the iambic pentameter that is the bedrock of English poetry. What was also involved was reimagining the action of the poem, so that it was alive from start to finish, and feeling his way into a style that in our time would seem as timeless as the original. After six or seven years of this, he felt, he said, that Homer was looking over his shoulder and he could ask him, "Will this do or won't it?"

The years in Italy were rich with the kind of family happiness he had been deprived of as a child. In 1961 he wrote, "We now have a house near Perugia, a tall old house near a road along a grand hillside looking out over the Tiber Valley. One of the towns sprinkled on the mountainside opposite is Assisi. The valley goes gently and is wide and the slopes are planted with olive trees." But lyric poetry doesn't thrive where there is no shade. In that same letter he said, "I understand your going back to Lincoln last year. I went back to Springfield one weekend in July in a rented Chevrolet, and I drove around the streets like the very ghost that was ahead of me on my bicycle forty years ago. The years intervening were like heavy plate glass between me and everything. The elms were gone, and the era, and the people. It is well that, as Yeats put it, all things remain in God."

He loved music, especially Bach and Schubert. He delighted in the beauty of women. His letters to friends were crammed with affection. His illness did not intimidate him, and, with the help of his wife, Penny, and his grown daughters and sons, he held the enemy at arm's length while, wandering around the house in his bathrobe or sitting up in bed, he put his affairs in order, and lived in joy.

The Quiet Man

Geoffrey Stokes/1985

From the *Voice Literary Supplement*, December 1985, 27-28. Reprinted by permission.

It is summer, 1912, in "Draperville," a small Illinois town quite like the one William Maxwell lived in as a boy. Mississippi cousin Randolph Potter, a young man we have reason to dislike, is visiting his northern relatives, the Kings, and has been bitten by their usually friendly dog. Convalescing more than is strictly necessary, he has come downstairs to the kitchen for a talk with the Kings' cook, Rachel:

"'The trouble with you,' Rachel said to him one day, 'is you want everything. And you don't want to do no work for it.'

"'That's right,' Randolph said, nodding. 'There's a crippled boy at home—Griswold, his name is—had infantile paralysis when he was small and the other boys used to pick on him a lot. I don't think he ever had a friend till I came along and was nice to him. Griswold's very smart. He notices everything, especially people's weak points, and that way, when the time comes, he gets what he wants. The other day . . .'

"Most people, when they are describing a friend or telling a story, make the mistake of editing, of leaving things out. Fearing that their audience will grow restless, they rush ahead to the point, get there too soon, have to go back and explain, and in the end, the quality of experience is not conveyed. Randolph was never in a hurry, never in doubt about whether what he had to say would interest Rachel. By the time he had finished, she had a very clear idea in her mind of the crippled boy who knew how to wait for what he wanted, and she also knew one more thing about Randolph Potter.

"Turning from the sink, she asked out loud a question that had been in the back of her mind for days. 'What you want to go and hurt that dog for?'"

This passage, from William Maxwell's fourth novel, *Time Will Darken It*, is close to forty years old, yet it presciently conveys the risky path his fiction has followed for more than half a century. Tell the story—tell it *all*, for otherwise there is no use telling any—but words are double-edged. At the end, they will expose *you*.

One understands why, having lived for so long with this fearful knowledge, Maxwell chose not to speak during our recent interview, but the choice was nonetheless odd. It was also extremely courteous, which may take a little explaining. He was exquisitely polite on the phone—concerned, it seemed, solely for my well-being. "Do you use a tape-recorder, Mr. Stokes?" he asked. For long interviews, I preferred to, I said. "Oh, dear," he sighed. "I'm afraid it just won't work at all. I mean, it won't get a thing. I talk very fast when I'm excited, and I'm from the Midwest and swallow all my vowels. I just don't see how it would work."

Forbearing to mention that I was understanding him perfectly well over the telephone line, I suggested that I simply take notes—but of course that wouldn't work either. "I go *so* fast," he apologized; couldn't I see my way clear to sending some questions to him which he would answer as quickly as possible? I thought not; the aim was for a conversation, an interchange. "I see," he said, "you want something, er, spontaneous." He said this, as befits a man aware of how dangerous words are, rather distrustfully. After a moment, however, he brightened. "I know. You can come along up here, and I'll sit behind the typewriter. When you ask me a question, I'll write an answer, then you can look at it and ask another. It will be just like a conversation. Besides," he paused, "I really think much better at the typewriter."

The Maxwells' apartment is on the eighth floor of an Upper East Side building at the edge of the river. His wife, Emily, was out when I arrived, and after a few moments of amiable chat in their thoroughly book-lined living room, he led me back through the kitchen (whose black and white floor I recognized from his fiction) to what had been designed as a maid's room. Maxwell, nearing eighty, is slight, even a little fragile in appearance, but he hefted his grandfather's Morris chair over to his desk, set a cup of coffee for me on its broad arm, then settled in behind the typing table that would roll between us for the next couple of hours. Perhaps a half-hour into this exchange (rather like what I imagine the pause-for-translation Reagan-Gorbachev chats to have been), I referred to "something you said—or wrote, or whatever—a few minutes ago."

"'Said,' I think," he said. "'Said' is right. This *is* a conversation, you know."

And so it was—during the course of which he "said" (the last time I'll resort to sanitary quotes) something that echoed his comments on Randolph Potter's conversation. "Part of the pleasure of storytelling is to arrive at a point where you can involve the reader's imagination to such a degree that at a crucial moment you can sit back and the reader will not only know what you mean but see it happening.

"I have a passionate pleasure in details, and hate it when people say 'To make a long story short'—I want a long story *long*—but at the same time, perhaps from writing lyric poetry, I also hate it when the writer has used eight words and three would have done the trick."

The passage we were discussing, whose slowly mounting horror is a close-to-perfect example of the storyteller's sitting back at a crucial moment, was also from *Time Will Darken It*. The Kings' four-year-old daughter, Abbey, at loose ends, "went upstairs to her room and got her celluloid animals—a duck, a green frog and a goldfish—and started down the hall to the bathroom. When she pushed the door open, Randolph Potter was lying in the tub in water up to his chin. Ab stood holding her celluloid toys, and made no move toward the washstand.

"'I've lost the soap,' Randolph said. He moved his legs gently so that the black hairs stirred with the current.

"'Can't you find it?' Ab asked.

"'Not without an extensive search. What have you got there?'

Ab held out the toys to him.

"'I have a duck at home,' he said, and sat up slowly. 'A live duck. The water parted, revealing the bald slope of his knee. 'I wish I had him here right now.'

"'In the bath with you?' Ab cried.

"'He swims round and round,' Randolph said, nodding. 'And when I lose the soap he dives for it.'

"'Why does he do that?'

"'Because he knows I need it.'

"'Why do you need the soap?'

"'For the same reason little girls need to ask questions they already know the answers to.' When he drew his hand out of the water, his fingers were closed around a cake of castile soap.

"'What is the duck's name?'

"'I call him Sam,' Randolph said, and glanced at the open door.

"Now that they had something to talk about, Ab pulled the toilet cover down and set the celluloid animals on it. Randolph began to soap his arms and chest. Where the soap went, Ab's eyes went also.

"'He follows me wherever I go,' Randolph said, 'And he likes raisins and crackerjack.'

"'What does he do with the prize?' Ab asked.

"'He wears it on a string around his neck. When he gets in the bath with me, I take it off so he won't lose it. And when he swims, he goes like this.' Randolph made a movement with his hands which churned the water around the tub clockwise.

"'I take a bath with my mother sometimes,' Ab said, drawing closer.

"There was a sudden upheaval in the tub and Randolph stood up, dripping, and began to soap his back, his belly, and his thighs. He saw where Ab's stare was directed. Having got what he wanted, he said, 'I don't think you ought to be in here with me . . . You better go now before somebody comes,' and watched the child's curiosity slowly turn to fear.

"In her desperate hurry to get away from the bathroom, Ab slipped and fell thump-thump-thump, all the way down the treacherous back stairs. Her screaming brought Rachel, who picked her up and moaned over her and rocked her in her arms.

"The world (including Draperville) is not a nice place, and the innocent and the young have to take their chances. They cannot be watched over, twenty-four hours a day. At what moment, from what hiding place, the idea of evil will strike, there is no telling. And when it does, the result is not always disastrous. Children have their own incalculable strengths and weaknesses, and this, for all their seeming helplessness, will determine the pattern of their lives. Even when you suspect why they fall downstairs, you cannot be sure. You have no way of knowing whether their fright is permanent or can be healed by putting butter on the large lump that comes out on their forehead after a fall."

This section, though it is only two pages of a 368-page book, is long, I know, but of the details that precede Randolph's standing, what could be left out? Not Abbey's toys, nor the steps by which Randolph draws her into his game, and surely not his glance toward the open door nor her pleasure at finding they had something to talk about. And neither is Maxwell's calculated reticence about what she saw mere prudery; rather, by drawing the readers' imagination into play—and we do, indeed, "see it happening"—he forces us to inform her experience with our own.

The astonishing thing is that I could have cited, to similar effect, a hundred other passages. Individually, they show he has a magic way with words; together, they stamp him as among the past half-century's few unmistakably great novelists. I'm talking here about people like Fitzgerald, who is as good as Maxwell, and Faulkner, who isn't.

This is a large claim to make and, for a while, an embarrassingly private one. Only a couple of years ago, when I did a Canadian Broadcasting Company panel show on the five best American novels since World War II, my fellow critics (a Canadian and a Brit) acted as though I was trying to pull a fast one when I proposed *Time Will Darken It*. Neither would admit even to having *heard* of Maxwell, and they ganged up to accuse me of showing off.

This was bizarre. Not only had he been the *New Yorker's* long-time fiction editor—quietly renowned for his work with Frank O'Connor, John O'Hara, Salinger, Cheever, and Updike—but by then, Maxwell's 1980 novel, *So Long, See You Tomorrow*, had won both the William Dean Howells Medal from the American Academy of Arts and Letters and an American Book Award, and he'd sat for a lovely *Paris Review* interview. Indeed, the earlier books—including *Time Will Darken It*—were gradually being brought back into print in David Godine's paperback line. No matter. He might as well have been invisible.

One reason, I suspect, is the nature of the final paragraph I quoted. Even for a novel of *Time Will Darken It*'s vintage, the homiletic address to the reader seems more than a little old-fashioned, and Maxwell's work is full of them. But on examination, the initial impression of mere quaintness is misleading; the passage may be profoundly moral, but it is not *a* moral. Indeed, as sermons go, it is perverse, for the shift to the present tense, to the general, is anything but reassuring. "Even when you suspect why they fall downstairs, you cannot be sure," is a long way from "the moral of this story is . . ." For if the meaning of the *story* is clear, what it demonstrates is that the meaning of everything that surrounds us is shrouded and unknowable. Even sunlit Draperville is more dangerous than we dare imagine—but having *seen* Randolph, just as Abbey did, how can we not imagine dangers all the time? How can parents ever let their children go? How can they—as Maxwell's mother did when he was young—allow themselves to sicken and die?

The last question has haunted Maxwell's work for years. It animated at least four of his books—*They Came Like Swallows*, *The Folded Leaf*, *So Long, See You Tomorrow*, and the nonfictional *Ancestors*—and accounts in part for the special place children have always had in his work. "In some ways," he says, "I think small children understand life better than anyone else, because there is nothing between them and it, no rationalization or second-hand ideas of what they ought to think and feel. I have found old age to be as lyrical as adolescence, which is to say emotionally bumpy, and at times like playing Russian sleigh, as you say to yourself I won't be doing this or that any more . . . The sight of a young person running fills me, for example, with complex emotions. I think what it would be to have legs that do that, and at the same time remember that I skipped a great deal of the time when I was young, because of an excess of energy that walking or running wouldn't quite dispose of. But certain impressions of a general sort do remain. Such as that old age is a kind of mine field that you walk through, expecting explosions. Cancer, strokes, a fall, arthritis, etc. It is something you share with your contemporaries, and therefore I find it easier to reach out to people on a deep level than ever before."

And yet, despite the enlightening experience of aging, he has (with the notable exception of *Over by the River*) tended to write of children not with a parent's eyes, but with a child's. At first, he talked about this as a mystery. After fifty years in Manhattan, "when I sit down to the typewriter, to write a story, long or short, I seem nearly always to find myself back in Illinois—which I left forever in my late twenties. I don't know why this is, but I do know that it is a requirement of my imagination."

But then he proffered a couple of interlocking explanations: "In writing fiction, a lot of the time a kind of impersonation occurs. The writer feels with a character, feels at times that he is that character. The feelings of children and adolescents have always seemed accessible to me. And perhaps in all these things the general is more important than it seems. I mean, I remember myself as a child, and understand my feelings, did in fact at the time. But my mother died when I was ten and I only see her as a mother, not as a woman or wife to my father. And my father I have tried to understand and sometimes succeeded and sometimes not. Certain acts forever remain difficult or impossible to explain. I should have asked him to explain them, but I didn't know what things would require explaining after he was no longer alive. What I am getting at is that one's parents are perhaps the key to the rest of the world, and my education is somewhat incomplete.

"There is something else," he added. "John O'Hara once remarked that people have an ideal age that they either are approaching or have reached or have left behind, and that means that they are, in certain ways, always that. The overmature child, the boyish old man. And no matter what their experience at any given moment is like, it is colored by their ideal age, so that they go through the experience in a certain way. Sometimes the incongruity is ludicrous, more often it is just mildly noticeable. Sometimes I feel like a child of six, and at others like a seventeen-year-old—as if, really, the greater part of my life were still to come."

Once, I recalled, in addition to a children's book, he published a collection of fables, some of which I've read to my daughter. Were these a father's stories, written to his children? No, "those tales or fables—they are a kind of cross between a fairy tale and a fable—began shortly after I was married, when I told my wife a story, after we had gone to bed, in the dark. She liked this very much and would ask me to do it, and sometimes I would fall asleep in the middle of something and she would wake me and beg me to go on. I never knew where they were coming from. When I began to write them down I sat in front of the typewriter and waited for the typewriter to produce them, a sentence at a time. Which it obligingly did. In some way they are free from the constraints that realistic fiction imposes. They are also more abstract. I don't think, in any case, that people could, or even should, write fiction if there is not somewhere in their makeup a delight in telling a story. I came from a part of the world where this was an ordinary social accomplishment. Maybe, come to think of it, *that* is why I always start from Illinois, where the immortal storytellers lived."

Though all his fiction is partly autobiographical, lately, I suggested, his *New Yorker* stories seem to have been moving away not only from abstraction, but from fiction itself, and toward memoir. "About halfway through my writing career it came over me that you couldn't improve on the way things were in actual life, and I began to invent less and less and try more and more to find a pattern in actual events that would have a meaning, as it exists in a work of art. This partly depends, I guess, on living a long time, so that you begin to see how things work out." The problem with this shift, however, is that "to some extent, if I go toward direct autobiography, I find myself repeating myself. Which is not the best thing to be doing. Sometimes I have wished that I had never written anything whatever before I was seventy, and then I would be able to come at, freshly, material I had already used in other fictional contexts. But if I had never written anything before I was seventy, I wouldn't have learned how to write, so I guess you have to take things as they are."

Yet taking things merely as they are is virtually impossible for an inveterate storyteller, and in almost the next breath, Maxwell qualified my description of his more recent work: "The fiction I have written in the last few years is not as a rule purely autobiographical—I mean the impulse was not to tell about my life. I have already in one way or another disposed of that material. What works is if I write about someone else using all the details that memory, my own memory, supplies, to explain that other person. This often involves using myself as a minor or sometimes major character, but the center of the experience is elsewhere."

The qualification seems fair enough, for however frail Maxwell the person, Maxwell the artist is at once child and man. Though he rarely *insists*, his books confidently distinguish between good and evil; but along with this calm voice of adulthood, they present the turmoils of childhood and adolescence with a freshness that is absolutely credible. He loves children, identifies with them, but fears for them with an earned knowledge of the snares that surround them. Because of that, the metaphor he chose to describe his own books was more meaningful than it would have been for most other writers. Toward the end of our conversation, he talked about having his offspring once again available:

"There was a period when every one of my books was out of print, and it seemed that they would remain in that limbo. In some way, I felt disowned. By my publisher, literally, even though I understood that publishing is a commercial enterprise and I was not a hot property. Twice in my life, this melancholy condition has been rectified, once by a friend, and once by a stranger. Brendan Gill, whose office was down the hall from mine at the *New Yorker*, spoke to Pat Knopf, and the result was a contract to republish *Time Will Darken It*, *The Folded Leaf*, and *They Came Like Swallows* in the Vintage Press. Though *The Folded Leaf* continued to sell about five hundred copies a year—the others much less—that wasn't enough to justify keeping it in print. And once more the books existed only in secondhand bookstores. Then Hilton Kramer spoke to David Godine about *The Folded Leaf*, and Godine offered not only to republish it but all my books. And he has done so, in a handsome form that gives me great satisfaction. All my lost children are or will soon be in print."

Given the economics of publishing, it's rare for any contemporary fiction to get a second chance, much less a third. That these books have testifies to the strength with which some of Maxwell's readers have loved his children. But now that they are alive, once more, in the world of literature, they run again the risk of the marketplace's indifference. This time around, I like to think, we'll be good enough for them.

Interviews with William Maxwell

Barbara Burkhardt/1991

Published by permission of The Estate of William Maxwell

The following three interviews, previously unpublished, were conducted in Maxwell's apartment in New York City and in his home in Yorktown Heights, New York. As described in the introduction, Maxwell typed the answers to my questions. The three interviews are grouped together here with the dates and locations noted.

November 23, 1991—Maxwell's apartment, 544 East 86th Street, New York City

Burkhardt: Mr. Maxwell, what compels you to write?

Maxwell: I have a melancholy feeling that all human experience goes down the drain, or to put it more politely, ends in oblivion, except when somebody records some part of his own experience—which can of course be the life that goes on in his mind and imagination as well as what he had for breakfast. In a very small way I have fought this, by trying to re-create, in a form that I hoped would have some degree of permanence, the character and lives of people I have known and loved. Or people modeled on them. To succeed this would have to move the reader as I have been moved. This is the intricate, in and out, round and round, now direct and now indirect process that comes under the heading of literary art.

Burkhardt: You have said, "Some realism is sordid and harsh and some is very emotional. In my novels I deal with the emotional type."

Maxwell: I don't think William Burroughs, for example—speaking of the other kind of realism—had quite that intention.

Burkhardt: Yes. And in light of your receiving the William Dean Howells medal for *So Long, See You Tomorrow*, do you think of yourself as having carried on Howells's realist tradition in any way?

Maxwell: When I read Howells I always expect more than I get, but I do recognize that we are working the same side of the street. I think my disappointment comes from the fact that he is (more than Henry James, say) limited by being a man of his period. As I am a man of mine. I don't feel any such disappointment when I read *Life on the Mississippi*. I don't think Howells's life was easy, or free from struggle, but (I am not entirely sure about this, I haven't read enough about him) I have a feeling that his struggle was partly to become a literary artist and partly to be accepted by the establishment, and he ended up being the establishment, didn't he? This is dangerous if you care about posterity. Though posterity—the belief in the rightness of the judgment of posterity—is no longer an easily held conviction. What reason is there to think that it is anything more than the taste of a different time? Posterity, Arthur Schnitzler said, is fifty years. Viennese flippancy, with a measure of truth in it.

I miss something in Howells, a sense of the tragic nature of life. Which may be nothing more than that he felt there were certain things that one couldn't write about, that he should have.

Burkhardt: After you wrote *So Long, See You Tomorrow*, you said, "Now I have nothing more to say about the death of my mother. I think forever. But it was a motivating force in four books. If my mother turns up again I will be astonished. I may even have to tell her to go away." In the years since, have you had to tell her to go away?

Maxwell: It has seemed to me that if I go on writing about the death of my mother, as I have time after time, somebody is going to rise up and cry enough. I especially felt this after writing the story "The Front and the Back Parts of the House." The trouble was that there was no way of making the reader feel what I felt when that black woman didn't respond to my embrace without conveying my emotional expectations. That is to say, I threw my arms around her because she had known my mother and was therefore part of the beautiful past. To forestall the indignant reader's objections, I have tried to approach the experience as if I had never written about it before, and even when using the same details use them in a different context or style, with more or less distance. For example, when I was writing the last section of *They Came Like Swallows*, I walked the floor in tears, which I had to brush away with my hand when I sat down at the typewriter to write the sentence I had just written in my head. That is to say, there was no distance at all. Now I try to do the same details but less personally, with my eyes on the other figures in the drama.

Burkhardt: Your father and older brother were very different from you. And, I suppose, in a fraternity, and in school in general, you were surrounded by other young men who did not share your interests. How did you stay true to yourself at a young age?

Maxwell: I might have felt peer pressure more if I had also been more accepted by other boys of my age. I was fifteen years old before I had a real friend—Spud Latham in *The Folded Leaf* is modeled on him. He liked me, I think, because I was different. He loved mavericks. It is also possible that I felt more of an outcast than I actually was. The simple truth is that I never learned how to throw a baseball, which was enough to make as much of an outcast of me as if I had been a character in a novel by Joseph Conrad.

My father, with my own good and future happiness in mind, exerted a considerable pressure on me when I was an adolescent to take up the pleasure of other people. I mean, when we went to work together on the L in Chicago (I did odd jobs in his office during school vacations), he insisted that I put *The Brothers Karamazov* aside and read the bridge column in the *Chicago Tribune.* If I didn't learn to play bridge, he said, nobody would ask me anywhere. Needless to say, the minute his back was turned I stopped thinking about bridge (and never learned to play it) in order to go on with *The Brothers Karamazov.* That the kind of life and the kind of people that I knew (from my reading) must exist somewhere, he had no inkling of. I have received invitations, but seldom—really never—to places where it was expected of me to play bridge.

I suppose my sense of that world I felt I would be happy in came from being so close to my mother in childhood. She had all sorts of pleasures not shared by her women friends, but they didn't keep her from enjoying the women who were not like her. And as I have got older (her influence, no doubt, working subterraneously) I too have found great pleasure in liking all kinds of people, including those with no aesthetic interests whatever.

But to go back to your question. I have stubborn Scottish antecedents, and about matters that are important to me, am not all that easily swayed. And after I grew up I was not judged by whether or not I could throw a baseball. The situation just didn't come up. Neither my father nor my brother had any pedagogical talent. They tried to teach me to throw, but not very hard. In college, in Urbana, in corrective P.E., a whole class of physical misfits was taught how to play baseball, and though I have trouble believing it, I actually pitched. A year later it was once more impossible. In short, the difficulty was not physical but neurotic.

Burkhardt: In *Ancestors* you describe how you "get out an imaginary telescope and fiddle with the lens until you see something small and unimportant. Not Lee's surrender at Appomattox, but two men, both in their late thirties, whose eyes are locked, as if to look up at the sky or an oak leaf on the ground would break the thread of their discourse." What has drawn you to examine the significance of small things?

Maxwell: I think I am drawn to examine the significance in small things out of a distaste for the grandiose. The inflated. When I encounter something really grand, such as, for example, the last two pages of Tolstoy's *Master and Man*, I am overwhelmed. The poet Louise Bogan was a friend, and lived decently, but frugally, in an apartment near the Washington Bridge. She used to say that the view of the Hudson River, between two bleak buildings, was all the view of the river she was intended to have. I feel my only chance to get anywhere near the vicinity of the grand and the tragic is through the modest means that have been given to me. This is not a feeling a major writer is likely to have. The epigraph of Louise Bogan's collected poems, *The Blue Estuaries*, is taken from Rilke, and reads:

> "Wie est das klein womit wir ringer;
> Was mit uns ringt, wie ist das gross . . ."

When I am writing a novel, the first draft especially, I write much that I know is flat, doesn't work, is irrelevant, and so on, and then suddenly there is a sentence that I know will stand, or a scene, or a moment. Anyway, I cut them out and put them in a folder. And try to find a place that they can be locked into, as the narrative proceeds. It is only a slight exaggeration to say that nearly every sentence in *So Long* was in ten other places before it finally settled down and stayed put.

Burkhardt: You've described this writing technique as close to that of the lyric poet. As you've said, "I work with very small things at a time and try over and over to find the proper frame for them." How do you find this proper frame?

Maxwell: In the beginning, probably because of my intense admiration for *To the Lighthouse*, I liked lyrical and poetical fiction. Which I can no longer read. Because of the easy surface and lack of concentration. And because the poetry is inappropriate to prose. The effects too easily come by. But in working from small details and doing what I can to derive a larger meaning from them I am in effect doing what poets do. And perhaps all it means is that my taste has become more refined. And I can't enjoy any novelist much who is without some quality of the poet.

Burkhardt: This reminds me of how Hemingway described his fiction as poetry written into prose. He said that "it is the hardest of all things to do." Do you agree?

Maxwell: I admire Hemingway's stories immensely and detest him personally, without ever having known him. I think what he did in refining prose fiction to the point where it could acquire the intensity of poetry left all writers after him in his debt. But his insisting on how hard it was I feel is self advertisement. He did something that it made him happy to do.

Burkhardt: You've said that one of your favorite first sentences is Stephen Crane's from "The Open Boat," "None of them knew the color of the sky." How would you describe your focus on the internal landscape and on what goes unsaid—and to what extent do you think you are like Crane in this regard?

Maxwell: I guess I focus on what you call the internal landscape because I am aware, in myself, of a simultaneous double communication—the conversation I have with my wife at the breakfast table, for example, and the conversation I have with myself, that is so continuous and so fleeting often that I don't remember what I have said to myself from minute to minute. But there are places where the two conversations overlap and places where they cast light on one another because of the discrepancy, and this is interesting if you are writing fiction that you do not want to be superficial or on one level.

I think what I love in Stephen Crane is his indirectness. He could have begun "The Open Boat" by saying that hour after hour they were bent over their oars and never looked up. Instead he wrote, "None of them knew the color of the sky," which in effect puts the reader in that boat, with his hands on the oars.

Burkhardt: Regarding your own writing process, I am particularly interested in the structure of *So Long, See You Tomorrow*. How did you so smoothly weave fact, fiction, and your memory through the novel?

Maxwell: In the beginning—in the manuscript that I submitted to the *New Yorker*, I mean—the novel began with the death of my mother and arrived at Cletus Smith when I was writing about my father's remarriage and new house. In short, when Cletus appeared as more than somebody in my school room. The *New Yorker* has published so much reminiscence that the editors felt their readers would think this was one more "I remember" piece, only of greater length, and simply never know what it was really about because they wouldn't read that far. So I rearranged the structure and put my cards on the table with the account of the murder at the very beginning. I could have written about the murder as a reporter would, in which case it would not have mattered who I was. But the impulse that gave rise to the desire to write that book was a sudden recollection of the meeting in the school corridor, at which I felt myself wince. And then I thought, "How odd that I should be ashamed of something that happened so long ago." So because of that the book really had two motivating elements—the murder of the father of someone I actually knew (which may unconsciously awaken God knows what Freudian repercussions) and my regret at not having behaved in a more human way. Which left me with two main characters. Cletus and myself. I wrote the parts that were concerned with the murder and the farm separately from those concerned with my mother's death and my life with my father and stepmother. And had simply no idea what to do about connecting them until one day I awoke from my nap, in the little house we have in the country, and saw, among the books on a desk near the bed, a book on Giacometti, and still in the land of Cockayne I opened it and read a letter from Giacometti to Matisse about his sculpture the *Palace at 4 A.M.*, and said "Oh, now I have my novel." I wanted to call the novel the *The Palace at 4 A.M.*, and would have except that Howard Moss, the poetry editor at the *New Yorker*, objected. He himself had written a play with that title. It had been produced in Cambridge. "How would you like it, he said, if I wrote a play and called it *The Folded Leaf*?" He had me there. But I still prefer the title I didn't use, because it says (or stands for) exactly what the novel is about.

Burkhardt: Particularly in *So Long, See You Tomorrow*, your writing flows from one character's mind to another's. Does assuming the viewpoint of different characters—including a dog—come naturally for you?

Maxwell: I can see how Henry James's belief that the narrative should have a single point of view was useful to him, but it would be a straitjacket. I feel essentially a story teller and claim all the privileges of the profession, and it is as easy to pass from one point of view to another as it is to take a drink of water. And as natural. If I were more intellectual I would see more readily the possibility offered by the straitjacket. It is second cousin to hallucinating.

Burkhardt: You said that when you were given your first story to edit at the *New Yorker*, you didn't really know what to do, so you "just cut out what [you] didn't like." Will you describe something about your first experiences editing and how your approach with writers evolved?

Maxwell: I was hired by the *New Yorker* not as a fiction editor but to "see artists"—that is, to be a kind of front man between them and the art committee, which met on Wednesdays. I would listen, and convey their suggestions and decisions on the following day. After about three months, during which time I spent many hours staring at a self-portrait of Thurber on the wall above my desk, Wolcott Gibbs came over with a manuscript in his hand and suggested that I try editing it. He didn't explain what editing was, so I treated it as I would a manuscript of my own in an unfinished state—that is I cut and rearranged and put in or took out punctuation, and to my surprise he sent it off to the printer. The next time I overshot the mark and in the end it required a good deal of teaching and observing of his and Katharine White's editing before I began to get the hang of it.

As I got older I came to feel that the temptation to "improve" a writer's work was suspect, and that the less one changed the better the editing was because it left in the writer's essential quality. During my last years as an editor I did very little editorial tampering, but it is also true that at that time I was working only with extremely gifted writers. Often, in the earlier period, I had to deal with writing that was substandard, even ungrammatical if the writer was a foreigner, like Wexburg or Bemelmans.

Most, as an editor, I tried to make sure that the writer said what he meant and meant what he said. And that he didn't use more words than necessary or reasonable—in short that it wasn't longwinded. Inevitably this had an effect on my own work, and it became more and more concise. I also began to feel that to say precisely what you mean in the only exact way of saying it is a kind of bliss.

Burkhardt: How did your being a writer affect your editing work?

Maxwell: Though I did my best to make the writers I worked with forget that I, too, was a writer, I never stopped identifying myself with them, and it was so painful to me to have to reject their stories that when, after forty years I retired and realized that I would never again have to reject a manuscript, I felt immense relief. With writers who were inclined to be touchy, I would call them on the telephone, after gearing myself up to it, and tell them as simply and directly as I could, what kept the story from being bought. Always, of course, hiding behind the editor of the magazine. Waiting for an answer is killing to writers, and at least I cut that down to a minimum. The writers, on the other hand, joined in in the fiction, and O'Hara, for example, always spoke as if I would have bought the story if it had been up to me and was always on the side of any story he sent me. Whenever possible, and it often was possible, I would study the unsatisfactory manuscript and see if there wasn't something that could be done to make it work. Very often there was.

August 27-28, 1992—Maxwell's home, Yorktown Heights, New York

Burkhardt: As an editor of fiction, and earlier of visual art, you maneuvered between the worlds of art and commercial publishing at the magazine. Can you describe the relationship between the two worlds as you experienced it?
Maxwell: The conditions at the *New Yorker* were, I think unique. One was never concerned with what the reader (hypothetical) would think, or how many of them would or wouldn't like a given story. All that I ever had on my mind, or was expected to have in my mind, was whether or not it was a good piece of fiction. That the magazine at that time was highly profitable was somebody else's affair. My own writing has seldom had any kind of runaway success, and so both as an editor and as a writer I was subject to my own literary conscience and never obliged to think in commercial terms.

Burkhardt: As a fiction editor, did you often help negotiate between writers and the general editor of the *New Yorker*?
Maxwell: The only conflict of any kind was between the writer's intention and what the magazine felt that, for its own special reasons, it wanted to publish. A great deal of the time they were identical, but sometimes they weren't, and all one could say was, sadly, that the thing, though good in itself, didn't fit the needs of the magazine. For example, Robert Lax once wrote a monologue about a man trying to get God to respond to his yearning desire for communication between them. I thought it was just as much fiction as *Anna Karenina*, but I suppose *New Yorker* readers would have been surprised to read it in the magazine.

Burkhardt: In your experience, is there a balance between the production of art, literary or otherwise, and the selling of that art?

Maxwell: No. It goes without saying that publishers these days tend to go in for the kill—the book they can sell tens of thousands of. Advertising is expensive. I don't know whether if Alfred Knopf, for example, dividing the advertising budget equally between all its writers, would go broke or not. Perhaps not. But I doubt if they are going to try the experiment. I also think there are so many readers for work of a certain quality, and that trying to sell two hundred thousand copies of Turgenev's *The Sportsman's Notebook*, which I sometimes feel is the most beautiful book ever written, would be a waste of time and money. The readers who deserve to read it will probably find it eventually.

Burkhardt: You have said that *The Folded Leaf* is your favorite novel you've written. Do you also believe that it is technically your finest work?

Maxwell: I think that, technically, my best novel is *So Long, See You Tomorrow*, because of the structure, and the fact that almost every sentence in it—this is an exaggeration, but has some truth nevertheless—was in eight or ten different places before it finally got locked into the place where it seemed to belong.

The Folded Leaf was a harder novel to write, and is, emotionally, deeper, I think. Also I was writing about a place and the story took place against a rather elaborate background—two, in fact—Chicago and Urbana. The whole time I was writing I had to struggle against the idea that this was a story that no one would want to read. I had a strong temptation to burn it in the fireplace, perhaps because it revealed more about me than I was comfortable revealing. I couldn't write about my own precise family background, because my father and stepmother would have been upset if I had; I tried this, in fact, and it worked, from the literary point of view, but I felt I didn't have the right to do it. So I invented substitutes, made my father somebody he wasn't, and a widower. Half the book is stark simple autobiography and half is invention, and at this point to save my life I can't always tell which is which. It was also a difficulty for me that I was writing about adolescents, and who would want to read about them? I don't think, when I am writing, of whether the book will sell or how many copies it might sell, but I do think of catching the reader, as if I were fishing, and making sure he doesn't get away. I thought of Booth Tarkington and Penrod, and agonized over how to make the life of two schoolboys worth the concern of an adult reader. So maybe I love the book for its difficulties. Louise Bogan, to whom it is dedicated, told somebody, just before she died, that she thought it was my best novel.

Burkhardt: Looking back, what are your thoughts about Lymie and Spud, the boys you created in that novel?

Maxwell: Edmund Wilson thought, or at least said, in his review of *The Folded Leaf*, that it was a weakness that I hadn't followed the inner life of Spud as completely as I did that of Lymie. I hadn't intentionally concentrated more on one than the other, but simply went where I felt most secure, and Spud was, I suppose, an extrovert and they not only don't say, as a rule, what they think and feel, they don't know, being as a rule predominantly physical.

The boy Spud is modeled on must have had earlier school friends, but I didn't. So it was a matter of intense happiness to me that there was someone who wanted my company. I don't know whether in the novel I managed to convey why this was. Though Lymie Peters got good grades in school he was not an intellectual and wanted things to be on simple terms. Spud surely felt inadequate, or he wouldn't have been so pugnacious, and didn't feel inadequate when he was with Lymie because he weighed a hundred and fifty-five pounds and Lymie weighed a hundred and eight, and Lymie never was condescending with anything he said. Together they felt safer against the world than they did individually. I think he was proud to have a friend who was the head of the honor roll, and Lymie enjoyed being the friend of somebody who could like any other boy in sight. But also Spud was extremely funny and original in his sense of humor, and Lymie appreciated just how funny he was. So did the girl who eventually completed the triangle.

Recently at a party in Oregon a man came and sat down beside me who wanted to talk about *The Folded Leaf*. He began by saying "Of course Lymie is homosexual and Spud is bisexual." I found it hard not to go and talk to someone else. Nobody now can quite believe how free from the explicitly sexual the friendship was. Open homosexuality, in the Middle West in the twenties, was extremely rare. They were spoken of, quite simply, by boys in locker rooms as cocksuckers, and this is not a term that Lymie would have found it possible to apply to himself. Or Spud either. I was writing about love, not sex, and if the reader doesn't believe me there is nothing more I can say about it.

Burkhardt: Yes, I understand. Students have come to see me after reading *The Folded Leaf,* unsure about the passage in which "something had burst inside and he felt a flow like blood." What would you tell them about the passage and what is happening? What was your intention?

Maxwell: I meant it to be the moment when Lymie, defeated in his will by physical strength he couldn't manage, became aware of the fact that he loved Spud—more than he ever had any other human being. More than life itself.

The thing happened in the second that he admitted defeat and not in Spud's tucking him under the covers before he left the room. It was the loss of his belief that he couldn't be made to do anything he didn't want to. The psychologist would bring up the word masochist, but I think we should shut the door on the psychiatrist and try to understand it without Freudian jargon.

Burkhardt: In the originally published final chapter of *The Folded Leaf,* Lymie has been released from the hospital and goes to plant wildflowers in the woods. Why did you decide to leave him in the hospital when you republished the book?

Maxwell: The last chapter in the novel as it was originally published is an addition, made at the instigation of Theodor Reik with whom I was in analysis at the time. My original ending was in the hospital, but without the two or three sentences that give a clue to how the lives of the two boys will turn out. Reik wanted something more didactic, something that would make Lymie home free, those were the terms that he thought in. Actually Lymie wasn't more free, he remained Lymie. Diana Trilling, in a review in the *Nation,* pointed it out as a weakness—the upbeat last chapter, and I wished I had had the strength to stick to my original intention. So when I had a chance to revise the book, I did—the first time for the Faber and Faber edition. When I finish a novel, I am usually exhausted and wide open to suggestions from people I trust, when I shouldn't trust anybody but myself.

Burkhardt: What reactions did you receive about *The Folded Leaf* when it was first published?

Maxwell: When he first read the novel, John Cheever remarked that it was clear how much better fitted for life Lymie was than Spud. I think he meant that one was open, an acceptor of people and experiences, and the other essentially closed, by the sense of self-protection. His mother's son, in short.

Burkhardt: In your mind, how did removing the originally published ending in the woods change the novel?

Maxwell: I feel that it is dramatically well constructed without the last chapter, and also it has the phrase "this childish game," which I wanted to convey that the whole experience couldn't have happened to people older than the three of them were.

Originally—because I rewrote the novel at least four times—it was simply a story about a boy who tried to commit suicide. In analysis, I came to understand that man is his own architect, and that Lymie Peters was not pathetic but largely responsible for what happened to him, though often without being aware of it. This increased the dimensions of the book, and there was a further enlargement as I came to see that what I had learned on the couch applied generally, and suddenly all people were interesting to me, more understandable, more human. And I also felt that the only escape from Penrod was to place the story in a setting that was realistic, rather than *Saturday Evening Post*. So the picture of the area in Chicago where Spud lives. And the details about the gymnasium, the house dances, the rooming house, etc. There was, by the way, no such rooming house.

That is to say, the antique dealer is a composite character from people I met in later periods of my life—especially John Mosher, who was a reader and the movie critic of the *New Yorker*. I did go home one night with an acquaintance who lived in an ordinary rooming house with a dormitory, and as the boys noisily came to bed one by one they would wake up a boy named Lymie and say, "Do you want to pee, Lymie? Do you need to pee?" That's where Lymie's name came from and probably something of his character. I never saw the actual boy.

Burkhardt: Your narrator in *The Folded Leaf* makes detached observations that suggest how the story is part of an infinite pattern in human life, that universalize the boys' experience. As you write: "At no time is it necessary to restrict the eye in search of truth to one particular scene." Why did you decide to use this narrative device?

Maxwell: I think it was partly the effect of my being in analysis, but I didn't want to use Freud's explanations and observations. I wanted to enlarge the experience by references to *The Golden Bough*, for example, and my own experiences from a later part of my life. I also wanted to say things without explicitly saying them, especially about the more introverted part of Lymie's character. I have all my life been an enthusiastic reader, and have read the same books over and over, and from the nineteenth-century masters, especially the Russians, but also for example, *Tom Jones*, I felt that a commentator was called for. Really this stems from a fear, I am afraid well founded, that I was working with small scale things that if I didn't give everything I had to them would end up seeming trivial.

Burkhardt: Why did you move away from this type of storyteller in your later works and increasingly use first person?
Maxwell: When I was younger, I tried to use the first person and couldn't. The result was inevitably loquacious and without form. I think I learned how not to be loquacious, how to construct a self that would pass with the reader, from reading E. B. White, who is so candid, but so, so disarming. If I had done *So Long* in the third person I wouldn't have been as close to the painful center of the book, or been able to be a witness as well as an actor. Perhaps the material decided this, without my having anything to do with it. It never occurred to me not to use the first person in *So Long*, or to use it in the other books.

Burkhardt: Last time we met, you commented on Edmund Wilson's critique of *The Folded Leaf*: that you didn't carry Spud's point of view through to the end. You said that you agreed with this observation, but felt that it would have been difficult for you to continue assuming Spud's viewpoint. Why do you think this would have been difficult for you in light of the diverse viewpoints you adopt in *They Came Like Swallows* and *So Long*?
Maxwell: It would have been hard for me to describe Spud's feelings all through the novel because, in the actual experience the book is based on, the boys were most intimate in high school; when they got to college other interests and attachments came between them, and though they saw each other every day, there were things they didn't talk about—Spud's feelings for Sally, for example. They were sleeping together, and this wasn't something where the cat had to have two tails. I think also that Spud's jealousy made him close up like a clam. In short, I was without the necessary information.

When I was older, and much more of an autobiographical writer, when I found myself in a position where I lacked information and needed it, I fought my way to it. I read books about farm life, looked at photographs (Wright Morris, for example) and tried by an effort of the imagination to arrive at what must be so. After about a year I suddenly felt confident that I knew exactly what Cletus's life was like and proceeded to write about it as calmly as I wrote about my own. I couldn't have done this with Spud, it just didn't occur to me—I was too caught up in the events leading to the suicide.

Burkhardt: Considering Cletus and *So Long*: you write toward the end of the novel that Cletus "walks in the 'Palace at 4 A.M.' In that strange blue light. With his arms outstretched, like an acrobat on the high wire. And with no net to catch him if he falls." Earlier, the Palace is described as a place with no windows or doors, where "what is done can be undone." What does the Palace represent to you? Do you think of it as a refuge or a threatening place?

Maxwell: Neither as a refuge nor a threatening place, but the place where the two boys, each in his own way, struggled to find a way of balancing over an abyss. It is the place where the soul of the person is in jeopardy and his finding his balance will save him from disaster (or if he fails) not save him. It is the crucial experience.

Like the boys playing on the unfinished house, the element of balance is everything. They could have fallen and broken their necks. At the end of the book, the experience they were trying to deal with could have overwhelmed them. And in Cletus's case I don't want to say whether it did or didn't. Any more than I mean to imply that the I of the story ever extricates himself from the death of his mother.

Burkhardt: Did the "I" extricate himself?

Maxwell: If he had, this "I" (me) wouldn't have gone on writing novels.

I think it is also possible that what the Palace means to me is the world of (exclusively) my imagination, where life can be and in fact has to be dealt with in the imagination's terms, not the reason's, or the heart's. It is therefore a construction, like the Piranesi prisons, full of bridges in space over arching each other, above the empty and dangerous air. The danger of falling is ever present. The hope of safety equally present. It involves an attempt at an acrobatic performance of a desperately serious kind, where failure would result in living death.

Burkhardt: The Palace also seems akin to the place inside yourself where you transcend boundaries imposed by life and create your stories. Perhaps a place where you reconcile the "double communication" you described to me last time. Is there such a place inside you? What is it like?

Maxwell: The closest I can come to describing the writing part of my mind is to say that in back of the house on Ninth Street, at the foot of a big elm tree, there was a sandpile, which I used to play in by myself for hours. What I built out of sand was whatever I wanted it to be. It was a world totally apart from the world of the house, or any other. When I write I start to tell a story, as a person about to swim across a river takes off his clothes and gets ready to dive in. It is an element that I dive into, and sometimes it sustains me like water, sometimes it doesn't, and I have to wait until another day or abandon the intention. It is a world I don't as a rule share until I have done what I meant to do, and am ready to tidy up the details. The idea that sustains me is a private one.

The imagination's terms are largely imagistic, the heart's abstract pure feelings. The imagination creates metaphors, to explain the situation and so solve it. The heart longs overwhelmingly and hopes by the power and force of its longing to achieve its end.

Burkhardt: You mentioned that when Zona Gale offered to introduce you to anyone in New York, you asked to meet Willa Cather—who was by then a recluse and the only writer Gale could not take you to. How were you influenced by Cather—particularly in terms of what has been called her "unfurnished" writing style?

Maxwell: Much though I admired Willa Cather's books when I was young, when I sat down to write the unfurnished style was not what I was after. I was saturated with lyric poetry, and I didn't mind if it showed. The longer I went on writing, the more of this I shed, until by the time of *So Long* and *The Outermost Dream* all in the world I was after was to say exactly what I meant, without lyrical embellishments. So in effect I ended up in Willa Cather's corner, though she got there by way of Flaubert and I by a feeling that the way to write was the way I remember people speaking in my Illinois childhood.

Burkhardt: Your friend E. B. White wrote that "the essayist is a self-liberated man, sustained by the childish belief that everything he thinks about, everything that happens to him, is of general interest." Do you agree and have you adopted a similar philosophy?

Maxwell: Concerning White's theory about the essayist, I think referring to one's own experience is a matter of self-reference. Some people (I included) do this every time they draw a breath, and can be and often are the world's worst bores. He, of course, wasn't. I think people who are or want to feel they are just like everybody else, tend not to do this. The ones who do do it often have not been allowed to feel that they are like everybody else, but this is not true of him. He led a charmed though not precisely happy life.

As for what White said, I think I do agree with him to a large extent. That is, when I am in doubt about a passage or an idea, and concerned lest it be boring, I say to myself, "If it interests me it will interest *somebody*," and go ahead and write it.

Burkhardt: In your last letter to me you wrote that sometimes Whitman is "a little, quite a little bogus, but when he is not bogus he is a marvel." What do you find bogus and marvelous in Whitman?

Maxwell: When Whitman says, I embrace multitudes, I am the this and the that, I find him bogus. When he writes about the death of Lincoln, I find him marvelous, inspired. I detest rhetoric. That is language that has come unmoored from feeling.

Burkhardt: Whitman ends *Song of Myself* by telling future readers that he stops somewhere waiting for us. When you are writing, do you think about future generations?

Maxwell: When I think about future generations I think it would be nice, it would be a justification, among others, for my having lived the life I have lived, but I never imagine them thinking about William Maxwell the twentieth century novelist; only about this or that book, which it would make me happy to think that they are moved by, as moved as a present day reader, because that would mean I had got my hands on something that is a constant of human life.

Burkhardt: You have said that preserving the past is central to what you do as a writer. Do you, like Faulkner, believe that the past overtakes the present? How so?

Maxwell: I do think—at least it is true in my case—that if you live long enough the past rises up and becomes a part of the present; it is all one thing, enormously interesting to the mind.

Burkhardt: Yes, and you mentioned that you hate the "plowing under of human experience, leaving no trace." What experience has made it so important for you to preserve the past?

Maxwell: I suppose that if my mother had lived and I had never experienced bereavement I would have grown impatient with her, grown away from her, and of course never stopped loving her, but I might—I am not sure—I might have let the past go and not turned into a preserver, but simply lived each day as it happened. I also think if I were offered the choice I would choose the life of the preserver. It has more emotional resonance.

Burkhardt: Do you feel that you have been categorized as a regionalist writer? What do you think of this label?

Maxwell: I don't feel that I am categorized as a regional writer because what I do with the characters is more important than where they lead their lives.

Burkhardt: In the preface to the new Quality Paperback Book volume, you write that *Time Will Darken It* was written shortly after you were married and that you "had had the feeling that, for someone as happy as you were, writing was not possible." Do you believe that unhappiness is a more natural state for writing? How is writing different for you when you are happy or unhappy?

Maxwell: I think in a state of pure happiness one doesn't want to do anything but be happy. Though one can combine it with other things, they are essentially an intrusion. A state of unhappiness can be escaped from for the moment, or sometimes cured, by writing, as (sometimes) the dreamer makes the dream come out right. Fortunately most of the time one is neither perfectly happy nor utterly unhappy, and in that neitherish state writing is as reasonable and available as any other kind of action, such as for example shaving or eating and drinking and sleeping.

In writing *Time Will Darken It*, a set of characters seized me and ran off with me. My function was simply to record what they said and did, rather than shape the goings on. My wife was as interested in their behavior as I was. I could have dreamed the whole novel. It had no effect on my feelings when I was not at the typewriter.

Burkhardt: What was it like writing about a troubled marriage in *Time Will Darken It* at a time when you were so happy with your own new marriage?

Maxwell: No marriage, happy or otherwise, is without conflict. A marriage without conflict would I imagine rather quickly dissolve. The conflicts in the story were stand-in for real adjustment that had to be made, happiness or not, before we could live together on any kind of easy acceptance. Love has so many planes of being—romantic, sexual, human, personal fantasy, and simple need. All woven together. Separate and simultaneous. Some element of the actual exists in the novel, but it is largely the work of the storyteller, who was a bystander interested only in not losing his audience.

Burkhardt: Into how many languages have your works been translated? Are there books that are popular in particular countries?

Maxwell: I am not sure I can remember how many languages my books have been translated into—French, of course, German, Spanish, Portuguese, Italian, Swedish, Japanese, Dutch—possibly other languages. I forget. I think I am more read in France than in the other countries, *So Long*, particularly, but also *The Folded Leaf*.

Burkhardt: Flaubert said: "The author in his book must be like God in his universe, everywhere present and nowhere visible." How would you respond to this statement, especially in regards to your narrators in *The Folded Leaf* and *So Long*?

Maxwell: Flaubert's devices worked for Flaubert, as James's worked for James, but I never have felt that they had any universal application, or that not to write like either of them or like Joyce, was to fail in one's literary obligations.

Burkhardt: What do you think are the advantages of being invisible in narrative and also of playing a role in your own story?

Maxwell: At the *New Yorker* one of my colleagues, Maeve Brennan, was fond of saying, "I'd like to have been a fly on the wall," about some incident. The invisible narrator has all the advantages of the fly on the wall. But the one thing he cannot do is bear witness to something. Even though he is a witness, the fly cannot put his leg on the Bible and by swearing make the reader believe that what he says is true. The visible narrator is a person in whom the reader can at the critical moment put his trust. As the reader of Conrad does in Marlow.

Burkhardt: Did you ever consider writing from your mother's point of view?

Maxwell: Oddly enough, I never have considered writing from my mother's point of view. When she was alive I saw things as she saw them, pretty much. I wasn't interested in how other people saw them. And when she was dead I incorporated her personality into my own, so how I see things is (unconsciously) how she also would see them.

Burkhardt: What life experiences have helped you write from a female point of view?

Maxwell: I couldn't have done Nora Potter's love for Austin King if I hadn't had access to the love letters of a girl, now dead. In short, I helped myself to the actual. In general, I have always been comfortable in the presence of women, and often what interested them seemed to me a reasonable thing to be interested in. Only a fool would be condescending with a woman, no matter which one.

Burkhardt: Bruce Bawer has written that unlike many writers you seem "never to have forgotten how a child's mind works." How do you believe a child's mind works?

Maxwell: A lot of the mental behavior of most adults is secondhand, and very little of the child's. Everything is seen for the first time, without (very often) any explanation. Things are what they seem to be, even if actually what they seem to be is not what they actually are.

Burkhardt: When you are writing from a child's point of view do you translate from your adult mind into what you remember a child's mind to be like, or do you place yourself in a childlike state in which you actually relive experience directly?

Maxwell: I think sometimes I call upon my child self, what I remember it to have been like, or some other child I knew when I was a child. But in general I don't think I have outlived any part of my life, it all seems to co-exist—childhood, adolescence, middle age, old age—no one of them any more remote than the other, or remote at all. It is easier for me to imagine what goes on in a child's mind while he is playing than it would be, for example, to imagine what is going on in Edmund Wilson's or George Bush's or Senator Moynihan's. In a pinch, though, I could do them, I think. Doing a child is easy as falling off a log.

Burkhardt: In the new Quality Paperback Book preface you write, "as a rule, unless real people have suffered a sea change and become creatures of the novelist's imagination, the breath of life is not in them." What do you believe can be more real about characters you create than people you meet in life?

Maxwell: I own the creatures I create and so easily believe in them. The man I am introduced to in the drugstore I don't own. He is a mystery from one end to the other. My friends also can astonish me, and I would hesitate to speak for my nearest and dearest. I never hesitate to speak for an imaginary person.

Burkhardt: Do you believe that balancing the life of solitude with life in society is an important conflict for your characters? If so, why and how?

Maxwell: I have never thought consciously about the conflict in my characters between balancing the life of solitude with the life among people. In my own life the conflict is ever present, adding up to innumerable failures. Because ultimately, no matter how fond of the person I am, I will desert them and go write—that is, enter a world where they cannot follow. With characters in a book, the moments of solitude are simply a way of entering more deeply into their natures.

Burkhardt: In your essay on Colette you wrote about your admiration for her work. You called yourself a "tongue-tied" fan. Now, do you enjoy being the object of admiration yourself?
Maxwell: I enjoy being admired, when it happens, but I put it out of my mind almost instantly, because to sit around thinking about how many people admire you and how much would be too silly for words.

Burkhardt: Last time we met, you described literary art as a "now direct and now indirect process." How do you decide when to be direct and when to be indirect in telling your stories?
Maxwell: The methods and devices of storytelling are largely instinctive. If one is dissatisfied with the results, one tries to do it over or uses some other method. It is a mixture of the conscious and the unconscious. Very much like painting or carpentry.

Burkhardt: In your story, "My Father's Friends," the character Dean Hill says, "I am interested in the writer—in what he is carefully not saying, or saying and doesn't know that he is." What is the importance of "carefully not saying" in your writing?
Maxwell: Sometimes I want an idea to come into the reader's mind without its seeming to have been put there by me, but rather by the events he is reading about. That way he becomes more of a sharer.

Burkhardt: Dean Hill goes on to say: "All forms of deception are entertaining to contemplate, don't you find? Particularly self-deception, which is what life is largely made up of." Do you agree? How do we deceive ourselves?
Maxwell: I do agree that life is largely self-deception. Eliot said human beings can't stand very much reality. Self-deception is one way of coming in out of the cold. Without it one would spend a large part of one's life wincing over past behavior.

Burkhardt: So much is written about your concentration on the Middle West. When you write about other locations—France, New York, the Caribbean—do you feel that your intent is the same? Do you approach writing about characters in these other locales differently?

Maxwell: I think at the moment one has the idea for a story one has with it the time and place—which are often not attached to it but the source of it. I suspect it is essentially a matter of where one's heart is. One's heart is more often than not in command, issuing instructions, making decisions that pass for rational but are really emotional instead. In writing the fables in *The Old Man at the Railroad Station* I was most of the time not anywhere. I was in the state of mind of storytelling. Though a number of them are based on actual experiences in actual places, they have been absorbed into once upon a time.

Burkhardt: In "The Holy Terror," you write that because your brother was so incorrigible, you became a more "tractable, more even-tempered, milder person" than it was your true nature to be. Were it not for your brother's temperament, what do you believe would have been your true nature?

Maxwell: I don't think I would be so soft-spoken. I might have been more given to pushing people around, though I don't admire people who do this. I might even, God forbid, have been given to tooting my own horn. Or I could have asked for more than my share. Or monopolized the conversation or have been unpleasant in any number of ways. In the letters of Joseph Ackerly there is a masterly description of E. M. Forster in extreme old age, making his way along the sidewalk, elaborately getting out of the way of passersby who weren't there. It is the extreme of what you are asking about. Over consideration can sometimes come at a rather high price.

Burkhardt: What was your life like when you first came to New York in the thirties? Did you ever have second thoughts about leaving the Midwest?

Maxwell: When I first came to New York my life was lonely, though I did have friends—a brother and sister who were the children of a doctor who lived and had his office on upper Madison Avenue, and an actor/photographer, who later became a director for CBS. For something like four years I spent every weekend with his family in Wilton, Connecticut. But I was working five days a week at the *New Yorker* as both an art and fiction editor, and when I got home at night I didn't want to have anything to do with people, having had so much to do with them all day long. I tried not to have a telephone, and when Mrs. White's secretary insisted I had one put in but didn't answer it when it rang, which it didn't very often do. I didn't go to the theater or the opera or buy paintings or go to museums. I just was caught up in my job. I also had insomnia. And used to try and fall asleep between the passing of one Sixth Avenue L train and the next. Unsuccessfully, I also walked at midnight.

Burkhardt: Since you write about so many actual people, many of them relatives, what types of reactions have you received from them?

Maxwell: About the reactions of actual people, my Aunt Maybelle, who sat for her portrait as Aunt Clara in *They Came Like Swallows*, made a point of saying she didn't buy my first novel because she was waiting for the second. I don't know how she arrived at this decision, but at the time she said it I was already embarked on the second, and knew that she wouldn't like the picture of her. But kept to my course, even so. I spoke to my father about it and he advised her not to read it, but she did anyway. Fortunately for me, she died before I saw her again.

Burkhardt: What are your personal guidelines as far as what you will or will not include when writing about living people?

Maxwell: I tried to spare the feelings of the French family that I used as a model, or perhaps I ought to say that I wrote about—with inventions and rearrangements, naturally—by not letting the book be published in England (because English books easily cross the channel) or translated into French. Inevitably a member of the family that I had never met came to America at the time the book was being talked about, bought a copy, read it and when she went home said (so far as I know) nothing about it to anybody. Years later they did see the book, and wrote to me, saying that I have been very "naughty" and could they please have a copy. Not long ago I wrote and asked if enough time had passed that the book could be published in France, and after due consideration they wrote back that it was a very good book but the answer was never. I have abided by their wishes. I don't know of any harm that I have ever caused by writing about actual people. But in identifying themselves with characters I did not base on them, people have hurt them-selves badly. Whether this is my fault or theirs, is the question. Some of it probably is my fault, for coming too close to home, in creating a composite character.

In writing about living people, I try to write about them as they would be in the eyes of the angels (who are of course not easily bamboozled) but not in such a way that would seriously expose them, to themselves or to other people. I have not, for instance described the scene in which my Aunt Annette tore up my Aunt Edith's will because she didn't like certain aspects of it regarding the share of her children versus my mother's.

In writing a novel I have always been seized by the subject, without a certain number of essential choices. Time, place, etc., given to me rather than chosen by me.

Burkhardt: You have said that you try to find the simple, natural way of saying exactly what you mean and describe this as a Midwestern trait. How does the direct, simple language of your childhood in Lincoln come into play with a novel set in France or a short story in New York?

Maxwell: I am not sure that, in writing about France, for example, or New York I do summon the speech of Lincoln people. I think it is only in the latter part of my life that it has come to be so important to me. The voice of the man writing about France is the voice of the man who made his living working on a magazine.

I think when I am writing about New York or a foreign country I tend to fall back upon my eyes rather than my ears. The writing becomes more visual.

Burkhardt: During our last visit, you mentioned that you could no longer read James, and in the *Tamaqua* interview you said that you would have liked to have taken the "Six Novels of Henry James" course at Illinois, but that at the time you had "no inkling of how deeply" his novels would one day command your attention. In what ways did James command your attention?

Maxwell: Even though I have trouble reading him now because of his embroidery and surface mannerisms, I did come to feel, reading him, that a strong structure is a very good thing for a novel to have. I have never felt that his insistence on a single point of view was of any value for me. Or tried to invent difficulties of understanding for their own sake. But my admiration for his sense of what is a story worth telling is endless. In my first novels I advanced from details one to another, rather than from an inner form that was dictating the events. I didn't consciously think of *The Ambassadors* when I was writing *The Chateau*. I wouldn't presume to put myself even in the position of imitating him. I was working from an actual experience, and I don't suppose he was.

Burkhardt: You have said that you were not suited for a position at the *New Republic* because you were "politically uninformed." Whether you still see yourself this way or not, what national or international events have most touched your life?

Maxwell: I had no interest, no real interest in politics until Adlai Stevenson, whose marvelous speeches made me into a responsible (after a fashion) citizen. When he was defeated it broke my heart. But I became a liberal Democrat and don't understand how any feeling person could be anything else. My wife finds this bigotry trying, though she is not herself a registered Republican.

Burkhardt: Your cousin Tom Perry mentioned to me that you attended a protest against the Vietnam War with Brookie on your shoulders. Can you describe this event?

Maxwell: I did walk in Vietnam protest parades, sometimes with my wife, but not with my older daughter who was also protesting but didn't want to do it with the family. I lay down in the mud in Central Park, between two strangers, and released a balloon into the sky with theirs. But in fact we did do this once as a family—all four of us, with candles in our hands, in front of St. Patrick's Cathedral.

Burkhardt: What about this issue compelled you to participate publicly when you are normally a private person?

Maxwell: I hate war. I hate the killing of young men, or, as it now is, everybody.

Burkhardt: In the *Tamaqua* interview, you wrote that you were originally planning on studying at the Art Institute of Chicago. Tell me a bit about your aspirations for being an artist. What type of art were you most interested in?

Maxwell: As a child I was never far from a paint box, and in high school in Chicago I had courses in illustration. I thought I would be an illustrator of children's books, like Kay Neilson, for example. My art teacher was very affectionate and kind, but she taught us how to make a drawing by working with photographs and taking a detail from this drawing and another from some other. This does not, of course, make one confident. It is really a kind of cheating. I don't think I would have made a very good artist. It was lucky I escaped.

Burkhardt: In 1932 you went to the Caribbean and in 1948 visited France with your wife. In the preface to the Quality Paperback Book Club volume you mention that you went to the Caribbean when it was the best time to go to Europe. How aware were you of the travels of other writers during the earlier part of the twentieth century? Say, Hemingway, Pound, and Dos Passos in Europe in the twenties and early thirties, and Hemingway's own later travels to the Caribbean?

Maxwell: I really wasn't very conscious of the American expatriate writers in the twenties and thirties. Glenway Wescott and Janet Flanner later became friends of mine, and I loved to hear them talk about Paris during the prewar period, but I think it may have been that when I had time I had no money and when I had money I had no time.

Burkhardt: How did your later travels influence your work?

Maxwell: *The Chateau* and two or three stories were the result of traveling in France, but I also traveled in England and Italy and Austria without anything coming of it. Then or with later trips. I think it is probably because we were always tourists, and if we had settled down in one place stories might have come of it. The experience of tourists is necessarily two dimensional.

Burkhardt: Does traveling, especially out of the country, provide a clearer perspective of home that is important to your writing?

Maxwell: In relation to "home," I am already out of the country when I live in New York. Being in France or Italy wouldn't change the perspective.

Burkhardt: Yes, I see. How has being "out of the country" in New York influenced you?

Maxwell: Living in New York made me want to preserve my Middlewesterness. When I went to the U of I, I was seduced into changes of speech, in imitation of faculty members I admired, that were not those of Lincoln—"resolyution," for instance. I did pick up a few habits of speech then that have remained. But in New York and especially at the *New Yorker* I was never consciously tempted—toward saying ahnt for aunt. I didn't want to lose my identity and simply be part of the *New Yorker*. I wanted to be the one who was an outlander. God knows why.

Burkhardt: So the experience of living away from Illinois made you want to preserve your own background. Do you think Americans in general have a sense of preserving regional culture and traditions?

Maxwell: I think Americans have weak memories. This results in a loss of all kinds of cultural flavors and values.

Burkhardt: Emerson believed that traveling is a fool's paradise.

Maxwell: I agree to the extent that one helplessly takes oneself with one wherever one goes. Garreta Busey, the banker's daughter, in whose house I lived, had worked in New York on the staff of the *Tribune* book section, and had been a nurse during the first World War and had traveled in Yugoslavia, but remained, in speech and attitudes as if she had never left Urbana. I admired this and probably copied it.

Burkhardt: Can you talk about how your wife, Emily, has served as your most trusted reader?

Maxwell: What most often happens is that in the first flush of finishing a story or a book review I take it to her to read, because I know she is interested, and she reads it very slowly and carefully and more often than not smiles and says, "I think this is going to be one of your best stories." So I climb down from the euphoria and go back to the typewriter and eventually she smiles and says she likes it and then, and then only do I know I have done it.

Burkhardt: About other relationships in your life: did you continue your friendship with Jack Scully after college?

Maxwell: Not really. He went off to medical school in Chicago and struck up a friendship with my father, but one night when my father went to his house (by that time he was married to "Sally") and Jack was rude to his wife, a thing my father was deeply offended by since his feelings toward women were invariably gallant, and he told Jack off, and ended the relationship.

Burkhardt: When were you able to let go of the friendship yourself?

Maxwell: I am not sure when I was—possibly the same year that I attempted to commit suicide—but I heard that Jack had appeared at the Theta house drunk and looking for me in order to beat me up. I knew he wouldn't have if he had met me, and was amused. What really brought the friendship to an end occurred about a month after the end of the novel—I expect you to know I am telescoping the book and life—anyway, he was in the same hospital with a strep throat, and "Sally" and I stood outside his window, talking to him, as the twilight deepened into dusk, and suddenly I sensed a return of his hatred for me—of the jealous rage. And turned and walked away, for fifty feet or so, thinking it has returned, after all that happened. I have to choose, or it will repeat itself over and over, and I chose in that instant to stop loving him.

Burkhardt: How did he and others from the University react to *The Folded Leaf*?

Maxwell: I was the best man at his wedding, which gave me pleasure, and once when I went to see them, after the birth of their only child, he held the baby upside down by one heel proudly to show me what he had done. But in later years when I was at the *New Yorker* he didn't call me. When I published *The Folded Leaf* I sent them two copies, and they sat up in bed reading it together, and "Sally," whose name was Margaret, thought I had been too harsh on his sister, and Jack said no, that was just the way it was. Beyond that he had no comment on the book.

Burkhardt: What happened to him in later years?

Maxwell: His philandering led ultimately to a divorce, a remarriage, etc. When he was about sixty-eight he had a massive heart attack and his doctor told him he must change his habits. He decided he wanted life on his own terms and didn't change them but went on smoking and drinking, and died in a car accident, of a heart attack. I was deeply surprised. I had thought he was immortal. I still find it odd that he who was so physically strong should have died before me. E. M. Forster, correctly I think, says if you have ever loved someone you go on loving them as long as you live, whether you see them or not.

Burkhardt: Last time we visited, you told me that, like Lymie, you attempted suicide in college.

Maxwell: I think that, partly from reading so much poetry, I had a poetic idea of a life after death in which I would be reunited with my mother, and I think that, unconsciously, this was exerting a pull, quite independent of the feelings that made me want not to go on living. But what I thought, at the time, was that I didn't want to live in a world where the truth has no power to make itself be believed. I don't feel that anymore. I have too much respect for the difficulty of arriving at the truth in the first place.

Burkhardt: How did Freudian theory and analysis with Theodor Reik help you to write about this experience?

Maxwell: Well I think it can—Freudian theory—open up possibilities, but it can also reduce or at least diminish the diversity among people and one ought to try to understand oneself by listening to one's own mind and trying to understand one's dreams. After a leg up, I guess I mean, the work to be done is by the person not the analyst. In writing, the effect of analysis is to shift the emphasis from what happened to why it happened, and this inevitably brings the action to a dead stop. I had a hard time breaking myself of the habit of looking for the why. The why is always there, but it should be felt spontaneously, and not be the driving force.

Burkhardt: Last time we spoke about the *Palace at 4 A.M.* in *So Long, See You Tomorrow*. As a metaphor, does it represent the place where these questions are worked out?

Maxwell: I don't think the Palace is in any way active, it is (metaphorically speaking) a place, a state of being and you could give yourself a second chance or you could fail utterly. It doesn't shut off any possibility. It is walking the high wire without any net to catch you and a fall can be mortal.

Burkhardt: In the *Tamaqua* interview, you mentioned spending a summer at the MacDowell Colony in Peterborough, New Hampshire. When was this? What was the experience like and how did it affect your writing?

Maxwell: I spent three months, July, August, and September 1935, at the MacDowell Colony. Robert Fitzgerald, who had become a friend at Harvard in the winter of 1930-31, was also there, which added immensely to my pleasure. We lived in the men's dormitory and his room was above mine, and I would hear with pleasure his footsteps crossing the ceiling. He was very poor and used to wash his shirts and underwear in the washbasin and hang them across the room on a string.

I had started to write *They Came Like Swallows*, and had done the first section seven times, while living at [Bonnie Oaks]. At Peterborough I did it for the eighth time and it stuck. Looking at it now I wonder what the difficulty was; the difficulty was that I didn't know how to handle narrative, or what form the book would take. I spent a lot of time talking to other people, going swimming in a park in Peterborough, and even I once climbed Mt. Monadnock, but the essential work got done. I mean I got past the block, into the second section, which I finished in Urbana, and the last section I wrote in two weeks, in a room at the Busey house, walking the floor and brushing the tears away in order to see the typewriter keys. It was only a little over fifteen years after the disastrous facts, and I hadn't achieved much distance from them. What I wrote later may move the reader more, but is written from a certain distance I had not then acquired.

The MacDowell Colony was a beautiful place ruined by an accumulation of rules which it was virtually impossible not to break. Without meaning to I broke all of them. The pasture gate was the worst. Don't do this, don't do that; thank God I can't remember what they were. Mrs. MacDowell was very old and had a toadying companion whose eye was forever out for infringements. Ordinarily I like old women, but Mrs. MacDowell and I didn't take to each other. I had the feeling that she didn't care all that much for anybody who wore trousers. On my birthday, Martha Graham was dancing in the town hall, and I got tickets for Robert and me, and then we learned that Mrs. MacDowell was giving a musical that evening and had invited people from the surrounding hills. The colonists were expected to attend. The colonists, or most of them, had tickets to Martha Graham, and were beside themselves. One of them was a friend of Graham and got her to start her performance late, and the musicians who were to play for Mrs. MacDowell planned an intermission, which would allow us to slip away unnoticed and go down to the village. In the intermission of Graham's recital (which struck me dumb with amazement) I was standing on the front steps of the hall with two girl dancers from Jacob's Pillow, when I saw Mrs. MacDowell drive by with her head out of the window counting the offending colonists. The rest of my stay was largely devoted to apologies, ditto everybody else, and in the fall when I went to a meeting of the MacDowell Association in New York, she saw me and turned her back, releasing me forever from what would have been a considerable obligation.

Burkhardt: Can you tell me more about leaving Lincoln to move to Chicago?

Maxwell: In the spring of 1924 my father and stepmother moved to Chicago so he could take up his new position, and left me behind with my stepmother's brothers and mother, to finish my freshman year of high school. Her brothers were very lively, generous men who treated me with great kindness, and were in the habit of stuffing ten-dollar bills in my pockets, and enjoying my enjoyment. I actually shared a bedroom with one of them that spring, and when he went to bed at night the last thing he did was hang his toupee on a bedpost. My stepmother's mother was also very kind to me.

When it came time for me to join my father and stepmother in Chicago, the uncles happened to be driving there on business and so took me instead of my taking the train. They stopped to see one of their gravel pits and then we drove into the city and they checked in at the Hotel LaSalle, whose mahogany and coffered ceiling far outdid any splendor I have ever seen. Then we took a taxi up Michigan Avenue to Rogers Park so I could see everything. Their enjoyment of my enjoyment I have never forgotten.

The neighborhood we lived in had a group of boys, but for several weeks they ignored my existence. Then my older brother, who was an easy mixer, struck up an acquaintance with a girl his age who had a brother my age, and this boy spoke to me, after which I existed. But it was very lonely for the first weeks at Senn High School. But again my brother made things easier, by a connection with one of those boys who linger in high school playing football past the age of twenty-one. He got me into a high school fraternity, which was illegal, but provided me with people to speak to, who knew my name. Little by little, I became more at home and ultimately very happy, since the school offered every conceivable opportunity.

Burkhardt: Could you talk a bit about your father's marriages to your mother and stepmother?

Maxwell: There was nothing about either of my father's marriages that I would have thought of trying to avoid. He was devoted and considerate and both marriages were happy. When I brought Emmy to Lincoln the first time she was distressed because he waited until he had finished watching a boxing match on TV before giving his attention to me. And for a day or two I thought, "Doesn't he realize what she is like?" The one day when we were alone he said simply, "There has been nobody like her in our family in three generations. She is like a star."

Women were the one place where his imagination functioned. The rest of him was practical. Or ethical. But he did also say seriously (and I listened seriously): "If you will only think of her first, she will always think of you first." I don't suppose this is always true, but in our marriage it proved to be.

Burkhardt: You grew up with two brothers, and you write a great deal about young boys. What was it like to switch to a predominantly female household as an adult? Did this in any way change your writing?

Maxwell: I have always felt comfortable in the world of women. As a child, I was often in my mother's bedroom when she and my aunt would be trying on clothes, and I was familiar with their corsets and the things on dressing table tops. Since I had no desire to kill animals, hunting and fishing—the guns and tackle that were so conspicuously a part of the men's world—were not interesting to me. I think it is possible that the reason so much of what goes on in my novels is domestic is a reflection of all this. Brookie told me not long ago that she thought I went into my room and played with a toy (my typewriter) which she was not encouraged to play with. Sometimes she did, and once I roared at her, when her finger and my finger struck a typewriter key at the same moment, and I was too absorbed to realize that she was even there. Tears, apologies under the dining room table. In general, they knew they could come and go and I sometimes wrote with them sitting on my lap. I don't mind interruptions. I like to write against a background of domestic activity.

Burkhardt: Do you watch television?
Maxwell: McNeil Lehrer.

Burkhardt: Who are your favorite singers?
Maxwell: Lemnitz, Kathleen Ferrier, Judith Raskin, Lucrezia Bori—in short lyric sopranos, and Flagstad, of course. And Marian Anderson, Schipa, John McCormack.

Burkhardt: Have you enjoyed any popular music?
Maxwell: Gershwin, Jerome Kern, Rodgers and Hart, and a little though not much of Rodgers and Hammerstein. Hammerstein is largely bogus. June is busting out allover indeed!

Burkhardt: If you could spend your day doing anything—other than writing—what would you do?
Maxwell: Talking to two or three people, among the living and dead. Robert Fitzgerald, for example. And William Meredith. And some young friends, like Ben Cheever, Dan Menaker, and Chip McGrath of the *New Yorker*. Alec Wilkinson, Joseph Mitchell.

Or gardening. Or reading a book that I am carried away by. One of the great pleasures is starting something just before bedtime and feeling the strong pull to read all night. Sometimes we have, as with *Heartbreak House*, finished at four in the morning. Gardening is a form of emptying the mind. You think only about what is a weed and must be pulled roots and all, without disturbing the surrounding flowers. It is unreflective, and free from anxiety or remorse or any emotional complication. It just is. Meditation could be a little like this, I don't know.

Burkhardt: What are your favorite foods?

Maxwell: Moussaka, lamb shanks, sweet corn, asparagus from the garden, peas, double lamb chops, stuffed baked potatoes, risotto with kidneys, fish broiled with fennel; in France, sour cherry pie.

Burkhardt: Tomato and bacon sandwiches? [We had just had tomato and bacon sandwiches, made by Mrs. Maxwell, for our lunch, and he told me they were among his favorite foods.]
Maxwell: Tomato and bacon sandwiches.

Burkhardt: Before you were married, did you go out in the evening?
Maxwell: No.

Burkhardt: What did you enjoy about being the president of the National Institute of Arts and Letters?
Maxwell: I remembered how kind the expression on Malcolm Cowley's face was when he handed me a check, before I became a member. And so, in giving awards, I tried to convey a similar warmth. I didn't have a carrying voice, and the deafer members would call "louder, louder," and I would have to say, "I can't speak any louder," until another friend advised me to speak to the person in the room who was farthest away from me and after that I had no more trouble. I hated to compose citations, and I liked to be able to plan evenings where writers I admired, like Eudora Welty and William Meredith and John Wheelock read from their works. Or there was interesting music. Committee work bores me. I never read from my own work.

Burkhardt: What were the most memorable performances you have seen in New York?
Maxwell: The performances I remember with most pleasure are the original production of *Our Town* and *The Glass Menagerie*, a form of *Die Fledermaus* in the early thirties, called *Champagne Sec*, The Ballet Russe de Monte Carlo, the Abbey Theater's *Playboy* and *The Plough and the Stars*. The best thing I ever saw in the theater was in London, and was Shaw's *You Never Can Tell* with Ralph Richardson.

Burkhardt: How do you celebrate Thanksgiving and Christmas now? How does this compare with the holiday celebrations of your childhood?
Maxwell: We don't much celebrate either now. The family is loosened, and other claims are felt by the children. It is a hit or miss affair, though Emmy tries. When we had more elaborate Christmases and the children

were small, I used to get bored watching people open their presents and one Christmas I worked on galley proofs, creating considerable displeasure on the part of everybody. As a bachelor, I couldn't get enough of Christmas. Also as a child. As for now, I have had it.

Burkhardt: Have you and your wife entertained often?
Maxwell: We don't entertain often. There was a time when we had a black housekeeper who liked for us to have company, and we did more. But it takes away from our work, generally, and requires a day or two to recover from it. I like people immensely but one at a time.

Burkhardt: You chose to leave Illinois and pursue a career as a writer, while your friend, Charles Shattuck, stayed in Urbana and became an English professor. Looking back, how would you describe the life choices you both made?
Maxwell: As a young man Charles went off with traveling players and the hardships he experienced cured him of an interest in the uncertainties. He has made a distinguished career out of his scholarly pursuit of the way Shakespeare's plays were acted, and he also was a director. I suspect a good one. He also enjoyed being part of *Accent*. I do not sense any regret or discontent with his life.

If I had my life to live over I would do the same thing that I have done. Without worrying. Which is a waste of spirit. I have been terribly lucky. I liked editing and working with writers and artists. And I liked writing my own books. I get a good deal of pleasure out of contemplating other people's talent.

Burkhardt: What kind of life do you wish for your daughters?
Maxwell: I wish for my daughters to be involved, to have a family to love, and work that fulfills them. And friends. And accomplishments to look back on with satisfaction.

Burkhardt: What were your favorite books as a child?
Maxwell: I moved from the Oz books to *Treasure Island*, and read them many times. Then it was J. M. Barrie. And then it was lots and lots of lyric poetry.

Burkhardt: Other than the *Palace at 4 A.M.*, have there been artworks that have particularly inspired you?

Maxwell: I am not sure I could point to any painting or artist whose work moved me to write something, apart from the *Palace at 4 A.M.* But I had a period when I loved Gauguin and lived with reproductions of his painting, and I have continued to love Bonnard and Vuillard. When I was working in the *New Yorker* art department I tended to derive the most pleasure from those contributors whose covers and "spots" were highly decorative, like Ilonka Karasz, Susanne Suba, and Christina Malmon, and though I admired the virtuosity of the ones who caught, in an almost photographic way, aspects of the city, I didn't love their work. Of the artists I became more intimate with Karasz, who lived in a ravishingly beautiful house near Brewster, New York. She and her husband, Willem Nyland, had built it with their own hands, adding room after room, as the house wandered, so to speak, up the hillside. They had lived in Java for a period, and had collected lamps, batiks, and furniture (which she had also designed) and the effect was like no other house on earth. If you will look through the *New Yorker* book of covers, you will find something like a hundred of them, and they got better, I think, when I was working with her, because of my excitement about her work. Artists, literary or otherwise, thrive on appreciation. She gave me many of her drawings and illustrations and when I married the house was uncomfortably (from Emmy's point of view) full of them, making her a kind of presence in the house. Like a previous wife, almost. So I took them down, but Emmy and I had a running argument about decorative painting against what we called easel painting, and in a short time I was converted to her point of view, and have remained there. But I wonder at the fact that, when I was working full time at the *New Yorker* and had more money than I knew what to do with, I didn't buy paintings, which were at that time extremely reasonable. One lives the life one lives, and it is a waste of time thinking about what one might have done. I am not indifferent to painting, in any case.

Burkhardt: Do you find that you appreciate the same qualities in painting as you do in literature?

Maxwell: Yes. I know I shouldn't, but I do much prefer a painting that is a painting of something, flowers, landscape, a portrait, whatever, to a painting that is an effort to convey what is going on in the psyche of the artist. I like pictures that I feel are like a descriptive passage in a novel.

Burkhardt: What was it like flying to Oregon recently after years of not traveling?

Maxwell: In the early days of our marriage when we went to Oregon it was by train, and delightful. The first time we waited in Harmon station in a blizzard so severe we weren't sure the train would get there from Grand Central Station, and I can still see it pulling in, amid the swirling snowflakes. We rode up the Hudson in a stateroom feeling unspeakably cozy, changed in Chicago in the morning, went to the Art Institute and then got back on the train to go to Oregon. It took as I remember three nights and two days. It was the next best thing to being on an ocean liner. Once, on a later trip, the air conditioning was failing as we were going through the Great Plains and we sat in our underwear reading Henry James's *Life of Hawthorne* aloud. At Salt Lake City and Boise, Idaho, one stepped down from the train and walked on the platform breathing a different air.

I find ordinary airplane travel squalid. There is no place to put your elbows, you can't walk up and down in the aisles, you are sometimes in uncomfortable physical proximity with strangers, etc. Who doesn't hate it? Also, going to Oregon takes about the same length of time as flying to Europe. This last time, in July, my brother-in-law had accumulated enough flying time to put us in first class, and it made the trip seem half as long, though first class was not as luxurious as I would have supposed. There was room. Two seats instead of three made all the difference. I would still prefer to go by train, the old trains, without muzak, and with pleasant dining cars.

Burkhardt: You have said that the Moderns were important to your work— and you came of age during the early years of Hemingway and the expatriate writers. Could you comment on the influence they had on you?

Maxwell: I didn't read and reread Hemingway, like most writers. I knew his books, but they didn't draw me in any way toward imitation, except his brevity. Which is no small except. Dos Passos's *Three Soldiers* I loved, and Cummings's "The Enormous Room," and I read Pound, and Eliot, but was more drawn to Elinor Wylie and de la Mare. I don't know why it didn't occur to me that I would love Europe. Possibly I was so satisfied by books like *The Counterfeiters* and *Le Grand Meaulnes* that I felt no need for anything more.

Burkhardt: You have mentioned several writers as your favorites now: Colette, Forster, Tolstoy, among others. Who have been your favorite writers at different points in your life?

Maxwell: Yeats. Arlington Robinson. Cummings. Wylie. De la Mare. Then later, it settled down mostly to fiction. I spent two years reading hardly anything but Colette. Another two years with Elizabeth Bowen. Then Hardy. Forster. Turgenev, Tolstoy, and Chekhov. James. When I finished Tolstoy's *Master and Man*, and came to the description of the dead horse with his mouth full of snow, I felt like getting down on my knees to Tolstoy. It struck me as as close to the center of existence as it is possible to come in writing. Nabokov, also, two years. It wasn't so much that I got something from them, though of course I did, as that they were the company I chose to keep at that time.

Burkhardt: In your work, and in interviews, you often describe what you love about Lincoln, Illinois. What do you like about New York City?
Maxwell: What I like about New York City is the people I know who live there. Actually, New York City is a European city, largely, and has a certain worldliness that makes me comfortable in it. It has an immense amount of inconvenience and now some danger. But I live a quiet life. It is where my books and records and family and friends and typewriter tend to be.

Burkhardt: Without worrying about putting labels on your religious thought, could you describe your spiritual or philosophical beliefs?
Maxwell: Religion, in the sense of a form put upon spiritual experiences and yearning has no appeal to me whatever. When I listen to religious leaders I think, "oh give me a break." I do not (emotionally anyway) rule out the possibility of other experience than this, and only a fool would fail to recognize that life is more than we believe it to be, as Zona Gale said so often on the flyleaf of books she gave me. I stopped going to church when I was fifteen. I found Mark Twain's *The Mysterious Stranger* in the school library and it made an atheist of me. I don't think it is really a profound book, but once lost, faith is not easily recovered.

January 3, 1993—Maxwell's apartment, 544 East 86th Street, New York City

Burkhardt: In the *Tamaqua* interview, you spoke about how some readers interpreted the ending of *Time Will Darken It* differently than you intended it. You said, "The reader can always walk off with the characters in a book and change their lives if he wants to." How would you describe the relationship between the author's intent and the reader's response?
Maxwell: I think often the reader reads because of a desire to live in another world than his own. He moves into the story and becomes emotionally in-

volved with the characters. If the writer has sufficient authority the reader doesn't question, or at least not very often, his account of what happened. But sometimes, if the emotions are touched on a deep level, the reader can protest, and insist, no it was this way, not that. Once at the San Carlo Opera in Naples, during a performance of *Bohème*, a singer was taken from the chorus to sing one line of the doctor when asked if Mimi, coughing on a bed in the last act, would get well, he sang that she would not, the whole audience rose up in arms and shouted, "What a bad doctor! Why don't you do something to save her?" I think usually when there is a misunderstanding like the one you mentioned, about the ending of *Time Will Darken It*, it is because the author has been over-subtle, or at least more indirect than some reader can accommodate. I think also that I meant to indicate something positive in Austin's arm, something beneath the ordinary level of thought, that would hold the marriage together. I could have said this, but it would have been more didactic than I care to be. I think that the author does bring characters to life through his imagination, and sometimes through something like hallucination, and that once alive, they can go their own way (and did, in *TWDI*) and that this leaves just as much room for differing interpretation and human behavior as actual life does. Now that you speak of it, I can remember disagreeing or disbelieving an author's statements about his characters. It is of course a proof of the validity of his art.

Burkhardt: How did you decide to use the passage from Tennyson's "The Lotus-Eaters" for the title and epigraph to *The Folded Leaf*?
Maxwell: When the book was done, Louise Bogan, to whom I had been sending the manuscript, chapter by chapter, through several versions, called me up and said, "I have the title for your novel," and read me the passage from Tennyson. In short it was a present from her.

Burkhardt: Why did you decide to use it?
Maxwell: Because it was a beautiful image for adolescence and the emergence from it. After a novel is done, it is usually extremely difficult to find an appropriate title, and you wish that you had spent a lot of time thinking about it earlier. Often the title isn't as good as it ought to be, because the author is tired and the publisher is breathing down his neck.

Burkhardt: Last time you told me that you feel *The Folded Leaf* is emotionally deeper than *So Long, See You Tomorrow*. Why do you think so?

Maxwell: I think because I lived through the suicide attempt in *The Folded Leaf* it seems deeper emotionally to me, but this may simply not be true for the reader. Lymie Peters leaning over the bathrobe to cut his throat in a tidy fashion and not leave blood all over the floor moves me, and so does his statement, "I did not want to go on living in a world where the truth has no power to make itself be believed." I think what it comes down to is a question of distance. In one case remembered emotions are driving the action, in another the author's shaping mind, which is certainly sympathetic, but not anguished.

Burkhardt: You also mentioned that while writing *The Folded Leaf* you had "to struggle against the idea that this was a story that no one would want to read." Why did you feel this way? Have you had similar feelings about other works?

Maxwell: Over my shoulder I kept thinking of Tom Sawyer and the Booth Tarkington Penrod stories, and of course the general attitude of people toward adolescents, mostly tolerant of their aberrations, and not really expecting behavior that anyone need take seriously. Puppy love, crushes, etc. In all the details, especially of the early part when the boys are in high school, I felt the need of some larger frame of reference than the lives of the two boys, and so I wrote about their parents, the bleakness of certain parts of Chicago, the initiation motif, etc., so that the action wouldn't seem small or trivial. I haven't had this difficulty with any other book.

Burkhardt: You told me last time that, just before she died, Louise Bogan told someone that she thought *The Folded Leaf* was your best novel. Why do you think she felt that way?

Maxwell: What Bogan actually said was "His best novel is dedicated to me." Her literary judgment was very sure, but on the other hand she never had a chance to read *So Long*, being dead when it was published. Possibly the fact that she read it, that it was written chapter by chapter and sent to her, so she saw it taking shape slowly and with great difficulty, made her more inside it. Possibly she was right: I think the structure of *So Long* is much superior, but in the end what gives permanence and importance to a work of fiction is how deeply it reflects human feelings. To know the answer one would have to be able to ask her. That she would have given one an answer I have no doubt. The only two comments, apart from keep on going, that she ever made were a complaint that the physical description (which I rewrote) of Spud was too conventional, and once when there had been a gap between the arrival of chapters, "Get that boy up off the sleeping porch." (I was temporarily stalled.) It was her idea, of course, that the first chapter, which I showed her thinking I had written a short story, should be the beginning of a novel.

Burkhardt: You've said that Theodor Reik wanted a more didactic ending to *The Folded Leaf*: he wanted something that would make Lymie more "home free." You told me, "Actually Lymie wasn't more free, he remained Lymie." What would have made Lymie free? Did Lymie ever become free?

Maxwell: Nothing. Unless you believe in the absolute efficacy of Freudian analysis. A boy who was no longer over sensitive, or subject to absolutes, subject also to neurotic impulses disguised as self-destructive or hostile ones, would not be recognizably the same person. Bogan quoted Goethe as saying—she did this out of a dissatisfaction with the upbeat last chapter—that maturity had to be achieved once more with every day we woke to. But who is Lymie? If you mean the boy in the book, I mean, in the revised chapter, to suggest that his troubles were by no means over. Not that they were solvable, and Spud's not. If you mean the author, the most freeing experience was marriage.

Burkhardt: Last time you said that in analysis you came to understand that "man is his own architect, and that Lymie Peters was not pathetic but largely responsible for what happened to him, though often without being aware of it." How was Lymie responsible for what happened to him?

Maxwell: Well, as I indicated in the novel, he was not stupid, and yet never took any precautions against arousing Spud's jealousy, and also failed to recognize it for what it was. If he had wanted to torment Spud he could hardly have gone about it better. Also, people in love have a choice, some choice anyway, about whether to give their whole hearts or to (for safety's sake) hold something back. In any case he should have thought twice before buying Sally those violets. At the same time that I say that, I also believe in the absoluteness of innocence. You could say I am of two minds about the matter of man being his own architect.

Burkhardt: Are we always responsible for our actions?

Maxwell: We are responsible for our actions but not for what other people make of them, especially people who are paranoid, for example, or caught in a pattern of behavior that systematically distorts the truth (i.e. congenital suspicion) about other people.

Burkhardt: Do you embrace the philosophy of naturalism: that we live under the auspices of an indifferent nature (or society), that we are pawns rather than agents in our lives?

Maxwell: I don't believe we are victims of a malign deity. I do think it would be unreasonable to expect Nature to care what happens to us, anymore than, apparently, it cares when the owl snatches the baby rabbit from its nest. "Pawns" suggests a game, especially of chess, and that implies a player with a personal interest in the outcome, even if it is only winning. People with money have power, often, over the lives of those who do not, and must work or starve. But this is on such a small scale compared to creation, and the starry universe. The only God I can imagine believing in is an unanthropomorphic creative intention. Whatever accounts for the astounding special adaptation of, for example, various insects and animals.

Burkhardt: Do you read your work after it is published?

Maxwell: From time to time. Sometimes I am dissatisfied. For example, I wish I could redo my first novel and make the Negro a more worldly character who would be beyond being upset by the scene in the screen tent. Sometimes I wish I had given Lymie Peters the father and stepmother I had, instead of that made-up race-track tout, but I thought it was unfair to expose my father's life, and if I had I could not have done it as understandingly as I could now, and therefore it wouldn't have been very good. The last time I reread *Time Will Darken It*, I saw a similarity in the climax with the climax of *They Came Like Swallows*, and wished I had kept it closer to the ground. These are not, any of them, very deep regrets, because the first novel is not terribly good in any case, and the other (*TWDI*) not spoiled by the resemblance. Louise Bogan cautioned me, I now remember, about the trap of the sensitive author, and that one must guard against it in making judgments about characters. Unknowing feelings of superiority.

Burkhardt: In "The Thistles in Sweden," you write: "I can always afford what I dearly want—or rather, when I want something very much I would rather not think about whether or not we can afford it." In this story, you were speaking of a gateleg table, but have there been other things you've really wanted and didn't think about whether or not you could afford them?

Maxwell: Yes, a ship's model that cost $200, in the late forties, and that was about all the spare cash we had. It was made by a Russian émigré who lived on Nantucket, whose models (on a larger scale) were owned by, among other people, Franklin D. Roosevelt. Mine is a little sloop, but perfection.

I thought if I owned it I would not have to strive for perfection in writing. But of course I went right on striving for the perfect sentence, structure, etc. after the ship's model was on the mantelpiece. I guess I haven't had objects put the finger on me as often as many aesthetes have.

Burkhardt: In the same story, you describe a group of friends who play a game on New Year's Eve in which they ask each other a series of questions. So I will put these same questions to you: "If you were a school of Italian painting or a color of the spectrum or a character from fiction, what school of Italian painting or color or character would you be?"

Maxwell: (a) Carpaccio (b) scarlet (c) the little boy who was cutting pictures out of a catalogue at his mother's feet in *To the Lighthouse*: James, I think his name was. The one who cried because the weather kept them from going to the lighthouse, and who was unnerved by his father's loud quotations from Tennyson.

Burkhardt: Your first novel appeared the same year as Fitzgerald's *Tender Is the Night*—and yet you are still publishing nearly sixty years later. What are your thoughts about longevity in terms of your literary career and your life in general?

Maxwell: On the merely practical level longevity depends on some publisher's willingness to keep your books in print. It also requires that they have not become dated. That readers of a later period find them interesting or moving. I don't think this is something the writer can contrive or bring about. He can only do his best, and hope that that will continue to interest. Writers fall into at least partial neglect because of the insufficiency of a certain kind of reader, which they enjoyed in their lifetime. Elizabeth Bowen, for instance. I think her best books and a great many of her stories are as good now as when they were written, but not the kind of writing the present day reader is looking for, apparently.

There was a considerable period when all my books were out of print, and half forgotten. I seem lucky at the moment, but have no idea how long it will last or if it will last at all.

Burkhardt: When was this period?

Maxwell: Between *Time Will Darken It* and *The Chateau*. Then I went from Harpers to Knopf and the out-of-print books were brought back in paperback. In the fifties.

Burkhardt: Last time you talked about balancing the life of solitude with the life among people. In "Self Reliance" Emerson writes that "the great man is he who in the midst of the crowd keeps with perfect sweetness the independence of solitude." Do you agree?

Maxwell: I have no understanding of what it is like to be Emerson's great man or a great man of any kind. I avoid crowds, clam up at parties, become restless, and keep looking at my watch in the hope that it will be time to go home. I am a one-to-one person, and consider any other kind of social exchange something to be put up with patiently. When I enter the world of people, I usually fasten my attention on the person I am talking to, forget my own concerns, and strive to, in Forster's phrase, connect. To understand the person on some unsuperficial level. I for the most part leave my solitary self at home when I am doing this. Gibbs once remarked that Thurber could sit at a party gazing into space, and later describe everything that happened. Possibly he was both solitary and socially present at the same time.

Burkhardt: You also said, "Self-deception is one way of coming in out of the cold. Without it one would spend a large part of one's life wincing over past behavior." Do you believe self-forgiveness can serve a similar function?

Maxwell: I believe that since we tend to live a fairly long time these days self-forgiveness is necessary, since the illumination of remorse is limited and repetitive. And it is a virtue to be happy.

Burkhardt: Is it easier to deceive ourselves than to forgive ourselves?

Maxwell: Much easier.

Burkhardt: E. B. White noted the significance of the Model T in "Farewell, My Lovely," and Fitzgerald has chronicled how cars suggest something about the moral character of the owners. Do you have any particular feelings about cars?

Maxwell: I have loved all the cars we have owned, especially a 1936 Ford touring car and our present SAAB. I don't like to sell cars when we get a new one, and have often found happy homes for the old ones. I used to dream about the Ford touring car before I was married and think it was probably the woman in my life.

Burkhardt: You have said that "the odds are on objects." And your friend E. B. White wrote a very humorous piece about the accumulation of objects,

"Good-bye to Forty-Eighth Street." Have you ever grown attached to any particular objects or possessions?

Maxwell: I am attached to countless objects and possessions. They are what make up my sense of home. Books, pictures, snapshots, clothes, classical records, the record player, the fireplace, the shapes of rooms, the light at various times of day. I could manage without any possessions but I would be lonely. What this might indicate about me is that at some time I had had a home I was deeply attached to and had it taken away from me.

Burkhardt: In one of our previous interviews, you mentioned how a feeling person approaches politics. Could you elaborate?

Maxwell: My highly prejudiced view is that the Democratic Party is the party with a concern for people, and that the Republican Party is concerned with property. By feeling person, I guess I meant a person with some imaginative ability to put himself in another's shoes. Not just a question of emotion, since one can be deeply attached to a piece of property in the individual instance, but the Republican attachment seems to me to be to generally property, wealth, etc. Not the place one calls home.

Burkhardt: We talked at length last time about your fondness for art and your own artistic endeavors. Have you ever been involved in an active way in music? Have you sung or played an instrument?

Maxwell: As a little boy I took piano lessons, but didn't much like to practice, and often went to peer at the clock in the hall, to see if the practicing time was almost over. In my fifties I took it up again, with a concert pianist who lived across the road from us in the country, and took lessons once a week for about five years, and practicing became an obsession. I got so I could play the simpler works of Mozart and Beethoven, but never up to time or with a pedal. I stopped when my teacher had a heart attack and I had to face the fact that my time would be better spent at the typewriter, since I was a fairly good writer and a poor pianist.

Burkhardt: We also talked about your taste in music, which leans toward the classical. Do you enjoy other kinds of music?

Maxwell: I now enjoy music that my father used to play, showtunes, mostly, from the 1900s on to the present, or rather, not the present, but say through Rodgers and Hart, Gershwin, Cole Porter, and Kern.

Burkhardt: Can you describe the way you respond to different art forms? Specifically literature, visual art, and music?
Maxwell: I respond to music emotionally, and get most pleasure from melody, being ignorant of the technical aspects of what I am hearing. I thought I wanted to be an artist when I was a boy, and in painting tend to respond to color and forms, but not in an abstract way. I like portraits, interior scenes, landscapes, still lifes, in what is I suppose a literary way—where at least half of the pleasure comes from what it is a painting of. I like Chardin, Boudin, Rembrandt, Degas, early Matisse, Gericault, Constables notebooks, Carpaccio.

Burkhardt: Why does the role of the preserver have more resonance for you than the role of one who lives each day as it happens?
Maxwell: A love of the world around me, and of the forgotten past.

Burkhardt: Do you enjoy novels that have been translated into film?
Maxwell: I don't think novels often translate to film, because of the time limitation. Something is always sacrificed, some essential theme or point or scene. For example, the ideas of the father in *A Room with a View* give the novel its depth, and they simply do not exist in the movie. They do exist in the movie of *Howard's End*. Forster's ideas, I mean. But I would rather read the book than see the movie, so something must have been lost. Most movies made from novels are a disaster. This one wasn't.

Burkhardt: What is your view of literary biography?
Maxwell: The best literary biography I know is Sylvia Townsend Warner's life of T. H. White. For a long while she simply treats the periods of his life, with, at the end of a chapter, a telling observation, and then as his life begins to go to pieces, she takes over, becomes more and more important as the interpreter of events, and the final, charitable judge of his efforts. I am also fond of Francis Steegmuller's life of the Grand Mademoiselle. Which is rather like a novel. But a brilliant treatment of a period and of the central character. Most present-day biographies seem out to get the subject and if possible destroy him or her. They are badly written, untrustworthy, and misconceived, and I mostly do not want to read them.

If the biography is unsympathetic or biased against the subject, and the subject is a friend, I become angry and indignant. Otherwise I am interested to learn facts about an acquaintance that I was ignorant of. For instance, Consuelo Kanaga was a neighbor in the country, and the catalogue for her retrospective show this March contains a long biographical essay about her earlier marriages, travels, etc., which somewhat oblige me to change the way I thought of her. But I see no excuse for the kind of biography that diminishes the subject.

Burkhardt: You have said that life is a privilege. Why do you believe this to be so?

Maxwell: I think that it is somehow unimaginative to consider the universe as the product of chance. I am inclined to say that it is the product of God knows. The evidence offered in Nature is so astonishing and so consistently on the side of an Intention. I did not escape the influence of seven or eight years of Sunday School and believe we ought to help each other when it is possible, that the self-centered life is a kind of living death, that life on any terms is a privilege, and that we ought to be grateful for it and use it to our best ability, and not be frightened or frantic when we reach the end of it. But instead stand, accepting, like a flower that has gone to seed. I am not much inclined to exercises in self-improvement. And don't find that I can believe in any formal religion or totally believe in any religious leader.

Burkhardt: Aside from literature, what are some of your passions?

Maxwell: Politics. Literary style. It was Adlai Stevenson's speeches during his campaign for president that made me aware of politics at all. I had a fondness for him because he was personally charming and literate and because he came from Bloomington, Illinois. He made me realize what side I was on.

Burkhardt: Do you think that your work at the *New Yorker* shaped your own writing in any way?

Maxwell: I have come to love writing that says what it means and means what it says, is free from clumsiness, is shapely and beautiful to the ear. Is not longwinded or repetitious. Is emotionally involving. Sheds a quick light. And becomes a permanent part of one's experience.

Burkhardt: Last time you mentioned that the only conflict at the magazine "was between the writer's intention and what the magazine felt that, for its own special reasons, it wanted to publish." With your own writing, were your intentions and what the magazine wanted to publish always identical?

Maxwell: For example, though they published a fair number of what I call fables, though they are not strictly that but once upon a time moral tales, or immoral tales, they do not want any more, and these pieces were all queerly at odds with the nature of the *New Yorker*. Too poetic or unworldly. Or something.

Burkhardt: You have expressed concern and dissatisfaction about how you portrayed the African American character in your first novel, and many years later you wrote about the story of Dr. Billie Dyer, the first African American physician from Lincoln. What is important to you about writing about black Americans?

Maxwell: I think a white writer writing about black Americans must call forth his utmost powers of sympathetic imagination, and even then the chances of success are not very good or are limited. The great problem is unconscious complacency. It can only be done on one's knees to the subject. Sentimentality is also a danger. And ignorance of details, since our lives are so little shared with them.

Burkhardt: I've asked before if you had ever considered writing from your mother's point of view, and you said that "when she was dead [you] incorporated her personality into [your] own." What aspects of your personality do you believe derive from your mother?

Maxwell: A surprising (to me) pleasure in sociability, a tendency to be fond of all kinds of people, easily, and for the fondness to become a part of my life, so that my cast of characters is larger than is sensible for a man of my age and habits. A quick sympathy for people in trouble. Tenderness toward children or anybody who needs being loved.

Burkhardt: You wrote to me that the story "The Way He Was" "more or less wrote itself so that [you] don't feel [you] deserve any praise." Last time we met, you spoke about the story "Love," in a similar way. How often have stories just come to you like this?

Maxwell: The "fables" used to, but don't seem to any more. Novels never, long stories, never.

Burkhardt: How is the satisfaction of writing different when a story comes easily compared to stories or novels you work and rework carefully until they are finally acceptable to you?

Maxwell: When I have worked hard, and reworked and reworked, I more or less know what I have. With a story that comes easily I find myself taking other people's word for what I have accomplished.

Burkhardt: How would you compare your own childhood in Lincoln with your daughters' childhoods in New York City? What was it like raising them in the largest city in America when you were brought up in a small town?

Maxwell: New York City is an amalgam of villages, and so to some extent, since my daughters walked to school, and to the places where their friends lived, it was like a small town. But of course in a small town everybody knows everybody else, roughly. Years after my family moved away from Lincoln, I went into a café, on a visit home, and had a glass of milk and a piece of pie and found I had left my wallet at home. As I was explaining to the proprietor, he said, "It's all right, you're William Maxwell's boy." This couldn't happen in New York City. When my daughters went to Lincoln, at the age of nine and eleven or thereabouts, they were enchanted with it and their young cousins. Everything about Lincoln was romantic to them.

Burkhardt: Can you describe the period in which you and your wife were waiting to adopt a child? How long was it?

Maxwell: Ten years. Recurring disappointment. Sadness, mixed in our pleasure in being with each other. Interest in other people's children that diminished noticeably when we had our own.

Burkhardt: Last time you mentioned that you "have always felt comfortable in the world of women." How did this ease affect your writing and your relationships?

Maxwell: I have often been aware that more often the writers who influenced me were women. Virginia Woolf. Elizabeth Bowen. Colette. Elinor Wylie. Bogan. Zona Gale was a kind of fairy godmother to me. Cather.

I think it has made it seem as easy and natural to be friends with women as it is to be friends with men. I am always aware of them as persons, not as sexual objects only. I enjoy, up to a point, their conversations. Am left behind when it comes to clothes, for example.

Imagining the Middle West: An Interview with William Maxwell

Bill Aull, Sandra Batzli, Barbara Burkhardt, James McGowan, and Bruce Morgan/1991

From *Tamaqua*, 3:2 (Fall 1992), 9–25. Reprinted by permission.

William Maxwell was born in Lincoln, Illinois, in 1908. His family moved to Chicago when he was fourteen, and he attended the University of Illinois from 1926 to 1930. After a year of graduate work at Harvard and two years teaching freshman composition back in Urbana, he turned to writing. His published work includes the novels *Bright Center of Heaven* (1934), *They Came Like Swallows* (1937), *The Folded Leaf* (1945), *Time Will Darken It* (1948), *The Chateau* (1961), and *So Long, See You Tomorrow* (1980); the short story collections *The Old Man at the Railroad Crossing* (1966), *Over by the River* (1977), and *Billie Dyer and Other Stories* (1992); and the family chronicle *Ancestors* (1971). Maxwell worked at the *New Yorker*, primarily as a fiction editor, from 1936 to 1976. He and his wife live in New York City.

The following interview was conducted between October 1991 and July 1992. Answers to an initial set of questions were received in person by Barbara Burkhardt, during her visit with Maxwell in November. Subsequent questions and answers were exchanged by mail. The questions were composed by Barbara Burkhardt, Sandra Batzli, Bill Aull, James McGowan, and Bruce Morgan.

TAMAQUA: Although much of your adult life you have lived in New York, your fiction is mostly set in the Midwest. How does the Midwest speak to you in ways that other locales do not?

Maxwell: I have earned my living in New York City, from the time I was twenty-eight until I retired from my editorial job at the *New Yorker* at the age of sixty-seven, and during that time lived in the city or in Yorktown Heights, which is forty-five miles to the north, in Westchester County. Since then, habit has kept me there, and it must surely be said to be my home, but it is not my imagination's home. My imagination's home is the dead center of the state of Illinois, and when I have an idea for a story or a novel, much more often than not it is located in that part of the country. Or, perhaps I should say a facsimile of it. For I was removed from Lincoln at the age of fourteen, and so my childhood and early youth were encapsulated, so to speak, in a changeless world. The real Lincoln that people now live in or drive through has never stopped changing, naturally, though I believe it retains much of what I feel to be its essential character. I was not present to observe or record those changes. I can only speak for the town and the people as I thought they were (which may have been far from the truth of things) during the years I lived there.

It is not so much that the Middle West speaks to me as that it speaks through me. It is extremely important that a writer have a voice, and mine, in so far as I have acquired one, is clearly a reflection of the simple, direct, often humorous, emotionally charged speech of the people I knew when I was growing up in Lincoln. It has got me into no end of arguments with copy editors who have a vision of correctness that I subscribe to also, but not all that much, and certainly not at the risk of losing the effect of a human voice.

One summer long ago when I was at the MacDowell Colony in Peterborough, New Hampshire, I drove to Lake George with another colonist, the violinist Sol Cohen, from Urbana. He was an impulsive driver and did not read the road signs carefully, and we got lost and at dusk found that we had been driving north when we should have been driving south and east. All around us were mountains, and I felt threatened by them. Only a flat landscape is reassuring to my unconscious mind. A landscape where you can see the horizon in all directions.

In terms of commerce the Middle West (or is it my father?) speaks through me in that I would not be comfortable running up debts. Both at home and in the Presbyterian Sunday school it was drummed into me that people should help one another when help is obviously needed. That, under no matter what circumstances, life is a privilege is perhaps a conclusion I arrived at on my own.

TAMAQUA: As a writer you surely want to reach the changing world of readers. How do you hope to do this with a fixed, unchanging locale that you speak of as your imagination's Lincoln, Illinois?

Maxwell: I am uneasy with generalities but I think it is safe to say that novelists are trying to express, through narrative, aspects of the truth—by the truth I guess I mean a statement that will stand up to careful scrutiny. If I started to worry about the change in readers from one generation to the next and how to hold onto them, I think I would give up and go work in the garden. When I am in doubt about whether some scene or situation is worth writing about, I tell myself that if it interests me then there is a fair chance it will interest others, and let it go at that.

TAMAQUA: In much of your work—such as *Ancestors*; *So Long, See You Tomorrow*; *The Folded* Leaf—the boundary between fiction and nonfiction is very difficult to define. How do you define that boundary?
Maxwell: Since Proust, or maybe I ought to say since *The Way of All Flesh*, fiction has had an obvious element of autobiography. It exists in Tolstoy but not obviously. My own feeling is that the distinction one should be aware of is that between reminiscence (that is to say, writing in which there is no structure apart from *I remember this* and *I remember that* . . . and the interest comes largely from the areas where the writer's memories duplicate or at least touch the reader's) and autobiographical fiction, which may, or may not, stick just as closely to the facts but contrives to give the experience a form, and to produce a literary effect. I know that *The Folded Leaf* is about half autobiography and half invention, but which half I am no longer certain about. It all seems like something that happened to me. And to Lymie Peters. I admire fiction writers who are, or at least appear to be, not dependent on their own lives for material. But I also suspect they are more dependent, often, than they appear to be, if the truth were known.

TAMAQUA: As a follow-up, did writing *Ancestors* allow you to come to terms with your past in ways that your fiction did not?
Maxwell: I think there is no question that writing *Ancestors* made me more aware of the wealth of material my elders offered me. Most of them loved me when I was a child, and in writing about them I got a chance to love them back.

TAMAQUA: In your interview with the *Paris Review*, you say, "During part of the time I was writing *The Folded Leaf* I was in analysis with Theodor Reik." How does such analysis of self influence the understanding of one's characters in fiction? Did therapy help you maintain distance from your characters? What can be accomplished in such therapy that cannot in writing?

Maxwell: The problem for a fiction writer in being psychoanalyzed is that it shifts the focus and primary emphasis from what happened to why it happened. And you cannot tell a story by advancing from why to why; you must, at the typewriter, keep why in the back of your mind and what happened in the front. Therapy made me think about myself and the reasons, conscious and unconscious, for my actions, until all interest in the subject was virtually exhausted, and with relief I turned and applied what I had learned to an understanding of those about me. To the degree that I understood them better than they did themselves (having nothing at stake emotionally) I suppose it created distance. Imaginary or partly imaginary or composite characters are still people. The fact that they exist in the writer's mind and not on the other end of the telephone or in the same bed is immaterial.

I don't know whether writing a novel about a man with a self-destructive tendency would cure the writer of that tendency, but I would think in the long run not. Nor does therapy always. All I know is that at a certain point in my analysis I suddenly found that I had an overwhelming interest in everybody around me. Writing would not have produced this, I think.

TAMAQUA: In addition to psychological analysis, writers also engage in technical analysis. How did the works of other writers help you to develop your style? Eliot said, "Immature poets imitate; mature poets steal." From whom did you steal?

Maxwell: Everybody in sight, when I was young. And without knowing it. More to the point than what Eliot said is Saul Bellow's "A writer is a reader who is moved to emulation." My first novel is riddled with echoes of Yeats, Elinor Wylie, Virginia Woolf, Walter de la Mare, whatever poets and novelists had aroused a response in me, including probably Byron and Keats. Ten years after it was published I reread it and discovered to my horror that I had lifted a character—the homesick servant girl—lock, stock, and barrel from *To the Lighthouse*. When I found myself writing about material that was my own, the echoes fell away.

I don't study other writers' work with an idea to analyzing their methods of plot, dialogue, or narrative. I am, when not a writer, a reader and go on binges. I spent two years reading hardly anything but Virginia Woolf. No, that is not true, I have read her intensively (though I can't any longer) over a much longer period of time. But it is true of Conrad, E. M. Forster, Colette, Isherwood, Elizabeth Bowen, Nabokov, Henry James, Sylvia Townsend Warner, Hardy, Isak Dinesen, Tolstoy, and Chekhov. But of course the reader is not deaf, dumb, and blind. I pick up ideas, even when half out of my mind with pleasure at what I am reading. I notice.

The only writer I have ever known who was not a reader is E. B. White. It took him three years to read *Anna Karenina* and I never heard him express any pleasure in the experience. As a child he simply looked at a pile of writing paper and felt an urgent desire to write on it.

TAMAQUA: Did your work as an editor of other people's fiction at the *New Yorker* affect your own writing at times?

Maxwell: Most of the writers I was in an editorial relation to at the *New Yorker* were very gifted. I had, in making sure that they meant what they said and said what they meant, to be partly inside their creative process. But I tried to keep my life as editor and my life as writer separate. On my *New Yorker* days I tried to make the writers I dealt with forget that I also wrote, and on my working days at home I forgot I was an editor, in the pleasure of dealing with my own words for a change. I certainly was affected by editing and corresponding with Sylvia Townsend Warner. About the others, I simply don't know.

TAMAQUA: The narrative strategy of editorial omniscience is used extensively and variously in your fictional works, ranging from the detached authorial persona in *The Folded Leaf* and *Time Will Darken It*, to the final retrospective chapter of *The Chateau*, to the author-as-character in *So Long, See You Tomorrow*. How and why has your use of this strategy evolved?

Maxwell: What you call the editorial omniscience I would call the storyteller. He has, traditionally, felt free to explain his characters, present them in full flood, and judge the consequences of their behavior, etc.

Part II of *The Chateau* (I suppose it is an epilogue, really) was made necessary by the awkwardness of the material. Formally the book ended when the Americans left Paris and said goodbye to the old Frenchwoman at the railway station. But it left all manner of threads hanging. Which troubled me. The biographer Francis Steegmuller is a close friend and read the manuscript and tidied up my French where it needed it and was a great help. But he also expressed a dislike for the Americans—that is to say, he found them rather foolish. Part II took the form of answering his objections and at the same time taking care of loose threads. And inevitably the narrative moved forward. I didn't figure this out in my head and then do it; it worked itself out as I wrote. I hardly ever figure anything out in my head. You could almost say that I would write just as well without a head.

Isherwood, I think, once said that the narrator of a first-person narration must also be a character himself. Something like that. Anyway, I felt I could not tell the story of Cletus Smith in *So Long* without making myself (the "I") also a character.

TAMAQUA: The last scene of *Time Will Darken It* has certain parallels with the ending of *Ulysses*: a married couple in bed, the husband asleep, the wife's thoughts casting new light on the novel's events. Were you in any way inspired by Joyce to write a Midwestern variant of *Ulysses*—or, of *The Dead*—with the switch at the end to the wife's point of view?

Maxwell: I never went on a Joyce binge, though I have of course read him. Most of him. I never read all of *Finnegans Wake*. *Ulysses* doesn't speak to my condition, to use a Quaker phrase that my colleague Joseph Mitchell is so fond of. *The Dead*, like *The Death of Ivan Ilyich*, one would emulate if, alas, one could.

TAMAQUA: At the end of *Time Will Darken It* Martha's revelation that she will leave Austin comes as a surprise when first read, though upon reflection it appears consistent with Austin's character and their conflict throughout the novel. How much of the surprise is a result of plotting, the subtle masking of their marital troubles, and how much is the result of the point-of-view shift?

Maxwell: It was not my intention in *Time Will Darken It* that the reader would think Martha King was actually going to leave her husband, though I see now how you could think that. In the first place, in that period women didn't often do that. But I meant it as a kind of working out of her feelings in preparation for forgiving him. His happiness in having her home was a kind of affront in that it meant he had already forgiven himself. In spite of a certain incompatibility of temperament, they were tied together for life. As I had imagined them. The reader can always walk off with the characters in a book and change their lives if he wants to. Though it would be a brave reader that dared to give *Madame Bovary* a happy ending.

TAMAQUA: Jefferson in *Bright Center of Heaven* characterizes the enduring legacy of slavery: racism, whether explicit or implicit; the desire, perhaps hopeless, of African Americans to have a culture free of white America's influence; the simultaneous advance and retreat of African Americans into white society. How were you attracted to such a subject so early in your career?

Maxwell: In an article in the *New Criterion* Bruce Bawer pointed out, correctly, that the black man in *Bright Center of Heaven* is totally unconvincing. The setting of that novel is taken from life, the characters largely but not wholly extensions of parts of myself. Sixty-five years ago, at the age of seventeen, I worked [at Bonnie Oaks], and during the summer a black man, the National Secretary of the N.A.A.C.P., came for a brief visit. I had never sat down to eat with a black person before and I observed that my appetite was unimpaired and that the other people present appeared to feel that there was nothing unusual in the occasion. Which left me without any climax for my novel, so I invented one, unsuccessfully. I would have done better to stick to what happened, which was nothing much.

At the end of my life I seem to be drawn to writing about black people, but in a very limited way, and, so to speak, on my knees before the subject.

TAMAQUA: As a professional writer who also was for many years an editor at one of the most influential publications of American fiction you have a unique perspective. How would you assess American fiction in the current era? Where is it going? How would you like to see it develop?

Maxwell: I haven't read enough current American fiction to be able to "assess" it, and I have no idea where it is going. The fiction I like is always concerned with character, with the behavior of men, women, children, and animals. I don't—I hardly ever—read criticism, and when I do I am not moved to emulation, as I have been by *The Common Reader* and the literary and biographical essays of Lytton Strachey. Which are not in the proper sense criticism, but literary divertissements.

TAMAQUA: What did your college education at the University of Illinois contribute to you as a writer?

Maxwell: Do you want a direct answer or is it all right if I go round Robin Hood's barn?

TAMAQUA: Why not?

Maxwell: Novelists are members of the phylum *Porifera*—that is to say, they are sponges that mostly soak up life. John O'Hara never went to college, and said he had never read anything back of Scott Fitzgerald. He regretted that his father hadn't been able to send him to Yale, but it was for snobbish reasons. I can't think of anything he lacked that Yale could have given him except social detail which he picked up anyway. As a young man he did not lead a sheltered existence. By the age of twenty-nine he was in full possession of his talent. I don't know what he would have made of "But to subsist in bones and be but pyramidally extant were a fallacy in duration."

I read for pleasure, all through my childhood, but my first encounter with literature came when I was a freshman in Lincoln High School and we were assigned *Treasure Island*. I reached the final sentence of the book and turned back to the beginning and went on reading. I read *Treasure Island* five times without stopping before I turned to something else.

Then we moved to Chicago. My English teacher during my senior year in high school had a friend at the main library downtown. Once a week a crate of books would arrive and we would dive into it. I sometimes read six or seven plays and novels over the weekend. Shaw, Barrie, George Moore, Galsworthy, de Morgan, H. G. Wells, Conrad—whoever was admired among contemporary writers in the year 1925. But about English and American literature in general there were dense areas, whole forests, of ignorance which my years at Urbana gradually reduced the size of.

When I graduated, I thought I was going to study at the Chicago Art Institute. My best friend, Jack Scully, had enrolled at the University of Illinois as a pre-medic. When September came, he was recovering from pleurisy and his father and mother thought that he was not well enough to start school. I offered to go down to Urbana with him and help him enroll. We put up at my older brother's fraternity house, which I had stayed in before, until Jack found a room, and what with one thing and another, including the full moon, we both accepted pledge pins from the fraternity and I decided to spend a year at the U. of I. and then go to art school.

My freshman composition teacher read off the names of those students who were to be transferred to "star rhet" sections—meaning that they didn't need as much grounding in grammar and syntax—and my name was not among them. I had never thought of becoming a writer but I had had things published in the high school magazine and enjoyed seeing my name in print, and I was a little disappointed. A day or so later a boy I knew said, "I saw your name on the star rhet list," so I went to the English office and found I belonged in Paul Landis's class. He was a big man with an immensely tall forehead and a beautiful reading voice. His struggles with the window shade were so ludicrous that the whole class sat laughing at him. But he was not a stand-up comic; he meant to teach us to write lucid English. He cured me forever of purple prose by reading one of my themes aloud in class as an example of how not to write. As he was reading he stopped to point out here and there a phrase that was not hopelessly bad, and this helped me to live through it. Just.

A few weeks into that first semester, I met him on the sidewalk in Urbana and he asked me to his apartment for a cup of tea. From that moment on, through all four years of college, he kept his eye on me. I couldn't have had a better mentor. He admired *Tom Jones* above all other English novels, and cautioned me that I ought not to read *Jude the Obscure* in any but the most cheerful surroundings. One day he offered me a copy of the Tauchnitz edition of *To the Lighthouse* that he had picked up while traveling in Europe, and said, "You may like this. I couldn't bring myself to finish it." What he suggested that I read, I read. What he told me it was perhaps unwise for me to do (I was given to flights of foolishness, dictated by one absolute or another), I found myself not doing.

Since I was only going to be at the university that one year, he pulled strings and got me into two advanced English courses. One was Clarissa Rinaker's course in "Dr. Johnson and His Circle." She was a high-strung woman with a caustic tongue, and scared me stiff. When I raised my hand and said that *Rasselas* was reminiscent of Oscar Wilde, her laughter at my misuse of the word reminiscent was not kind and it was unnecessarily prolonged. But I did end up loving Johnson and Boswell and Joshua Reynolds and Dr. Burney and Mrs. Thrale and the whole opinionated crew. The other course was on the English Romantic poets, under Bruce Weirick. We were required to write a ballad, an ode, a sonnet, etc., so that we would have a less distant feeling toward Coleridge and Wordsworth, and some faint idea of how poems are made.

Weirick was in his fifties, and the most popular teacher in the English department. He was at his best when he was dealing with the infinite variety of Byron's *Don Juan.* From the side he looked like a question mark. With his tilted cigarette holder, his eyebrows raised suggestively, his rasping ironical voice, his delight in wickedness of the milder kind, his stock of double-edged epigrams, he was catnip to the young. His interest in them was personal and genuine. They called him by his first name, and there were usually two or three of them sitting around in his apartment in the late afternoon. His door was left unlocked and you could go there and play his records and read his books when he wasn't home. He inquired into my plans and then told me that I would be happier and more secure financially as a professor of English. He could be very persuasive. I gave up the idea of becoming an artist and stayed on in Urbana.

Landis suggested that I major in languages because they would be useful and you didn't need to take a course in Shakespeare in order to read *King Lear.* He then saw to it that the English courses I did take were taught by men and women he admired. Richard Lattimore was a student at the university at the same time I was, and long afterward he remarked that there were several brilliant young men in the English department who didn't realize how extraordinary they were. I had no basis of comparison and simply took them for what they appeared to be, men who knew a great deal more about literature than I did.

Jacob Zeitlin grew up in New York City, but never spoke of it. He had a short black beard, sad dark eyes, and thick bright- red lips. He looked like a minor prophet. If he ever made an injudicious statement I am unaware of it. He taught courses in seventeenth-century prose, the English essay, and American social and literary criticism. He had embarked on a translation of Montaigne, now listed in the *Columbia Encyclopedia* as one of two standard modern texts. He also had a running feud with an overly rigid colleague, and a Ph.D. candidate being prepared for his oral by one of them was sure to meet with trouble from the other. Zeitlin had no small talk, and when everybody else in the room was in gales of laughter over some piece of faculty gossip, he sat with an abstracted look on his face and hummed. During the brief period when he attempted to learn how to drive a car he was a danger to himself and the landscape. Though the Modern movement was not much felt in Urbana, in Paris on a sabbatical he saw James Joyce, sitting by himself in a box at the Opera, enthusiastically applauding a performance of *La Gioconda*.

Harold Hillebrand's most important course was a survey of tragedy from the Greeks to O'Neill. His book on the Elizabethan boy actors was both scholarly and readable. I cut a minor exam in order to skip up to Chicago and see Gordon Craig's *MacBeth*, thinking he would be pleased with me for being so enterprising, and instead he gave me an E and showed no interest in my impressions of the production. It didn't occur to me at the time, but possibly he didn't think all that much of Gordon Craig's innovations. Outside of class his manner was sardonic, and faculty wives pretended to be afraid of him. His innumerable acts of kindness, especially to students who were hard up or stranded somewhere, he was at some pains to keep people from knowing about. He was a bachelor and lived with his mother, who had been a Washington hostess. Their Christmas party, with the house decorated with holly and mistletoe, and with a fiddler for the Virginia reel, was the high point of Urbana entertaining. The first time I was invited there for dinner, a fifteen-pound roast turkey was brought onto the table, for three people. Also there were finger bowls, which I just barely knew what to do with. Old age had made Mrs. Hillebrand a little silly. Her matchmaking was blatant, and once when I was sitting across the table from her she remarked that the maid had seen bear tracks in the back yard. He seized his napkin and burst out, "For God's sake, Mother, try to keep the madness in the family." In his course on writing the one-act play, the emphasis was not on the literary but the practical. The two plays I wrote for him were both later produced in the University Theater and, to my surprise, worked on the stage. After I was out of college I wrote several full-length plays and—possibly because he was not looking over my shoulder—none of them worked. I think in each case they were trying to be a novel.

If H. S. V. Jones were to have, under provocation, raised his voice it would have been extremely shocking. With his lips pursed and his head slightly askew, he lectured so exquisitely on the structure of *The Faerie Queene* that he seemed to have strayed out of the sixteenth century. His very syntax conjured up the spring flowers in a miniature by Nicholas Hilliard. The scabrous parts of *The Canterbury Tales* we did not discuss in class. On the other hand, no shade of disapproval was cast on them by him. He said once that he longed for a study with only one door, but it was a Jane Austenish joke at the expense of his affectionate wife and daughters.

Weirick taught a course in contemporary poetry called "From Whitman to Sandburg," in which he devoted several weeks to the Good Grey Poet, though Whitman was born in 1819 and died in 1892, and so was not very contemporary. Trumbull Stickney, Robinson, William Ellery Leonard, Sandburg, Masters, Vachel Lindsay, Elinor Wylie, Edna St. Vincent Millay, Amy Lowell, the Pound of the translations from the Chinese were held up for our admiration, and a fair number of poets not worth serious consideration, like Joyce Kilmer and Eugene Field, were considered even so. The Pound of the *Cantos*, Eliot, William Carlos Williams, Wallace Stevens, and Gertrude Stein were made fun of and dismissed as "the lunatic fringe."

I would have done better to take Caroline Tupper's "Six Novels of Henry James," but at that time I had no inkling of how deeply *What Maisie Knew*, *The Princess Casamassima*, *The Ambassadors*, *The Wings of the Dove*, and *The Golden Bowl* would one day command my attention. Miss Tupper was from Charleston, South Carolina, and there were times when her upperclass accent presented difficulties to a middle-class Middlewesterner, until you got the hang of it. A mirror, for example, was a "mirá." My happiest memory of her is of an occasion when a graduate student brought a copy of *Transition* to her "at home" and read aloud, to half a dozen people, several pages from *Finnegans Wake*, then known as *Work in Progress*. By slightly unhinging your mind it was possible to guess that what we were hearing about was the fornication of two grasshoppers. Miss Tupper sat smiling and impervious to the indecencies.

Leah Trelease I never studied with but came to know and love when I was a graduate student embedded in medieval literature. I think Mrs. Wharton was her specialty. She had beautiful, luminous, melting brown eyes and the gift of charging the atmosphere around her with humor and radiance. For many years she was courted by an unromantic looking but witty business-man from Champaign, and eventually married him. He was as much an anomaly among the professors as Bottom the Weaver in Titania's bower, but more than able to hold his own conversationally.

And there were others—men and women from the Romance Language and Philosophy and Classics departments. They made up a delightful so-ciety, from which undergraduates were not excluded. I was never again to meet anything like it. It constituted a large part of my education in manners, and was always there in my mind to draw on when I wanted a certain kind of dialogue, a lightness of tone.

I am afraid that, after all this, I haven't answered the question you asked, but another question, which you didn't ask.

TAMAQUA: How would you advise young, aspiring writers to prepare themselves to be writers? As English majors? Creative writing classes? Jour-nalism? What general advice could you give?

Maxwell: I have never taken a course in creative writing, or been a profes-sional journalist, and so can't speak of them. A writer is a reader who is moved to emulation. Read, read.

TAMAQUA: In your unfinished novel *At the Pension Gaullard* there is an odd mixture of intimacy and alienation between the islanders and the young American; they care about him, and—apparently—he cares about them, but they are often startled by the foreignness of each other's lives. Relation-ships in *The Chateau* are similar, but among more complex, fully developed characters. Could you comment on the relationship between *At the Pension Gaullard* and *The Chateau*?

Maxwell: I don't think there is any. If there is something similar about them, it is accidental. Or perhaps I should say unintentional: I didn't have the ear-lier fragment in mind when I wrote the later novel. Or set out consciously to do what I earlier failed to pull off. The mixture of intimacy and alienation could be just the way I ordinarily see things.

TAMAQUA: Under what circumstances was *At the Pension Gaullard* written? Why didn't you finish it?

Maxwell: It was only after I had worked for the *New Yorker* for several months that I was given a chance to read and edit fiction manuscripts. The job I was hired for was "seeing artists." On Tuesdays they left their work, usually submitted in the form of a rough sketch, with the receptionist, and it was looked at the following day by the Art Meeting. On Thursday I returned the artists' portfolios to them, explaining which ideas had been approved (in which case they were to make a finished drawing) or rejected. I became friends with a number of them, including the Hungarian artist Ilonka Karasz, who did a great many covers and decorative spots for the magazine. She also designed wallpaper and fabrics. She and her Dutch husband, Willem Nyland, were half a generation older than I and lived sixty miles north of New York City in a very beautiful house they had built themselves. She asked me to write something that she could illustrate and so in 1942 I began this novel.

She had never seen the West Indies, where the story takes place, but she and her husband had lived in Java, and she was perfectly at home with tropical houses, landscapes, and flora. She did several charming pictures, in egg tempura on scratchboard, which I wish I now owned. They were in so many brilliant colors that I think it is likely most publishers would have considered them too expensive to reproduce. Later I wrote a book for children, *The Heavenly Tenants*, which was published in 1946 with her illustrations. It has just been republished this year after being out of print for nearly half a century. She also did a number of dust jackets for my books.

TAMAQUA: As readers of your unfinished novel, we have many questions about the story. You may not be able to answer them—or else you would have finished the story. But, for example, why *is* the "young American" on the island?

Maxwell: I wish I knew. Also, what was preventing him from going home to Wisconsin, where he so longed to be? Again I have no idea. You could say I had painted myself into a corner. Or you could equally well say I hadn't quite managed to externalize my own experience.

In December 1932, I took a freighter down the Windward Islands with Martinique as my ultimate destination. I had written a novel, *Bright Center of Heaven*, that had been submitted to Harper and Brothers by a friend who knew the trade editor. I had also read a book by Lafcadio Hearn about Martinique and thought it would be interesting to go there and perhaps write about it. The city Hearn wrote about, St. Pierre, had been destroyed by a volcanic eruption in 1903. I stayed in Fort de France. I spoke only rudimentary French and the natives spoke patois. I had nothing to do all day except wander around looking at what there was to see. That month seemed as long as a year under ordinary circumstances in America.

When I got a letter from a friend in Urbana telling me that Harpers was seriously considering my novel and waiting for Cass Canfield to return from Europe, I thought I ought to hurry back and at least be nearby when he arrived at his decision. Which turned out to be favorable. I was twenty-four at this time. If I had stayed longer in Fort de France, I might have stumbled on the material I needed ten years later to go on with this unfinished book.

TAMAQUA: What about the boy, Michel? How will the American's relationship with Michel be resolved?
Maxwell: I don't think, considering the difference in their ages, that it will be. Friendship doesn't always have to be resolved, even in fiction; sometimes it just is.

TAMAQUA: How will the boat trip turn out?
Maxwell: I am afraid they are still and will be forever on that boat. I was hoping the volcano would erupt again and provide me with a dramatic ending. So far it hasn't happened.

I did actually go from Fort de France to Trois Islets with a boatful of native people who were attending a funeral there. In my white linen suit I was very conspicuous, but would have been even if I had dressed in black like them. After the funeral procession had gone twice around the public square and disappeared into a very old church, I walked around in the fields at the edge of the village, certain that every rustle in the long grass was a fer-de-lance. Later I went by bus over the mountains to St. Pierre to make the acquaintance of the volcanologist, only to discover that that day he had taken the coastal steamer to Fort de France.

I could have made the young American a would-be writer looking for material to write about, but it seemed too prosaic to be interesting. I have since come to the conclusion that nothing is too prosaic to be interesting if looked at long enough and hard enough.

Irwin Shaw once remarked that writing a novel was easy. You made a list of the characters and an outline of the events and then sat down and did it. But I have never known—not entirely anyway—when I sat down to write a novel what was going to happen to the characters or how the book would come out. I just felt I had hold of an experience of a certain size and complexity and that it would sustain investigation for several hundred pages. This is, of course, a wasteful way of going about it. But a novel in which I knew beforehand what was going to happen wouldn't interest me to write. I need to wrestle with the material, like Jacob with the angel, until I win its blessing.

Why didn't I finish this one? Once, one of my colleagues at the *New Yorker* found himself standing beside Harold Ross at the urinal and when Ross asked him why he hadn't written any stories lately, nervously answered, "Because I lost the slight fancy that sustained me," and fled. I guess that's what happened to me.

Past Perfect

John Blades/1992

From the *Chicago Tribune*, 5 March 1992, Sec. 2, 2. Copyrighted 3/5/1992, Chicago Tribune Company. All rights reserved. Used with permission.

NEW YORK—Unlike Ernest Hemingway and many other native Illinois writers who left their hometowns with scarcely a backward glance, William Maxwell has never stopped looking back.

Born in Lincoln in 1908, Maxwell settled in New York in the middle 1930s, becoming a revered fiction editor at the *New Yorker* magazine, a literary minister to J. D. Salinger, Eudora Welty, Frank O'Connor, and three famous Johns: O'Hara, Cheever, and Updike.

All the while he was at the *New Yorker*, editing the words of those and other writers, Maxwell was slowly crafting his own distinctive body of fiction, most of which nostalgically focused on Lincoln. "I guess what it amounts to," says Maxwell, who left Lincoln when he was fourteen, "is that the older I get, the closer I come to home."

Bypassed by time, fashion, and interstate traffic, along with so many other central Illinois towns, the Lincoln of today is not the same place that Maxwell so lovingly recalls, a community that was "touched with a bloom, a golden dust," as he put it in his 1971 memoir, *Ancestors.*

With his new book, *Billie Dyer and Other Stories* (Knopf), Maxwell has again returned to the "Earthly Paradise" of his boyhood, which is how he describes Lincoln in that innocent era, before blight destroyed the vaulting elms and the automobile displaced electric trolleys and horsedrawn carriages.

Why, three-quarters of a century later, does Lincoln have such an obsessive but elegiac hold on Maxwell's memory and imagination?

As he does in responding to most such questions, Maxwell takes his time. He is sitting in his small, somewhat untidy office, at the rear of a commodi-

151

ous apartment on Manhattan's Upper East Side, where he has lived for more than thirty years.

After nearly a minute's reflection, Maxwell smiles apologetically and rolls a sheet of paper into his portable electric typewriter, explaining: "The typewriter's my friend. I think better on it than I do offhand."

For perhaps five minutes, he types on the noisy, antiquated Smith Corona. Occasionally he pauses, a contemplative finger touching his upper lip, then strikes the keys again, his long, expressive fingers moving like tree roots photographed in fast motion. When he's done, he wheels the typewriter around with his answer.

"To begin with, it was a very pretty town," he has written of Lincoln, "with elm trees meeting over the brick pavements, and a great deal of individuality in the houses, and the people as well. And because I left it when I was still a boy, my early memories are not overlaid by others, so the Lincoln of the first decades of this century is very vivid to me."

Now almost eighty-four, Maxwell has had ample time to rummage through the past since retiring from the *New Yorker* sixteen years ago. The words and the memories don't come easily, but he persists.

"The past is really quite central to what I do," he says, speaking now in a gentle, measured voice, "the desire to preserve as much of it as possible, the feelings and details of life as it was lived."

"The one thing I hate more than anything else about life," he says, elaborating on an especially wistful passage from his new book, "is the plowing under of human experience, leaving no trace."

Halting the plow

Billie Dyer is another effort to halt the plow. Though called fiction, the book is as close to fact as his memory permits, Maxwell says. It is told in his undisguised first-person voice, and his mother, father, brother, and various aunts, uncles, friends, and neighbors make appearances, with many of the stories recalling episodes in the true memoir *Ancestors*, though seen from slightly different angles. In that case, why call it fiction?

Back to the typewriter. While Maxwell composes, his black cat, Genji, climbs into an available lap for a mid-morning nap. Hunched over the Smith Corona, Maxwell is an austere, almost frail figure. His glasses low on his nose, a few white hairs standing out on his head, he types purposefully, precisely, totally absorbed by the words that materialize on the page.

A few minutes later, he has his answer, which reads, in part:

"I came to believe that life itself, untampered with, always has a profound meaning and interest, and the less you rearrange the details the better, but unfortunately unanswered questions abound, and sometimes they are not questions that the writer has a right to avoid answering, artistically that is, and it has driven me to fall back on my imagination."

For anyone acquainted with Maxwell's prose, his reliance on written, rather than spoken, words should be no revelation. It helps explain why his words are so slowly, carefully, sparingly shaped into sentences and paragraphs, in novels such as *The Folded Leaf, Time Will Darken It* and *So Long, See You Tomorrow*, winner of an American Book Award, as well as such short stories as "Over by the River," one of his rare works of fiction set in Manhattan.

Asked how he came to this austere but evocative prose, Maxwell speaks of the Hemingway influence ("Who could not be affected by his style?"), then credits the directness of his ancestors. "When I was a child, the people around me said exactly what they meant, in a simple language. What I long to do is find the simple, natural way of saying exactly what I mean. That's definitely a Midwestern trait, I like to think."

Looking back on the years Maxwell was his editor at the *New Yorker*, John Updike also mentions Maxwell's Midwestern taciturnity, remarking that one of his "rare qualities was that I never heard him say anything silly. Everything is to the point. There's a wonderful economy in his mind, very direct."

"He made the whole process a learning process for me," Updike says, recalling his first meeting with Maxwell ("kind of Fred Astairish, slight but graceful") in 1954, shortly after he had his earliest stories published in the *New Yorker.* "He was a good editor because he wasn't trying to shape you into somebody else. He was trying to draw out of you the best writer you could be."

"He was very good at not doing more than was needed," Updike says. "There was always a lot of fiddling, and a lot of the fiddles came not from him but from [*New Yorker* editor William] Shawn. And Bill would occasionally assist me in ignoring them."

As Updike's graceful prose would indicate, he required far less fiddling than most other writers, Maxwell says. Citing Updike's critical essays as well as his fiction, Maxwell calls him "the brightest person I ever encountered . . . at the present moment our only first-class writer, on any scale of magnitude."

Adding some spice

Maxwell is equally admiring of John Cheever, who was "simply a wonderful writer," he says, but an enigmatic person, "much too complicated to go into." The increasingly erotic nature of Cheever's stories caused editorial problems at the *New Yorker*, Maxwell says, even a comparatively inoffensive description of a man "with love in his heart and lust in his trousers."

"Shawn wouldn't allow the reference to lust," Maxwell says, "and I was beside myself. It seems very old-fashioned now, but then it was unacceptable, and there was nothing I could do."

Like Cheever, John O'Hara was inclined to stir some spice into his *New Yorker* stories, Maxwell says, which resulted in a "running battle with [founding editor] Harold Ross about the sexual innuendoes, a tradition that survived through Shawn." Now, he says, that attitude of sexual modesty is gone.

Maxwell's take on O'Hara doesn't square with that of Brendan Gill, a longtime New *Yorker* staff writer who, in his memoir, *Here at The New Yorker*, portrayed the novelist and short-story writer as a belligerent drinker, snob, and "master of the fancied slight."

"I was aware that he could be unpleasant," Maxwell says, "but he was never unpleasant to me. He was a changed man when he stopped drinking. And he had a rare tenderness for women in his fiction."

Perhaps because his own outlook is so much more charitable, Maxwell didn't recognize many of the *New Yorker* colleagues that Gill drew (and quartered) in his jovially abrasive memoir.

Maxwell does agree with Gill about the obnoxious character of one famous *New Yorker* writer, James Thurber, who, he says "could be very, very unpleasant. But he could also be terribly, terribly funny."

Though he doesn't share many of Gill's personal judgments, Maxwell calls him "one of the colleagues who gave me the most pleasure. There was a period when he and I and Maeve Brennan, an Irish girl who was very witty and charming, had offices side by side. And there was so much laughter that it bothered Shawn, and he moved me because he didn't think it was good for the general morale of the office to have that much laughter."

Settling in Manhattan

Maxwell considers himself blessed that fortune led him from the bucolic streets of Lincoln to the urbane sanctums of the *New Yorker* at the "very rock bottom" of the Depression. After Maxwell's mother died and his father remarried, the family moved from Lincoln to Chicago, where William graduated from Senn High School, then went on to get his degree at the University of Illinois at Urbana-Champaign.

By the time he settled in Manhattan in 1936, with a $200 bankroll, Maxwell had already published one novel, *Bright Center of Heaven* (now mercifully "buried under a rug," he says), and had another, *They Came Like Swallows*, ready for publication. He had also sold several stories to the *New Yorker*—all of which led to a $35-a-week job on the magazine, not as a writer or a fiction editor but as an assistant in the art department, who "sat in on meetings and told artists what changes they wanted."

Eventually, Maxwell moved into the fiction department, under the estimable Katharine White. Though he always found the atmosphere around the *New Yorker* extremely congenial, he spent only three days a week in his office, an ideal arrangement that allowed him time at home for his own novels, stories, essays, and memoirs, which now total thirteen volumes.

Still back home

After White's departure, Maxwell inherited one of the magazine's (and the world's) most illustrious but hermitic writers, J. D. Salinger, with whom he has kept in touch, even though Salinger's last *New Yorker* story appeared in 1965. "We talk once a year, every two years, or letters go back and forth," Maxwell says. "To the best of my knowledge, he's never stopped writing. It must be quite a pile by now."

If compulsory retirement hadn't caught up with him in 1976, Maxwell might still be keeping office hours at the *New Yorker*.

"I always shaved with pleasure on the days I went to work there," he says. "But when I left, I really left. I still have colleagues there whom I love and see from time to time, and through them I hear things. But I'm not emotionally involved with what goes on there now."

Though Maxwell hasn't been satisfied with any of the many books about the *New* Yorker, he doesn't begrudge the writers their views. And, he says, "I wouldn't dream of writing my own. I don't feel any emotional need to. I don't feel the same about the magazine's past as I do my own."

By contrast, Maxwell has never really left Lincoln. His emotional ties have endured for eight decades, though he has been less and less inclined to visit the community in person. The last time was more than ten years ago, when he attended his stepmother's funeral.

"The older generation are all gone now," he says, "and I don't like to travel. I don't like airplanes. I like to stay home with my typewriter."

"I used to dream of going back and buying the family house and living there. But I knew that it wasn't a place where my wife would be particularly happy," says Maxwell, whose two grown daughters live in New York.

"You have to look at the past with appreciation rather than trying to re-live it literally. But you can live it in your imagination to your heart's content."

Radio Interview with William Maxwell on KMOX Radio, St. Louis, Missouri

KMOX/1992

Broadcast April 8, 1992. Reprinted by permission.

KMOX: He has received the Brandeis Creative Arts Medal, the American Book Award, and the Howells Medal of the American Academy of Arts and Letters. Mr. Maxwell grew up in Lincoln, Illinois, just up the pike here, just up Highway 55. Those of you listening in the Springfield area will know Lincoln very well. And Lincoln, Illinois, is the setting for the stories in Mr. Maxwell's new work, *Billie Dyer and Other Stories*. It is a privilege to welcome William Maxwell to KMOX in St. Louis. Mr. Maxwell, good morning.
Maxwell: Good morning.

KMOX: You've done pretty well for a guy from Lincoln, Illinois, haven't you, now?
Maxwell: It's a wonderful place.

KMOX: You recall Lincoln with nostalgia, but also as a place where all of the good, and, in fact, the not-so-good parts of life, the closed ideas, the lack of tolerance, perhaps? Billie Dyer, the subject of your first and the title story in this book, a most distinguished gentleman, and yet, who remembered him in Lincoln, Illinois?
Maxwell: We've got some terrible interference. Can you forgive me while I answer the door?

KMOX: Oh, sure. He has to answer the door in his apartment in New York, because, of course, many people are coming to his door to seek his autograph, saying, "Is it true you're really talking to St. Louis?" Well, it's possible. Again, the former *New Yorker* magazine fiction editor William Maxwell now answering the door, and taking cards and letters from people who heard that he finally made KMOX. Kind of a rite of passage for excellent writers. You can win all sorts of awards and medals, but it's not until you get that first appearance on the—
Maxwell: The ringing has stopped.

KMOX: Who was there?
Maxwell: Nobody. Somebody pressed the doorbell, and then went away.

KMOX: A practical joke. How do you remember Lincoln, Illinois, Mr. Dyer? I'm sorry—Mr. Maxwell.
Maxwell: It's an honor to be called Dyer, because he was a great man. I remember through my boyhood's eyes so that everything is related to school and my bicycle and the people—my aunts and uncles and family friends who were loving, so there was a kind of affection over everything, I guess is what I'm trying to say. Because I left there when I was fourteen years old, and I saw it in an atmosphere of affection. And I think of it now in an atmosphere of affection. I do think it's not quite like other towns. When I was little I thought everybody was slightly larger than life size and in some strange way they seemed to be that way, because in a town of 15,000 or 16,000, most people know who they are, who their parents were, and it gives them a kind of mythical quality. Long after we'd moved away, I was in Lincoln and I went into a diner to have a piece of pie and a glass of milk, and found I'd left my wallet at home. The man who ran the diner said, "That's all right, you're Will Maxwell's boy." And I hadn't been there for ten years, but he knew who I was. Don't you think it's remarkable?

KMOX: It certainly is remarkable. You spent certainly most of your professional career and you now live in New York City. Those sorts of things wouldn't happen in New York, would they?
Maxwell: Well they have to divide up into neighborhoods. In a neighborhood they would happen, but neighborhoods change perpetually, and they don't have very long memories because so much is destroyed by new buildings. No, they wouldn't happen in New York.

KMOX: Is this somewhat common, though, among people who grow up in small towns that move to the big city? They wax nostalgic about small town life even though they want to get out of it at a very young age. There's something about that. You hear Garrison Keillor kind of mention the same thing.
Maxwell: It's very strange. I think there's a force driving people out of small towns, very much like the force that drives the baby out of his mother's womb—out, out, out. As a young man I went out looking for something to write about. I went to the West Indies on a freighter and I was looking, looking for the things that a writer writes about without knowing that they were right there where I came from.

KMOX: But maybe they weren't there until you'd lived an entire life.
Maxwell: I think that's right.

KMOX: At the *New Yorker*, you were editor, friend, perhaps even mentor to some of the greatest names in American Letters, J. D. Salinger, Eudora Welty, Frank O'Connor, John Cheever, John O'Hara, John Updike.
Maxwell: Yes, I knew and loved all those people.

KMOX: Can I ask you who your favorite writer of not just perhaps those six individuals, but who you regard as the top writer in America today, or even over the course of American writers?
Maxwell: I think I'd rather not answer the question. I think I'd rather say Tolstoy.

KMOX: Tolstoy. Are you in touch with Salinger at all?
Maxwell: I hear from him occasionally, once a year or so. We haven't seen each other for several years, but we have not lost touch with each other.

KMOX: Did you ever get into an argument with someone whose fiction was being edited by you?
Maxwell: Yes.

KMOX: Typically, how did that work?
Maxwell: Well, sometimes it was based on a misunderstanding. For example, it was the habit of the *New Yorker* to put things into proof, into what they called working proof, and then edit from that. And once John Cheever sent in a story that seemed to me to have two endings, and I wanted him to

see what it would look like without the second ending, so I stayed up and typed it out without the second ending, meaning that if he didn't like it we would simply put it back the way he had it in his manuscript. He misunderstood, and thought that was the way it had to be, and there was indeed a terrific argument, but it was printed the way he wanted it.

KMOX: There are now thirteen volumes of William Maxwell stories, essays, and memoirs. Are you working on volume fourteen, Mr. Maxwell?
Maxwell: I'm working on a story. If there are enough of them there will be another volume, but I don't think of stories as part of a larger collection until they sort of form it of themselves.

KMOX: Form it in and of themselves. For those of us in the Midwest, particularly those of you who may have grown up in a small town, and remember the people there, perhaps as you grow older you remember even more sharply than you did when you were younger.
Maxwell: I think that's true.

KMOX: We recommend *Billie Dyer and Other Stories*. Mr. Maxwell, thank you very much for joining us here on KMOX this morning.
Maxwell: It's been a pleasure.

An Interview with William Maxwell

David Stanton/1994

From *Poets & Writers Magazine*, May/June 1994, 36–47. Reprinted by permission of the publisher, Poets & Writers, Inc., 72 Spring Street, New York, NY 10012. www.pw.org.

At age eighty-five, William Maxwell's appearance is at once endearing and a bit disconcerting. He is thin and slightly frail, and on his head grow solitary white hairs. Yet he is also energetic—enthusiastic, at times even agile in a boyish way. Dressed in a pale green suit with a yellow knit tie, he answers the door of his Upper East Side apartment with a slightly uneven but reassuring smile.

Maxwell has lived in this Manhattan apartment for over twenty-five years—a period that accounts for less than half of his career as a publishing fiction writer. (He and his wife, Emily, also own a house in Yorktown Heights, New York.) His first novel, *Bright Center of Heaven*, appeared in 1934. (Maxwell now dismisses the book—long out of print—as hopelessly imitative.) Since then he has published six more novels; three collections of stories, including his latest book, *Billie Dyer and Other Stories* (Knopf, 1992; Plume, paper); a fascinating, semi-imagined history of his family, *Ancestors* (Knopf, 1971); and a collection of essays and reviews. (Except where noted otherwise, all of Maxwell's books are available in paperback from David R. Godine.) His novel *So Long, See You Tomorrow* (Knopf, 1980) won an American Book Award (now known as the National Book Award), and he is considered by many to be among America's greatest writers, though his readership remains limited.

Maxwell is better known, in fact, as a *New Yorker* fiction editor—one who, from 1936 to 1976, helped shape the work of John Cheever, Eudora Welty, John O'Hara, John Updike, and countless other celebrated writers. Joining on as an assistant in the magazine's art department soon after his arrival in

New York, Maxwell became part of its celebrated editorial staff—Harold Ross, William Shawn, and Brendan Gill were just a few of his colleagues.

Maxwell's own writing has changed both much and little over the years. In early books such as *Time Will Darken It* (Harper & Bros., 1948), which the *Boston Globe* called "as near to perfection as it is possible for a novel to be," Maxwell seemed more willing to describe at length and to speculate about his characters' motivations, and even their futures. *So Long, See You Tomorrow*, however, is a mere 135 pages and says much simply by what it leaves out. Yet one can fairly easily spot a Maxwell sentence—deliberate in tone yet informed by sympathy, precisely paced, and essential to whatever paragraph it calls home. Maxwell admits that the evolution of his current, almost-skeletal style was largely influenced by his work as an editor; yet he also claims that, during his years at the *New Yorker*, he became increasingly inclined to leave stories alone, assuming that the writer had good reasons for whatever he had done.

If Maxwell's style has changed over the years, his subject matter for the most part has not. Nearly all of his work takes place in the Illinois of his youth and has its roots in the death of his mother in the influenza epidemic of 1918, when Maxwell was ten. From his second novel, *They Came Like Swallows* (Harper & Bros., 1937), right through *So Long*, this loss has been his muse. It is amazing how much he has remembered and set down about this cherished period—a childhood that ended halfway through.

Maxwell's office, where this interview takes place, is well lived-in yet also surprisingly makeshift. His desk is a wooden card table, his work light a Tensor lamp mounted on what seems to be a rolling hospital IV stand. There are bookcases and file cabinets, several tidy stacks of magazines and folders, a small bed, a television, and a photocopier. His typewriter is a 1980s-style Smith Corona sitting on a classic wood-and-metal typing table the kind that forces your knees together. On the wall behind his chair hang his daughter Brookie's painting for the cover of *Over by the River* (Knopf, 1977), his first collection of short fiction, and a small Walker Evans portrait of the poet Robert Fitzgerald, Maxwell's longtime friend and advisor.

As I am setting up my two tape recorders, explaining with embarrassment that I like to "cover" myself in case one fails, Maxwell asks if I would mind if he typed his answers to my questions. At first I assume he means to use the typewriter to think with; but no—he wants to type out his complete answers, without saying a word into either of my machines. Apparently this has been Maxwell's practice for some time, but I have not read of it in any of the articles about him. I am taken aback, but Maxwell says, "Try it for a while."

For most of the next two hours, I sit in a comfortable green chair and watch Maxwell type. While working he is completely immersed, unaware of my eyes trained on his face or wandering about the room. After completing each answer, Maxwell turns the typewriter table toward me and allows me to peruse his work. On a few occasions I ask him to expand this or that aspect of an answer, and he graciously obliges. The final product is a cogent interview with the *um*'s and *uh*'s already eliminated, but also lacking some of the intangible virtues of a spoken interview—the offhand remark, the facial expression that leads to a follow-up question.

After the session, Maxwell seems more at ease. When I tell him I felt guilty watching him do all the work, he replies, "It must have been very boring for you." As we are walking out, he takes me to the window of his spacious living room; through the fog one can see the East River and the Triborough Bridge. It is obviously a view he treasures.

After talking with him, one feels that there are two Maxwells—the precise, business-like writer and editor, and the retiring, apologetic, cordial man. Yet they are also one—Maxwell is as committed to a sense of now-rare civility and decorum as he is to the perfection of words on the printed page. One wonders if there will still be such writers—or human beings—in another hundred years.

Q: First, I wonder if you could say a little about why you prefer to conduct interviews in this way—typing out answers to questions spoken by the interviewer.

A: Some while back I had a couple of rather bad experiences with interviewers, partly because I am inclined to mumble and partly because the interviewer didn't remember accurately what I said, and the results were distressing to both of us. When I read somewhere that Vladimir Nabokov didn't talk to interviewers but would answer questions that were submitted to him in writing, I thought of this way—of answering on my typewriter in the interviewer's presence, so that he would carry away with him the facts as I saw them, and whatever my ideas at that moment were. It makes his work easier and saves me from having to go back and correct misconceptions, or see them published and not be able to do anything about it.

Q: You have written so much about your childhood—a childhood that began in the era of the horse-drawn carriage—I wonder how writing fiction has changed your view of memory.

A: I suppose it isn't true, but I sometimes wonder if I skipped what is referred to as infant amnesia—that is to say, the point when children of five or six forget nearly everything that happened to them and start all over again. I remember things that happened (and that nobody could have told me about) when I was just barely able to stand up. And things I used to think happened when I was four proved to be when I was three. I don't think my memory is any more reliable than the next person's, but there is a great deal that I do remember, correctly or otherwise. Within the last two or three years the quality of my remembering seems to have changed, and it is as if the past and present were all one, that the past is present; and I do not simply remember something that happened long ago but am living it. For example, soon after my mother died, I stopped being able to remember her face clearly, and now it has come back to me.

Q: You have distinguished in other interviews between the storyteller and the writer—the storyteller being fanciful and the writer more literal. Could you say more about the difference between the two?

A: The storyteller, as I think of him, is the inheritor of an ancient tradition, and his effects are to a considerable extent spontaneous and surprising even to him. I think of the writer, as distinct from the storyteller, as a person with many threads on his mind that have to be woven together in a way that is aesthetically successful and intellectually responsible. He is given to rewriting, to worrying about style, and his job is essentially to find the form and meaning that are inherent in the material that, to all intents and purposes, has chosen him.

Q: You have said elsewhere that your favorite authors make writing seem "as natural as speech, and for the best writers it is all one thing." Yet your own technique, as I understand it, is to clip sentences from paragraphs and save them until you find a place where they fit. Why does your own, very deliberate method seem to conflict with the "naturalness" you admire in other writers?

A: Ordinary speech, if the speaker is an interesting person, holds one's interest partly because it is spoken, but when it is transcribed proves to be repetitious and often has dead spots, when the speaker is communicating by his expression and tone of voice rather than by the words. I have a concept of a literary style based on ordinary speech in its syntax and variety of sentences, but that is carefully pruned of the dead wood—is alive, laconic, says what it means and means what it says, and is the result of hard labor, and owes half its meaning to its carefully planned context. I know when I write a good sentence, but often it comes in the midst of a passage that is only partly in focus, or just plain dull, and so I cut the good sentence out and save it for another context. It seemed to me when I finished *So Long, See You Tomorrow* that half the sentences had been in nine or ten different places, tentatively, before they found the right one and were locked in. I can imagine a very clear mind (John Updike's, for example) that would know right away where the sentence belonged, but I operate more by trial and error, because I don't always know what I am trying to do, what the material demands.

Q: Since you have been an editor as well as a writer, I wonder how you feel about seeking advice from editors on unfinished work.

A: In my experience it is dangerous to show a long piece of writing in an unfinished state to a publisher. John Cheever did it with *The Wapshot Chronicle*, and the editor's less-than-enthusiastic response kept him from finishing the book for at least ten years. There are, of course, exceptional editors whose responses can be trusted, but on the whole it is safer for the writer to keep the project to himself until he is satisfied with what he has written, and in a position to argue about suggested changes: I have tended to be so tired when I finished a novel that I listened to editorial suggestions more than I should have. In the case of *The Folded Leaf*, I combined two characters because the editor at Harpers thought the story line should be strengthened. When it was republished I put everything back the way I originally had it. With *The Chateau*, an editor at Knopf argued strenuously that the long coda was a mistake. In the end I turned to Alfred Knopf who said, "Have it the way you want it." Now, if I opened the book and the coda was missing, I would feel like shooting myself.

I have sent stories that had reached the stage of a second or third (or tenth) draft to a friend who has several times proved helpful. So, for that matter, has Roger Angell, the editor at the *New Yorker* that I submit stories to. But I don't send him a story unless I think it is right, and then I don't feel bad when it is rejected. I just think the magazine and I had different ideas about it. Or sometimes, I see that they were right and the story wasn't really all that good.

Q: It seems, though, that you have often given your works-in- progress to specific people—friends more than editors—for their reactions. In the case of *The Folded Leaf* [Harper & Bros., 1945] for example, you sent numerous drafts to Louise Bogan [the poet and *New Yorker* poetry critic]. Could you describe the role of these outside readers in your work?

A: My friendship with Louise Bogan was, and still is, very important to me. Her literary standards were so high and her judgment so strict. I was eleven years younger than she was, and open to whatever she held out to me— Rilke's *Duino Elegies*, the songs of Mahler and Hugo Wolf. I showed her what I thought was a short story and she said, "Go on." My story turned out to be the first chapter of *The Folded Leaf.* And because it was her idea that I should pursue the situation of the two boys I sent her each chapter as I finished it, through four versions. Once when I was stuck, and a longer time than usual elapsed between chapters, I got a postcard from her saying, "Get that boy up off the sleeping porch." Over a period of four years she made only one criticism—about a physical description which she thought not fresh enough. When I finished the book she gave me the title.

The most important living reader I have is my wife. When I think I have finished something I take it first to her, sometimes in a state of unjustified euphoria. She has good literary judgment and a good sense of when I am or am not doing my best work. Often she has said, when I was quite pleased with something, "I think this is going to be one of your best stories," and so sent me back to the typewriter. At various times in my life the opinions of certain people have been important to me—of Zona Gale [the novelist and playwright]; of the poet and translator Robert Fitzgerald; of certain *New Yorker* writers like Shirley Hazzard and Francis Steegmuller and Mavis Gallant; of Sylvia Townsend Warner, whose letters I edited; of now one friend and now another, depending on the material. When I came home from France in 1948 [Maxwell spent four months there during the summer] I walked into our house in the country and, with my hat on my head, sat down to the typewriter and typed out a page of ideas for a novel, and tacked it to the bookcase and never looked at it during the ten years I was writing *The Chateau.* [*The Chateau*, published by Knopf in 1961, is a novel based on Maxwell's experiences in France.] Toward the end of that period my wife and I struck up a friendship with Elizabeth Bowen [the novelist and short story writer], and she asked to read the manuscript of *The Chateau.* And then she and I took some sandwiches into a quiet part of Central Park, and she told me everything that was on that (original) page, which she of course had never seen, and so I knew that I had accomplished what I set out to do.

I don't have tens of thousands of readers, but now here and now there some connection is made, judging by the letters that come from strangers, and this is of course gratifying. I wouldn't know how to handle a large audience. It would confuse me about who I am.

Q: Can you tell me a little about your early life as a writer. When did you write your first stories?
A: The first story I published was in my high school magazine, and it was about an aristocrat who, during the French Revolution, hid in a grandfather clock. It must have derived from my reading, and wasn't followed by anything for about ten years. In college I wrote poetry that was, I am afraid, rather noticeably under the influence of Elinor Wylie and Walter de la Mare. During the year that I spent as a graduate student at Harvard I met and became friends with Robert Fitzgerald, who was the real thing, and I came to the conclusion that, though I loved poetry, I was not a poet.

When I was a graduate student at the University of Illinois, I was living in the house of a member of the English department, Garreta Busey. One day she got a letter from a friend on the Yale faculty asking her to do a forty-page condensation of the life of Thomas Coke of Holkham, an eighteenth-century agriculturalist. He introduced in the House of Lords the bill to recognize the American colonies, but his major work was the improvement through breeding of strains of sheep and cattle. Miss Busey asked me to work on the assignment with her, and while she did the agricultural parts, which interested her but did not interest me, I condensed the passages about Coke's life. The biography contained a good many details about the life of the period—for example, there was his aunt, Lady Mary Coke, who divorced her husband because he was a scoundrel (unheard of—the divorce, I mean), and dressed her servants in pea-green and silver livery, and when she was depressed used to fish in the ornamental goldfish pond, and in her old age slept in a dresser drawer. In short she was a character in what might have been a novel. She also suffered from the delusion that the Empress Maria Teresa was trying to take her servants away from her. I wrote about her, about the balls, the great houses, etc., with so much pleasure that when the job was done I turned to and wrote my first novel, about the goings on on a Wisconsin farm that I had first-hand acquaintance with. I also, when I was working on that farm, met Zona Gale, who was a kind of fairy godmother to me, and made me feel that it was a wonderful thing to be a professional writer.

After my first novel was published, I naturally wondered what else I could write about, and the "what else" turned out to be my mother's death. Many years later, I was having lunch with Pete Lemay, who was the publicity director at Knopf at the time, and he told me about Willa Cather, whom he had been taken to see. Not many people were, since she was a recluse. After he had described her, I said, surprised by what he had told me, "Whatever do you think made her a writer, do you suppose?" and he said, "Why, what makes anyone a writer—deprivation, of course."

Q: I wonder what deprivation led you to be a writer. Was it your mother's death?
A: Well God knows it was a deprivation. Probably the answer is yes. If you search in the background of any serious writer, it isn't very long before you come upon a major deprivation of one sort or another—which the writer through the exercise of imagination tries to overcome or compensate for, or even make not have happened.

Q: In the story "The Front and the Back Parts of the House" [from *Billie Dyer*], which I gather is largely true . . .
A: It is entirely true.

Q: . . . you deal with the anger of someone who thought she recognized her husband in a character in one of your novels. I wonder if this kind of experience makes it more difficult to escape into the fantasy of fiction. Do you ever worry about the effect your writing will have on your friends and family?
A: I do sometimes worry about using material taken directly from life, but my worrying is inconsistent and arbitrary. I never worried about writing about my Aunt Annette's husband, who could easily have sued me for invasion of privacy, but when I wrote about the French family in *The Chateau* I suffered the torture of the damned—but that didn't keep me from writing about them. After the book was published I refused to let my British publisher have it, lest it hop the Channel. One member of the family happened to have a son in school in America and came for his graduation just at the time the reviews were appearing. She read the book and went home and didn't tell anybody about it. After a number of years the other members did discover the book, and wrote me that it was naughty of me but could they please have a copy. Over the years we have discussed whether it was all right to allow the book to be translated and published in France, and they finally

came to the conclusion that it was not, ever, and, since I was very fond of them, I have abided by their decision.

Q: In "The Holy Terror" [also from *Billie Dyer*] you tell another true story about a horrifying incident in which your brother lost one of his legs—an incident you have written very little about. And I am also struck in your work by how little you reveal about your father, emotionally, as compared to your mother, even though she died much earlier. I wonder why you have written so little about some aspects of your childhood and so much about others.
A: My brother's accident figures in *They Came Like Swallows.* In that novel, written when I was in my late twenties, I put down what I believed at the time to be true. My Aunt Annette read the manuscript and though she knew it was untrue didn't correct me, probably because she couldn't bear to tell me that she was the person who was driving the carriage, not her husband. The true story is in "The Holy Terror." As for my father, unlike my mother he was not dead and I owed him some consideration, especially since he had no real grasp of the nature of literary writing, of literature, and I didn't want to write about him in a way that would make him feel exposed or that I had no feeling whatever for his natural desire for privacy. In any case, I am under the impression that I *have* written revealingly about him, in *They Came Like Swallows, So Long, See You Tomorrow,* "The Value of Money," and "The Front and the Back Parts of the House" [both stories from *Billie Dyer*]. As for why I have written so little about some aspects of my childhood and so much about others, surely it is a matter of psychological pressures, often unconscious. In any case, a writer is chosen by his material, not the other way round.

My brother's affliction, as it was called, certainly colored my childhood and had, in all probability, psychological effects I wasn't conscious of. In any case, it was a fact in my growing up. My father was too, of course, but he was away three nights and four days of every week. As a small child I loved him as much, or something like as much as I loved my mother, but he was not really fond of children—when I was an adult he confessed once that he enjoyed my brothers and me more after we were grown. And of course we were of completely different temperaments. As I have grown older my view has become more charitable, less colored by the Oedipal conflict. But it is hard to do much with the emotional life of people who are essentially practical. My father was romantic in his feelings toward my mother, but about everything else, a matter-of-fact business man. I should say, though, that he took seriously his responsibilities to his sons, and at certain critical moments advised us seriously, in ways that were important. For example, when I took my wife home for the first time, I thought for several days that he didn't appreciate what she was like, until he said, when we were alone together, "There has been no one like her in our family for three generations. She is like a star." And then he went on to say, "If you will always think of her first, she will always think of you first." It is a good way to keep marriages out of the divorce court. At least, there have been no divorces among my father's children.

Q: I sense a theme of atonement in *So Long, See You Tomorrow* and in your more recent stories an attempt to redress a variety of past mistakes. Is this a recent development in your work of a longstanding subject?
A: As a child I went to Sunday school until I was fifteen or sixteen; with that much exposure to Calvinism (it was a Presbyterian Sunday school) it would be odd if I didn't feel guilty about what were obvious failures toward other people. That is to say, I have a standard of behavior that I try to live up to, and when I fall below it, I am troubled. In my old age I have twice written letters of apology for ancient lapses from kindness or proper behavior, and felt better when I did it, though the person I wrote to, in both cases, had no recollection of the offense. I don't think, though, that in general I am guilt-ridden. I just try to behave decently, and regret the occasions when I didn't do what I feel I ought to have.

Q: A point that has come up numerous times in this interview is the way in which your fiction straddles the boundary between fiction and nonfiction. I wonder if you could talk about the differences you see between the two genres.
A: For me "fiction" is not whether a thing, the thing I am writing about, actually happened, but rather in the form of the writing. Half of the details and characters of *The Folded Leaf* are based on actual events, half are invented, and when I read the book now I am no longer sure what I invented and what is a memory. Later on in my writing, I came to feel that life is the most extraordinary storyteller of all, and the fewer changes the writer makes the better, provided that you get to the heart of the matter. But with events that occurred so long ago that there is now nobody you can go to and talk about them, I think it is only sensible to fall back on one's imagination, which is supported by the experience of daily life. The important distinction is between reminiscence, which is a formless accumulation, and a story, which

has a shape, a controlled effect, a satisfying conclusion—something that is or attempts to be a work of art and not merely an exercise in remembering. The reader far too often wants to know if a story actually happened, in which case it is not, for him, fiction. But that isn't how I see things. Instead of giving himself to the story as a story, he wants his curiosity (which is pointless) to be satisfied. I admire writers who don't have to depend on actual experience for their material and storytelling, but I am not one of them.

Q: Having spent so many years as a writer, I wonder if you have any other advice you might give an as-yet-unpublished young writer.
A: Publishers have to be concerned with the bottom line, and magazines have their own purposes, which do not always exactly coincide with the writer's, and so ultimately the writer must trust his own judgment about what he has written. What has kept me going throughout my life is reading—the strength and example of other writers whose work I read with wonder and admiration. Conrad, for example. I don't see what any unpublished writer can do except have for himself the highest standards he can imagine, and hope that the quality of his work will be perceived. The payment at best usually doesn't amount to a living wage, but the satisfaction of being a writer is considerable. The double life—that is, to have another means of support—is maybe better than a life devoted exclusively to writing, with the wolf at the door.

The literary agent Diarmuid Russell, who was the son of the Irish poet AE, once remarked that there was no end of talented writers and what really mattered was energy. Certainly it is vital to literary work. But so is belief in oneself and one's talents. So is the love of writing itself, for itself. Of giving form and, where possible, beauty to the filling out of an idea.

A Modest, Scrupulous, Happy Man

Harvey Ginsberg/1994

From *New York Times Book Review*, 22 January 1995, 3, 20. Reprinted by permission.

This week, sixty-one years after the publication of William Maxwell's first novel, *Bright Center of Heaven*, Knopf is publishing *All the Days and Nights*, a collection of his short stories. It is to be hoped that its appearance will at last bring to this remarkably modest man the popular recognition that has so far escaped him during one of the most distinguished careers in contemporary American letters.

His own work comprises six novels, three previous collections of short fiction, a family history, one book for children (with a second on the way) and a collection of essays and reviews. In addition, he was, for forty years, a fiction editor at the *New Yorker*, where the authors he worked with included Eudora Welty, Shirley Hazzard, Vladimir Nabokov, and Mary McCarthy, and where he was familiarly known as the editor of the three Johns—Cheever, O'Hara, and Updike.

When I met him last November at his East Side apartment, Mr. Maxwell had been home for only two days after a two-week hospital stay for treatment of kidney stones. Nonetheless, he appeared to be in splendid health and, in a classic tweed jacket, looked like nothing so much as the 1950s ideal of an editor or of the college English instructor he had been for two years in his youth. I am tempted to say that despite a slight stoop, his body was as wiry as an athlete's, but that would be misleading, since he once confessed to a *New Yorker* colleague that as a schoolboy he had made forty-two errors, allegedly by "actual count," in a baseball game when pressed into service at shortstop instead of being allowed to occupy his customary position in right field.

This year Mr. Maxwell and his wife, Emily, will celebrate their fiftieth wedding anniversary, and one can tell from the dedications in several of his books how central her role in his life has been. They met when she applied for a job as poetry editor at the *New Yorker*, a title that did not exist at the time but which was one of several hats Mr. Maxwell then wore at the magazine. She didn't get a job. But with his usual brevity and a twinkle of rare self-satisfaction, Mr. Maxwell stated, "She was very attractive, and I pursued the matter."

Although many of his best stories are set in New York and one of his novels is set as far away as Europe, Mr. Maxwell's abiding fictional world is the small town of Lincoln, Illinois (sometimes called Draperville or, in one instance, Logan, in his books), where he was born in 1908 and where he lived until he was fourteen, a place that would, in his own words, provide "three-quarters of the material I would need for the rest of my writing life." Of all the questions I asked him, the only one to which he typed a reply, as if to insure that the answer not be garbled in my notes, was how he would decide in a given novel whether to call the town Lincoln or Draperville.

"The change from Draperville to Lincoln as the background for my fiction was, I think, because originally I felt that what I was writing was fiction, that is to say a mixture of things I had experienced or known about with events that I felt free to imagine if the novel or story required it. Gradually over the years I came to have such respect for the storytelling aspects of life that it more and more seemed a good idea to stick closer to what actually happened, and the result was certainly that the fiction became more autobiographical. It seemed simpler when I was writing about actual people as I knew them to use Lincoln. This doesn't mean I had moved over into reminiscence, because reminiscence is largely an accumulation of things remembered, whereas I wanted the material to have the shape and form and effect of fiction."

Referring to Lincoln, he has written, "Nothing of any historical importance had ever happened there, or has to this day"; yet for him, the town "was the Earthly Paradise, the apple that Eve prevailed upon Adam to eat being as yet an abstraction." But two far from Edenic events did take place in the decade and a half he lived in Lincoln. These tragedies profoundly affected his life and recur repeatedly in his books: his mother died in the influenza epidemic of 1918-19, and his brother lost a leg trying to climb aboard a moving horse-drawn buggy.

The circumstances of his mother's death and the halcyon years preceding it are the subject of his second novel, *They Came Like Swallows* (1937), and are movingly, if more briefly, described in three of his other books. In an essay on Colette, Mr. Maxwell wrote: "If orphaned children were allowed to deal with their grief in an otherwise unchanged world, they would probably, in time, extricate themselves from it naturally, because of their age. But the circumstances always are changed, and it is the constant comparison of the way things are with the way things used to be that sometimes fixes them forever in an attitude of loss."

He acknowledged to me that he was thinking of his own boyhood and of his mother.

One of the many things that make Mr. Maxwell so extraordinarily sympathetic a writer is his understanding of the ways in which fear of what might happen can have as great an influence on us as events that do occur. The fears he ascribes to an old woman in his 1980 novel *So Long, See You Tomorrow*, and to Austin King, the honorable young lawyer who is the protagonist of the 1948 novel *Time Will Darken It*, are strikingly similar, right down to locking the front door against bogymen. Even in the 1961 novel *The Chateau*, which fictionalizes a holiday in France taken by the Maxwells shortly after World War II, his hero and heroine are repeatedly concerned over what may befall them during the rest of their trip. With a smile, Mr. Maxwell remarked to me that their worries "were not without reason." Besides, "if people don't worry, they have no imagination. The world is not a safe place."

For Mr. Maxwell, childhood is a time in which self-invented terror can lurk in any corner. One of the two young daughters in "Over by the River" (the story chosen to open *All the Days and Nights*) is preternaturally afraid of tigers, but her father unquestioningly accepts her phobia. The same misinterpretation of a colorful picture of a man in a nightshirt who is dreaming of a steeplechase is shared by Austin King's four-year-old daughter, Ab, in *Time Will Darken It*, and by Maxwell himself, posing as the narrator of the short story *A Final Report*, who remembers his childhood. To both children the man is in danger; the horses will land on the bed and trample him. And yes, there really was such a picture in a neighbor's house in Lincoln, and growing up, Mr. Maxwell did fear for the safety of the dreamer.

Quite apart from the similarity of an old woman's and a young man's fears, the duplication of a picture, the refrains of a mother's death and the amputation of a brother's leg, the amount of material from Mr. Maxwell's Lincoln childhood that appears, reappears, and then reappears again in his writings is noteworthy. A very short listing would include such accounts of family horror as a grandfather who suffered a gruesome and protracted death from a ferret bite ("It may have been a rat bite," Mr. Maxwell told me, "but it was, in any case, a horrible death"), a ne'er-do-well uncle who lost an arm in an automobile accident and a young woman who was severely burned while attempting to start a fire with kerosene, and even far more benevolent details—like the furnishings of an aunt's house and a next-door neighbor who is invariably a veterinarian.

Many writers, of course, reuse the same materials. A ready example was provided by Mr. Maxwell himself, who had been rereading Mark Twain's *Life on the Mississippi*—"a perfect book to take with you to the hospital"— where, in the first hundred or so pages, we get both the Shakespearean actors and the feud that later appear in *Huckleberry Finn*. But with a smile Mr. Maxwell agreed that he was consciously describing himself in one of the twenty-one "improvisations" (short fictions "written for an occasion," he said) that conclude *All the Days and Nights*. In it, his protagonist is a man "who made his living telling stories . . . If it was a familiar story he was telling, he added new embellishments, new twists, and again it would be something he had never told before and didn't himself know until the words came out of his mouth, so that he was as astonished as his listeners, but he didn't show it. He wanted them to believe what was in fact true."

Mr. Maxwell's books may seem to tell everything about the Lincoln years, but they reveal nothing at all about his life as an editor. No man may be a hero to his valet, but Mr. Maxwell was certainly a hero to two of his assistants at the *New Yorker*, Fran Kiernan and Jane Bernstein. What struck me most was that, quite independently, they used almost exactly the same adjectives to describe him: "trusting and generous," "very supportive," "gentle but strong."

Throughout his tenure at the magazine, he enjoyed a loose arrangement that was mutually beneficial. He was granted much leave time for his own writing, and eventually worked a three-day week in the office, punctuated at noon by a twenty-minute lunch at the nearby Century Club and a short nap. He began as an assistant to Katharine White, the head of the fiction department, and it says much about their propriety and respectful formality that several years later, when writing to each other, they began their letters with "Dear Mrs. White" and "Dear Mr. Maxwell." To the question "Do you miss the old days at the *New Yorker*?" he unhesitatingly replied: "Very much. Sometimes I still have dreams about them."

For the most part, he typed (badly) his own editorial letters or worked with his authors in person or by telephone, surely one way of endearing yourself to an assistant. His correspondence with authors still remains in his possession because "they were always losing things at the *New Yorker.*" My own suspicion is that William Maxwell the editor regards the correspondence to be as intimate as love letters and not to be pried into by the curious.

In a 1982 interview with the *Paris Review*, he said that he learned from Katharine White that "It is not the work of an editor to teach writers how to write . . . Real editing means changing as little as possible." When Fran Kiernan, who later became a *New Yorker* fiction editor in her own right, was still his assistant, he told her, "It's important to learn when not to use your pencil."

In *Here at the New Yorker* (1975), Brendan Gill describes a trip Mr. Maxwell made in 1960 to see John O'Hara and, with strong misgivings, to read, by demand and on site, three O'Hara stories. Two of the stories did not pass muster; fortunately, the third, "Imagine Kissing Pete," proved to be one of O'Hara's best. Then there was the time he took the train to Ossining, New York, to tell John Cheever that the magazine was rejecting one of his stories; Cheever was furious, not at the rejection but at Mr. Maxwell's courtliness in thinking the news needed to be broken in person. And once, when William Shawn, contrary to all magazine policy, edited Mary McCarthy without showing her the alterations, Mr. Maxwell himself exploded in wrath.

It was Mr. Gill who played a crucial role in the major change of Mr. Maxwell's publishing career. In the late 1950s, David McDowell of the then newly formed publishing house of McDowell, Obolensky, approached Mr. Maxwell about bringing out an omnibus volume of his work. Mr. Maxwell found the idea congenial but heard no more about the plan until McDowell referred to it much later in a postscript to a letter about *New Yorker* matters. Believing that McDowell was mixing oranges and apples and that it was inappropriate to confuse his editorial and his authorial roles, Mr. Maxwell then approached Harper, his longtime publisher, to test its interest in the project. When Harper declined, he took his problem to Mr. Gill ("Brendan knew everyone"), and within forty-eight hours had met Pat Knopf, who agreed to reissue both *The Folded Leaf* and *They Came Like Swallows* as Vintage paperbacks. Mr. Maxwell has been published by Knopf ever since. (The omnibus finally appeared in 1992, when the Quality Paperback Book Club reissued *Time Will Darken It*, *The Chateau*, and *So Long, See You Tomorrow* in a single volume.)

And perhaps the appearance of *All the Days and Nights* will at last bring Mr. Maxwell the popular recognition that has so far escaped him. All but one of his works of fiction are currently in print. The exception is his first novel, *Bright Center of Heaven* (1934). When I told Mr. Maxwell I had been unable to track down a copy through out-of-print book dealers, he seemed visibly relieved and referred to it as a novel that should be "pushed under a rug," one that "does little but show the influence of writers whom I admired at the time."

Such editorial scrupulousness is further revealed in his thoughts about *All the Days and Nights*. What pleased him most about it "were the stories that were omitted," he said, acknowledging that he is "always happiest with what isn't there," an opinion that will hardly startle readers who have long recognized his refusal to use two words when one will do, or even one word when that word might be superfluous. However, rereading the stories he did include did provide some surprise for Mr. Maxwell, most notably in the form of sentences he liked but could not remember having written.

One of his other satisfactions is in knowing that "a lot of poets read my books, and I originally wanted to be a poet." But does he join his fans in lamenting that he is not more widely known? After all, his honors include the American Book Award, the Brandeis Creative Arts Medal, the William Dean Howells Medal of the American Academy of Arts and Letters. (He was elected to the academy in 1963, serving as its president for three years.) He considered the question for a moment and then countered with a question of his own: "Why should I let best-seller lists spoil a happy life?"

Tribute to Francis Steegmuller at the American Academy of Arts and Letters

William Maxwell/1995

From *Proceedings of the American Academy of Arts and Letters*. Second Series, No. 46. New York, 1995. Reprinted by permission of the American Academy of Arts and Letters, New York City. Delivered at the Academy April 4, 1995.

I met Francis Steegmuller when the *New Yorker* bought a story of his and gave it to me to edit. Since it needed editing the way a cat needs two tails, my connection with him remained slight. To explain what changed this I have to go all the way around Robin Hood's barn. When Francis graduated from Columbia he went straight to Paris. There, in the studio of the cubist painter Jacques Villon, he met Beatrice Stein, an American girl who was Villon's pupil. She had red hair and the warm heart that often accompanies it. She got polio when she was an adolescent and it left her with an atrophied leg, unable to walk without crutches. When she came of age her mother said to her, "You can stay home and I will take care of you, or you can go abroad on your own and have a life."

She and Francis continued to see each other when they returned to New York and he got a job at the *New Yorker*, writing for the *Talk of the Town*. But then she went off to Vienna to study painting. Knowing that she had other suitors, Francis asked for a leave of absence but didn't explain why he wanted it. Harold Ross thought it was because he didn't care very much about the magazine and fired him. This was, of course, a stroke of good fortune, because Francis's talents lay elsewhere. He and Beatrice Stein were married in Vienna.

One evening in the mid-forties, as Francis started off to a literary cocktail party, she said to him, "I've made a beef stew. If you meet anybody there that you like talking to, bring them home to supper." Home, at that point, was a suite of small rooms in the Hotel Ansonia at Broadway and Seventy-Third Street. After the introductions, Francis took my wife's coat and mine, and produced a bottle of champagne. The stew was delicious. And the four-way friendship that instantly sprang into being turned out to be life long.

It was impossible to know Francis and not love him. Large people tend to be good-natured and Francis was, very. I never heard him raise his voice in anger. On the other hand his disapproval was formidable, and he did not lightly put it aside. When I wrote a novel about Americans traveling in France his careful and detailed criticism was of great help to me. He was, almost from infancy, a Francophile. His mother said that before he was nine he had all but worn out the section on France in the family encyclopedia.

The French values of clarity and style and order inform everything he ever published. There was no clutter on his desk or in his study or in his mind. He typed the final manuscript of his books himself, using black type-writer ribbon for the text and red for the footnotes. Those pages I saw were elegantly typed and had no handwritten corrections.

Bea died of cancer, in 1961. Francis's grief and despair were so great that I was afraid he would never emerge from them, but after a while Fortune took pity on him. At another literary cocktail party, the Scottish novelist Muriel Spark said to him, "Francis, come with me—I want you to meet Shirley Hazzard."

A new life opened for him in his late fifties, and lightened both their spirits. He and Shirley Hazzard were married standing in front of the fireplace of a house Francis had taken in Sharon, Connecticut, with a few friends to witness the ceremony. Though they were different temperamentally, they were often like one person—for example, in the disciplined way in which they wanted to live. They divided the year between an apartment in Manhattan House and an eighteenth-century villa on the outskirts of Naples, with a view across the water of Mt. Vesuvius. There was also a pied-à-terre on the nearby island of Capri. They led a very productive writing life; during these years he won the National Book Award for his *Cocteau* and she won the Book Critics Circle and the American Book Awards for *The Transit of Venus*. And they were very happy. Their shared pleasure in reading, in art, in travel, in the company of friends, resulted in a closeness he thought the most important thing in his life.

The sweetness of Francis's nature is attested to by the fact that he remained on intimate terms with three highly irascible men—the novelist Graham Greene, the British art collector and critic Douglas Cooper, and the most difficult of all, a Frenchman, the son of a provincial doctor, born in Rouen in 1821, who died in 1880, twenty-seven years before Francis was born.

Francis once remarked, "Only one person stands between me and the authorship of *Madame Bovary*." I saw that he was only partly joking. That person, now residing on Mt. Parnassus, has reason to be grateful to him. What happens in Francis's translation of *Madame Bovary* is what happens when a century or more of repeated varnishings are removed from a painting and the original bright colors are once more revealed.

To appreciate the quality of his translation of Flaubert's letters, all that is necessary is to read the same letter translated by someone else. All in all, as biographer, translator, editor, annotator, and critic he served the master on eight occasions, over a period of fifty-four years. Long before this immense body of work was accomplished Francis was wearing, in the buttonhole of his lapel, the thin red ribbon of the Légion d'Honneur.

Just when one had come to think of him, because of his biographies or partial biographies of James Jackson Jarves, Guy de Maupassant, and Flaubert as most at home in the nineteenth century, by his life of the Grand Mademoiselle he established himself with equal authority in the seventeenth; with Mme. D'Epinay and the Abbe Galiani in late eighteenth-century Paris and the Kingdom of Naples; with Apollinaire and Jean Cocteau in the twentieth. Cocteau was considered to be of slight importance until Francis dealt with the quality and range of his accomplishments. The book has been mined ever since for interesting figures of the period.

The biographer deals with people frozen in time; unless he is lazy or a fool, they cannot escape him or succeed in covering their tracks. It is, needless to say, not merely a question of digging up the facts. There has to be a moral tone one can trust. In Francis's books there is no trace of the vindictive attitude toward the chosen subject that afflicts so many current biographies and that will speedily consign them to oblivion.

A Conversation
with Author William Maxwell

Linda Wertheimer/1995

From *All Things Considered*, National Public Radio, 8 February 1995. Reprinted by permission of National Public Radio, Inc.

LINDA WERTHEIMER, Host: Here is the beginning of a fable read by its author, who is eighty-six years old, himself a storyteller.

WILLIAM MAXWELL, Author: [reading from his book] "Once upon a time there was an old man who made his living telling stories. In the middle of the afternoon, he took his position on the steps of the monument to an aging intellect, in a somewhat out-of-the-way corner of the marketplace, and people who were not in a hurry would stop and sometimes those who were in a hurry would hear a phrase that caught their attention, such as 'in the moonlight' or 'covered with blood,' and would pause for a second and then be spellbound."

LINDA WERTHEIMER: William Maxwell was a fiction editor at the *New Yorker* magazine for forty years. He has published six novels, three collections of short stories, and other books. His newest collection of short fiction is called *All the Days and Nights.* It includes a story published in the '30s and at least one from every decade since.

Many of the stories are about reconciliation or about age. Asked about the differences from the earliest to the most recent, Mr. Maxwell says the earlier ones were simpler. "As you grow older," he says, "you do see things in a more complicated way." In addition to the short stories, there are twenty-one little fables at the end of the book. Mr. Maxwell calls them improvisations.

WILLIAM MAXWELL: Actually, they began because my wife liked to have me tell her stories when we were in bed in the dark before we were falling asleep. And I didn't know where they came from, but I just said whatever came into my head and sometimes I would fall asleep in the middle of a story and she would shake me and say, "What happened next?" And I would struggle back into consciousness and tell her what happened next. And then I began to write them for occasions, for Christmas and birthdays and things like that. And I would sit down at the typewriter and empty my mind entirely and see what came out on the typewriter, and something always did. And from the first sentence a story just unfolded.

LINDA WERTHEIMER: Why don't we take turns here and sort of whet the appetite a little bit for these little fables because I wanted to ask you about these first sentences. I'll read one. This is the seventh of the improvisations and it's on page 345.

[reading from book] "There was a man who had no enemies, only friends. He had a gift for friendship. When he met someone for the first time, he would look into the man or woman or child's eyes and he never afterward mistook them for someone else. He was as kind as the day is long and no one imposed on his kindness."

And then you take the next one.

WILLIAM MAXWELL: Yes.

[reading from book] "There used to be, until roughly 150 years ago, a country where nobody ever grew old and died. The gravestone with its weathered inscription, the wreath on the door, the black arm band, and the friendly reassuring smile of the undertaker were unknown there. This is not as strange as it at first seems. You do not have to look very far to find a woman who does not show her age or a man who intends to live forever."

LINDA WERTHEIMER: I like that one a lot. Here, I'll read the next one.

[reading from book] "Once upon a time there was a man who took his family to the seashore. They had a cottage on the ocean and it was everything that a house by the ocean should be, sagging wicker furniture, faded detective stories, blue china, grass rugs, other people's belongings to reflect upon, and other people's pots and pans to cook with."

Is the beginning of a story like this, is that the most important thing?

WILLIAM MAXWELL: Yes, there would be no story without it, and I am astonished that there always is a story, but first it has to come out of the absolutely empty mind. It's mysterious. I think it invokes the ancient storyteller because storytelling was once a profession, of course. And it is in direct contact with the unconscious mind, and I've never exerted any shaping influence upon it. Sometimes when they were done I would cut unnecessary words, but I never tried to reshape the story or make it into a different story.

LINDA WERTHEIMER: And it's a different process from writing the real short stories, the ones that are included in the—that you've published.
WILLIAM MAXWELL: Yes.

LINDA WERTHEIMER: It's a different process from that?
WILLIAM MAXWELL: Yes, it is totally different. With real stories I feel responsible. I feel that I must shape them. I feel they must be plausible. I feel that it must have the breath of life and I work like the devil over them. And these, no work is involved at all, I'm really a kind of medium to which they appear.

LINDA WERTHEIMER: In this collection which you've just published, *All the Days and Nights*, there are stories here that are older than I am. "Young Francis Whitehead" is the oldest story, published in 1939, and you return, I noticed, in the collection several times to that kind of theme of young people separating themselves from their families and their families not understanding what their role is if their children and the young people are gone and that sense of loss.
WILLIAM MAXWELL: And the young people not really knowing either but trying to find the way. I think it's part of an inevitable growing up, don't you?

LINDA WERTHEIMER: Mmm-hmm.
WILLIAM MAXWELL: And very painful both to the children and to the families, and then fortunately they come back again when they get older. A reconciliation they face sometimes when women have children, sometimes when men go into middle age. Sooner or later if there was love in the first place there is reconciliation in the end.

LINDA WERTHEIMER: There's a little tiny story called "Love" that you wrote in 1983, but it was about a much earlier time, about a little boy whose schoolteacher dies of tuberculosis.
WILLIAM MAXWELL: It was a very odd experience. It's the only story I ever wrote that wrote itself. I don't mean improvisations, which do write

themselves, but the story, and it was as if it had already been written in my mind because one sentence followed another and I saw no way of changing or improving it. And I just stood back and said, "Well, I've had a breakthrough. Now I know how to write and things are going to be easier from now on." But I hadn't had a breakthrough. I didn't know any more about writing than I had before. It was just that that material, because it was way back to my boyhood, settled itself in my mind into a permanent form and all I had to do was say it.

LINDA WERTHEIMER: You also write a fair amount about age.

WILLIAM MAXWELL: I do think being an old man is the most interesting thing that's ever happened to me because of all sorts of strange experiences, the opening up of memory, which I expected, and of the enjoyment of life being progressively greater instead of diminished by age. That was a surprise. And memory is perhaps the most remarkable part of all because you live in the past, you live in the present, and you, like everyone, live in the future. Only when you're old, they pass so easily into each other without any effort at all so that the past is quite as real as the present, and the future is, of course, problematical and that's interesting. But I've enjoyed good health and that's meant that life has continued to be interesting.

And I've also had one amazing experience in the night in the dark in bed. I suddenly was able to remember in detail the house I grew up in and left when I was twelve years old. And I went from room to room seeing things that I hadn't remembered for seventy years and more. And being able to look as if I were actually there, as if the house was actually there, I saw that level of the bookcase, I saw pictures, I saw empty rooms, I saw furniture, and could look at it as long as I wanted to. It was as if some shutter had slipped back in my mind and I had absolute, total memory of the past.

And when I'd had enough, I just willingly let go of it, but it was a marvelous experience and it makes me believe that everything is fair, absolutely everything. The whole of our lives is accessible at the moment when we are open to it. And it's—memory is a great blessing and a great delight and privilege.

LINDA WERTHEIMER: William Maxwell's collection of short fiction is called *All the Days and Nights*.

Remarks on Receiving the Gold Medal for Fiction, American Academy of Arts and Letters

William Maxwell/ 1995

From *Proceedings of the American Academy of Arts and Letters*. Second Series, No. 46, New York, 1995, 56. Reprinted by permission of the American Academy of Arts and Letters, New York City.

When I was a small boy, among my worries was the house I was born in. It wasn't as nice as the house we were by that time living in and it didn't look very substantial to me, and I was afraid it would no longer be there when the time came for them to put up the plaque.

Over the years my expectations moderated. And I came to realize that where I belonged, and where I wanted to be, was not in the White House but among the storytellers.

I rejoice in this honor, which I did not expect, and which it comes as somewhat but not entirely a surprise that I could be thought to deserve. I wish that I had written *The Great Gatsby.* I wish that I had written *In the Ravine* and *Ward Number 6.* I wish that I had written *The House in Paris.* I wish that I had written *Sportsman's Notebook.* But the novelist works with what life has given him. It was no small gift that I was allowed to lead my boyhood in a small town in Illinois [Lincoln] where the elm trees cast a mixture of light and shade over the pavement. And also that, at a fairly early age, I was made aware of the fragility of human happiness.

An Interview with William Maxwell

Kay Bonetti/1995

From *Missouri Review* 19.1 (1996), 81–98; 19.2 (1996), 84–95.

William Maxwell is the author of six novels and five collections of short fiction, most recently *All the Days and Nights: The Collected Stories*, published in 1994. His 1980 novel, *So Long, See You Tomorrow*, won the American Book Award. He is also the author of a family history, *Ancestors*.

Maxwell was born in Lincoln, Illinois, where he lived until the age of fourteen, when his family moved to Chicago. After graduating from the University of Illinois and a brief stint in graduate school, Maxwell went to New York to seek his fortune as a writer. He was hired by the *New Yorker* in 1936, where he spent the next forty years as a fiction editor and occasional essay reviewer. The writers he edited include J. D. Salinger, John Cheever, John O'Hara, Harold Brodkey, and Delmore Schwartz.

This interview was conducted by Kay Bonetti in November 1995 in New York City for the American Audio Prose Library.

Part I

Interviewer: Could we start by getting on the record some of the details of your chronology and your life? You were born in 1908 in Lincoln, Illinois?
Maxwell: Lincoln was a small town of twelve thousand people. My mother's father was a judge. My father's father was a lawyer. Behind them on both sides were country people. My father's father died just as he was beginning to make a career for himself, but my father's youth was rather poverty stricken. So he was always careful about money all his life, and preparing for a rainy day that never came. The pattern of our family life was that he came home on Friday afternoon and left Tuesday morning, and traveled the road with a heavy suitcase full of printed forms, which he used when he was

visiting local insurance agents. My mother and father, insofar as I'm able to say, were very much in love with each other. When he came home on Friday afternoons we were always waiting on the front porch—he was embraced with affection when he came home. We lived in a big old house with rooms that were hard to heat. I have a vivid memory of my father in October stuffing toilet paper in the cracks around the windows to try to save fuel. His salary when I was a little boy was three thousand dollars a year. On that he kept a carriage horse, and we lived in this extremely comfortable house, in a comfortable way. He put half of it away and bought a farm with it. I don't know how this was done. My mother must have been cooperative, though. She was not frugal like his family, but she was careful.

My brother lost his leg when he was five years old, when I was only a baby. My mother's sister came by the house one day in a horse and carriage and stopped in front on her way to do an errand of some kind and my mother came out to talk to her. My older brother asked my aunt if he could go with her, and she said no, but he began to climb up the wheel to get in with her anyway and she didn't see it. When she finished the conversation and flicked the whip, his leg slipped down into the wheel and was broken. What happened is that the family doctor was a drug addict. In those days they dispensed their own drugs, so he had access to morphine or whatever. It was a simple fracture that anybody could have set and that would have been the end of it. But he didn't set the leg at all and gangrene set in and they had to cut it off.

Interviewer: This is a secret that you were asked to keep from your brother, according to one thing you have written. Is that fact or fiction?

Maxwell: It's true. I assume he never found out. It wasn't a subject I ever discussed with him because he couldn't bear for anybody to pity him. And people didn't because he was so accomplished physically. He could do wonderful things. He won the tennis championship, the singles, when he was in Scout camp, with his wooden leg dragging across the court. He played football. I saw him once climb up to the high diving board and jump off. What took more courage than the physical part of it was that in his bathing suit, his poor stump was exposed. He faced up to that, did a nice dive and that was that. He was a very brave and remarkable boy.

Interviewer: What about your other brother? Your mother, as is well known because of your work, died of the Spanish flu in the big epidemic in 1918 when you were ten, two days after giving birth to your younger brother.

From what I can discern, you use your older brother time and again in your work, but you don't seem to write much about the younger brother.

Maxwell: We weren't with each other very much. My mother's sister said that my mother's dying words were, "I don't want the Maxwells to have my baby." My mother's other sister wanted to adopt him, but my father wanted to bring up his own children. He did his very best. He had a series of housekeepers, which was very hard. His life after my mother died hardly bears thinking about, it was so sad. After two and a half or three years he remarried and his second marriage was, I think, as happy as his first. But in the meantime, while my little brother was small, he spent a good deal of time with my grandmother, my father's mother. She became so attached to him that through one thing or another he spent several days a week with her. Then when he was about three, my father got a promotion and was moved to the Chicago office, which meant we had to leave Lincoln. My grandmother threw herself on her knees and said, "Will, it will kill me if you take this child away from me." He didn't have the heart to do it. So, my brother grew up in a different household and I don't have the daily memories that I have of living with my older brother who shared the same room with me while we were growing up.

Interviewer: You first went to college at the University of Illinois, and then you thought that you wanted to be a professor, so you went on to graduate school. Is that right?

Maxwell: It wasn't quite that simple. I really, from childhood, meant to be an artist. In high school I took art classes, and I was enrolled in the Art Institute in Chicago when I finished high school. But my best friend in school had been a lifeguard during the summer, and he caught pleurisy. His father and mother were afraid to let him go off to school—he was enrolled in Urbana, at the University of Illinois—because they didn't think he was well enough. I said "I'll go down with him, and we can stay in my older brother's fraternity house." Which we did. In the end I didn't want to leave my friend, and I thought the campus looked so exciting. I stayed that freshman year, and in the course of the year I met a very persuasive English teacher, who said, "An artist's life is very uncertain, and a professor's life is pleasant and guaranteed. Why don't you do that?" In the end I decided to be an English professor.

Interviewer: Then what did you do?

Maxwell: I graduated from the University of Illinois and went to Harvard for a year. I wanted a Ph.D. from Harvard because I liked the fact that their robes were lined with scarlet. But I had a block on the German language. I think it was because when I was a little boy the papers were full of cartoons of Belgian women with their hands cut off and children on bayonets. I had no trouble learning French or Greek or Italian, not too much trouble with Latin, but with German a total inability to memorize the vocabulary. I plugged along, taking things I liked and could manage, like Medieval French literature, and then began to teach freshmen by way of earning a living. After about two years I read a very lightweight novel called *One More Spring*. It was about some people during the Depression who decided money was not what they wanted and lived happily in a toolhouse in Central Park. For one reason or another it gave me the impetus to throw off the traces, and I resigned my teaching job at Urbana in 1933 or 1934, at a time when there were no jobs anywhere, in the whole United States. And I began to write.

Interviewer: Why? What happened?

Maxwell: Nothing is ever simple, of course. As a graduate student I lived in the house of a woman who was on the English faculty. She had lived in New York and been on the staff of the *Herald Tribune* book section under Stuart Sherman. She belonged to the outside world, really, not academic life. She had a friend who was a history professor at Yale. And he sent her—it seems very odd—he wanted a forty-page condensation of a two-volume life of Thomas Coke of Holkham, who was a great agriculturist and also a member of Parliament who introduced the bill to recognize the American colonies. These books arrived, and my friend asked me to take on the job with her. She was interested in the agricultural parts and I was not. So I got to do the rest about social life in the eighteenth century. Coke had an aunt named Lady Mary Coke, who was an object of scandal. Her husband was a boor, and instead of putting up with it, she divorced him. She must have had money, because she continued to live in style. She corresponded with Horace Walpole and dressed her servants in pea-green and silver, and when she was melancholy she used to fish for goldfish in the ornamental pond. She suffered from the delusion that the Empress Maria Theresa was trying to take her servants away from her. In her old age she slept in a dresser drawer. I found all this irresistible. When that job was done I sat down to write a novel.

Interviewer: Where did you go?

Maxwell: I had worked as a boy at [Bonnie Oaks] that was not an ordinary farm, but more like the farm in *The Cherry Orchard*, and I began to write the novel while I was actually staying there. I was given a room in what had once been a water tower, but was remodeled. On the first floor there was a room with a piano, for Josef Lhevinne, the great Russian pianist, who used to come there. On the second floor was his bedroom, and on the third floor was a little study with a fireplace, and a chaise lounge and chintz curtains, a very pleasant place among the treetops, and I would sit there writing this book. Several of the characters were just various aspects of me. It was the story of a black man coming to spend a weekend among white people. It was meant to be a comic novel, and it is funny, I guess, in places, but the trouble is, the black man is no good. I finished the novel that summer, and one of my professors at Illinois had a sister who had worked in publishing. She sent it to Harpers, and they took it. That was the beginning.

Interviewer: *Bright Center of Heaven.*

Maxwell: Yes.

Interviewer: In an essay you wrote about E. B. White, you said that when he went West as a young man, he was approaching his destiny by going as far as he could in the opposite direction. You eventually went to New York, and it seems to me that in going East you were approaching your destiny by going as far as you could in the opposite direction as well. Your heart's material is home, the Middle West.

Maxwell: That's perfectly true. In those days the literary world was so strongly centered in New York. When I was at Harvard I'd seen New York and liked it very much. The first time I tried to get a job there I failed because there were no jobs, and my letters of introduction usually ended in the person I had a letter to crying on my shoulder. The second time I got a job with Paramount Pictures, reading novels and writing a summary that would indicate whether they were good material for the movies. Meanwhile I'd had interviews. I'd gone to the *New Republic* where I had an introduction. They soon found out that I didn't know anything about politics. Then I had an introduction to the *New Yorker*, which had published one of my stories. It just happened that Wolcott Gibbs was tired of seeing artists and wanted to extricate himself from the job. I came at a fortunate time, job-hunting.

Interviewer: Your job was to judge the art coming in?

Maxwell: No. Just to deal with the artists. They brought their work in on Tuesday. There was an art meeting later that day. The decorative "spots" were looked at on Wednesday and the artists came back on Thursday and you told them what was bought and what wasn't bought.

Interviewer: By artists you mean. . . .
Maxwell: Cartoonists. And the cover artists, the spot artists. The cartoonists were always respected as very good artists.

Interviewer: So that was your first job at the *New Yorker*.
Maxwell: Yes. I had an interview with Mrs. E. B. White who was the fiction editor and art editor. In the course of the interview she asked me how much money I would want. I had been told that if I didn't ask for thirty-five dollars a week they wouldn't respect me. I took a deep breath and said, "Thirty-five dollars a week." She smiled and said, "I expect you could live on less." And I could have lived on ten quite easily.

Interviewer: What year was this?
Maxwell: Nineteen-thirty-six. That night I had dinner in a Chinese restaurant and they wouldn't let me have a table to myself. I was feeling low. Summarizing trashy novels (twenty-five pages minimum, five carbons, payment five bucks) didn't seem a life worth living. I thought, "There's no place in the world for me. Absolutely no place." I went home to the rooming house and under the door was a telegram that said *Come to work on Monday at the salary agreed upon.* I think if you absolutely hit bottom there's nowhere to go but up.

Interviewer: What was the salary agreed upon?
Maxwell: Thirty-five dollars a week. I paid thirty-five dollars a month for a one-bedroom apartment. And you could get a very decent meal at the Automat with lamb chops and baked potatoes and salad and dessert for a dollar.

Interviewer: I take it that at this point you needed to have a day job to support your writing.
Maxwell: I'm pretty sure I could never have supported myself by writing because I was too slow and too much of a perfectionist. The first novel had been published with pleasant reviews. They published a thousand copies and it went into a second edition, but only sold a hundred of that second

thousand. The rest were all remaindered. I sat down and began a second novel, which was *They Came Like Swallows*. It isn't a very long novel. I did the first section seven times, most of it at that farm in Wisconsin. The eighth time I was at the MacDowell colony, and that time it stuck. It was in the hands of the publisher when I went to the *New Yorker*. It was a Book-of-the-Month-Club choice, to my profound astonishment. The first payment was eight thousand dollars, which was so much money that I went into Wolcott Gibbs's office to tell him and could hardly walk, stunned by the overwhelming sum.

Interviewer: That was a lot of money at the time.

Maxwell: It was a lot of money. All the time that I was working as an editor I was writing, and the stories were published as a rule in the *New Yorker*, except that people kept resigning ahead of me, so that I kept getting promoted, and doing more and more demanding work, so that I wrote less and less.

Interviewer: At the beginning of *All the Days and Nights*, you tell a story about yourself at the age of twenty-five, which must have been that first time that you went to New York, trying to get on board a ship to be a sailor because you had read that that's really what you ought to do, to go out and get some experience. If you wanted to be a writer, you went to sea first.

Maxwell: Preferably on a four-masted schooner.

Interviewer: Right. To learn to write. You said that at that time, "Three-quarters of the material I would need for the rest of my writing life was already at my disposal." I would like to know, when did you discover that?

Maxwell: I don't remember whether I had written *They Came Like Swallows*, which was of course that material, or was about to. For a long while I was writing stories for the *New Yorker* that were sometimes about New York, sometimes about France. I couldn't write about the Middle West really because Ross had a map of what was possible to publish in the *New Yorker* in fiction. The stories could be about Florida, they could be about Hollywood, they could be about the East Coast—wherever, presumably, *New Yorker* readers went was what the fiction had to be about. Which rather tied my hands, and was a good thing. Because when I was free to write about the Middle West—eventually, after he was gone, they did accept stories about the Middle West—I was old enough to deal with the material. It was as if that was really my imagination's home.

Interviewer: You have been quoted as rejecting the idea of there being a *New Yorker* style or school of writing. And yet, what little I've managed to read about the kinds of restrictions, and the things you've just mentioned, would tend to belie that denial on your part.

Maxwell: Not seriously. I think if there is something characteristic of *New Yorker* fiction, it's that tendency to eliminate the dead spots. Also, for the story to proceed sentence by sentence, and not paragraph by paragraph. You can write fiction just as well in which you make your point in the course of a paragraph. In *New Yorker* writing you make it every sentence, and before you go on to the next one you've made the point in that one. It's very economical.

Interviewer: And yet John Cheever and John O'Hara—two writers closely associated with *New Yorker* fiction—both insisted that the stories they would write they would write for the *New Yorker*, and if you wouldn't take the bloody things they couldn't get anybody else to take them. I think they were saying that they wrote them with the *New Yorker* in mind, and if the *New Yorker* wouldn't take them, there was nobody else publishing that type of fiction. Was it the length? That the *New Yorker* was always publishing longer stories, perhaps?

Maxwell: They slowly got longer. When I first went to work there twelve pages was considered a very long story. Eventually it got up to fifty pages, or even a whole novella. It took a long while.

Interviewer: In talking about the three-quarters of all the material you needed for the rest of your writing life, was the other fourth a matter of learning the trade, the craft, and learning to recognize the right material?

Maxwell: Yes. It takes a while before you know how to deal with your material. I remember once having a conversation with Irwin Shaw over the fact that I was taking such a long time over a novel. He said he always made an outline for his novels and then just did it. I would begin with a metaphor, really. The metaphor for *They Came Like Swallows* was a stone thrown into a pond making a circle, and then you throw a second stone and it makes a circle inside the first circle, as it's getting bigger, and then you throw another stone inside those other two. I made the novel on that structure. In *The Folded Leaf* I saw myself walking across flat territory, such as you'd find in eastern Colorado, toward the mountains. I knew that when I got to the suicide attempt I would have the novel. That's where the heart of the novel was. So I just kept getting closer to the mountains by creating scenes. I never wrote an outline for any novel. Sometimes I would run into serious trouble. In *Time Will Darken It* I couldn't decide whether the hero went to bed with the young woman from Mississippi or not, so I wrote it both ways, and continued to write it both ways, chapter after chapter after chapter. It was like a fork in the road. I finally faced the issue and decided that in the year 1912, he wouldn't have. So I threw away all the rest of it. It was a wasteful way of going about it, but I had to discover the form from the material. I didn't have a clear idea, usually, of what I was up to.

Interviewer: When you speak of yourself as a child there are always these wonderful scenes where people are driving in a carriage out in the country. And you've said that as a boy you always loved houses. Do you have any thoughts about the mix of the town and the country as an important element in your writing life?

Maxwell: I've always lived in New York City a very circumscribed life and tried to lead the life I would have if I'd lived in Lincoln. This was not particularly a conscious determination, it's just that I grew up in a small town and it marked me for life. The love of home is I suppose partly because I had it taken away from me. But I loved it before it was taken away from me just as much. We've lived for more than fifty years now in a place in the country—I've lived partly in New York City and partly in northern Westchester—and the place in the country was not built by us. It was one of the very early prefabricated houses. After I married, my wife began to do something about its box-like nature. Every time we had a child we remodeled the house to make room for the child. Little by little it came to fit our family life, as it was at that time. I know that it isn't practical for either of my children to live there, and it wouldn't be for my wife after I died. Somebody else is going to live in that house. But it's painful. I don't mind dying. I just don't want to leave the house ever. I'm so deeply attached to home.

Interviewer: How did you meet your wife?

Maxwell: She came to the *New Yorker* office looking for work. She wanted to be a poetry editor. She loved poetry. There was no poetry editor as it turned out. She was lovely to look at, but I was in analysis, and at sort of that standstill state that you get in therapy. I did take her telephone number—I guess I just automatically took it. A year later I sat up in the middle of the night and looked her name up in the phone book and it wasn't there. Then

I went to the files in the office and it was there. I trumped up some excuse to see her, because I had never forgotten her. She was indeed very beautiful.

Interviewer: You were already living in the country as a bachelor before you married.
Maxwell: Yes. I moved to the country so I could garden and rented a house in Yorktown Heights. I remember sitting and being conscious of the darkness outside the windows. I'd lived in the country before but always with other people, and it was very black outside the window. Then I moved from one rented house to another until the present one.

Interviewer: All in the same area?
Maxwell: All in the same road, within half a mile.

Interviewer: You've spoke of the "sublime confidence" that you must have in order to write a novel. I wonder too if that couldn't be courage. The picture you've painted of yourself is of the over-sensitive kid, the second son, the one who wasn't his father's son; you were the mother's child. Yet what you've done with the material of your life—the kind of exposure that you've subjected yourself to—seems astonishing to me, the courage that it must take to use this kind of material in your fiction.
Maxwell: I've never seen it like that, but I have learned that I am my father's child as much as I am my mother's. When I was six years old we went to Bloomington, which was thirty miles away, where my mother's sister lived. There was a park, and in the park was a lake. You could rent bathing suits and swim. My father in his bathing suit and I in mine went into the water, and he taught me to swim by putting me on his hand, my face down in the water. I had absolute trust in him, so far as anything of that kind was concerned. I knew that if he said something he would do it. He wouldn't play tricks on me. He told me how to move my arms and legs, what to do. I did what he told me to and suddenly had a moment of doubt. I looked back and he was standing thirty feet away from me in the water, smiling. I think what my father gave me was a trust in life. I don't think it's courage, so much as just trust in life. The only danger is not to do what you want to do. Courage—I certainly don't have much physical courage.

Interviewer: But your material, the work, is the inner life laid bare—your grief as a child.

Maxwell: I think this is the motivation behind a great deal of fiction—I didn't want the things that I loved, and remembered, to go down to oblivion. The only way to avoid that is to write about them.

Interviewer: There's a piece of yours that was reprinted in *All the Days and Nights*—"The Front and the Back of the House," I think it's called. The story is that you approached an African American woman who had worked for your parents when you were a little kid, and you hugged her and she rejected you. This hurt and haunted you, and you couldn't figure out what was going on.

Maxwell: It wasn't so much that she rejected me as that she didn't move. It was like hugging a fencepost—the total absence of any response was distressing.

Interviewer: But the point seems to be that in this piece you confront, for the first time, the fact that you've made a fictional world out of your childhood and your life, and that you had no intention at all, in *Time Will Darken It*, of drawing the housekeeper, Rachel, from this woman. And yet, she had read the book and thought you had, and she was very offended by the material in the novel, that wasn't at all her—this rotten husband who was abusive, and in fact trying to abuse her daughter so that she had to go away.

Maxwell: When I look at it now, to save my life I can't always decide which is real and which is imaginary. As I got older I came to have such a respect for life and to believe that the way things actually happened really couldn't be improved on. Even the names of people can't be improved on. So I began to change less and less, and this involved writing more and more about real people, but of course by that time they were mostly dead. I tried to protect them if there was anything that I thought would be painful to them. Sometimes I suffered the torments of the damned about describing real people—where I was sure that I was perhaps causing pain. But in this struggle, the artist won out. There was a point at which I would not give up something which I knew was right aesthetically.

Interviewer: In that particular piece it's as though it had never dawned on you that anybody back home read your books.

Maxwell: I was under the impression that they didn't. They do read them more now, but in those days they didn't very much. A few friends of the family put their name on the list at the public library; but I think in general they didn't read books, so why should they read mine?

Interviewer: A lot of writers say that when you do draw characters from real life, they never recognize themselves. In the case of this woman, who in real life was Hattie, it hadn't been her and yet she thought it was. Has this often proved the case with you?

Maxwell: Sometimes. In *The Folded Leaf* I first described Lymie Peters as having a father and a stepmother. I used my father and stepmother and their social life as a background because it was so incongruous with him, temperamentally. And then I thought, this really isn't fair, my father isn't a literary man and he really won't like being in a book. So I made him a sporting character instead, which my father was definitely not. When I went home, a friend of the family said, "Why did you make your father like that?" People want to identify characters with actual people.

Interviewer: To refer again to your statement that a novel requires "sublime confidence," where did William Maxwell get that confidence?

Maxwell: Long after my mother was dead I took my wife home for a visit and we went to see one of my mother's friends, who was ill. She'd known me ever since I was a small child, and she said, "Your mother told me one day, 'I have such confidence in Billy.'" I was so startled, because I was a very small child, frail and given to tears. Where was this confidence? What was the basis for her having confidence in me? I have no idea. In general, I think confidence has to have come from being loved. She kept me alive by loving me so much. If anybody loves you a lot, there's a small piece of ground to stand on. So maybe that's it.

Interviewer: It wasn't a matter, then, of learning your craft as time went on? Were you more confident with each novel that you wrote?

Maxwell: No. I've never known what I was doing. Only the feeling that the material is in the end your friend, if you give yourself up to it entirely. For example, when I had the idea for *So Long, See You Tomorrow*, what floored me immediately was the fact that I had never lived on a farm. My father had a farm and we went to it occasionally when I was a little boy, but the farmer's children stood off to one side and I was shy and they were shy. I never played with them. I don't think I ever even went inside the house. I saw farmers, but I never lived on a farm. It bothered me so much that I spent a whole year looking at photographs, reading books about farmers' lives, to get inside this closed place. Then one day I thought, "Oh, well. I can trust my imagination, I can go ahead. I know enough." And I did, to my surprise.

Interviewer: In *So Long, See You Tomorrow*, you've plowed into a narrative method that flies in the face of all the conventions in literature that at least your generation believed in.

Maxwell: I had to follow the material. As you get older you take more chances, of course. The more unconventional it seemed to have to be, the more pleased I was with how things were going. It was a hard novel to write. I used to find that sometimes in a paragraph there would be one good sentence and the rest was worthless. So I would cut out the good sentence and put it in a folder. I would say that in a large part of that novel every sentence had been ten other places before it settled down and locked into place. It was much, much, much worked over.

Interviewer: By this time, when you were writing *So Long, See You Tomorrow*, we had seen the surge in what was called parajournalism, with Truman Capote's *In Cold Blood*, and all the work Norman Mailer did in that form. Now it's like time has come round to meet you at last. We just call it fine prose, and people teach classes in "creative nonfiction." Were you ever affected by these kinds of things with respect to your choice of form?

Maxwell: Did I worry? Oh, sure. I've worried many many times over novels. I worried most over *The Chateau*, I think, because I was afraid it wasn't a novel at all. I did worry about the structure, and think, "What you're doing you really can't do." Nevertheless I went on and found a way to do it.

Interviewer: We haven't talked about *The Chateau*. You say that you weren't even sure that it was a novel?

Maxwell: Yes. I was afraid it was a travel diary because it followed so closely the experiences of my wife and me during a four-month period in France in 1948. It was a novel in which nothing more profound happened than hurt feelings. I put all the ideas I had for this book on a sheet of paper and tacked it on the bookcase behind me, and never looked at it during the ten years that I was working on the novel. After I'd been working maybe nine years, the Irish short story writer, Frank O'Connor, who wrote for the *New Yorker* and who had become a dear friend, came to the country with his wife and asked how I was getting on with the book. I said, "I'm not getting anywhere. I have a grocery carton full of various versions." He said, "I'd like to read it." I was horrified. I wasn't in the habit of showing my raw material to anybody. On the other hand, as his editor I had seen his rough drafts for what I think is a masterpiece, *An Only Child*. I couldn't very well say, "It's all right for me to see your rough drafts but you can't see mine." So he drove off with the grocery carton, and he and his wife read through all the versions. Then he wrote a perfectly wonderful letter in which he said he didn't understand what I was up to. But in the course of the letter he assumed that it was a novel; he didn't assume that it was a travel diary at all. What he said was, it was really two novels. A great weight fell off my shoulders. I thought, "If it's two novels, anybody can make them into one." So I did.

Interviewer: That book has been compared, I think terribly superficially, to Henry James: the American innocents meeting the deep, dark European decadence. One of the ways that comparison is really not so remote is the fact that you are willing to fly in the face of what was the current convention about narrative method. What I find so remarkable about your work is the confidence with which you just dispense with those kinds of expectations. At the very end, in the epilogue, you just flat out address the reader directly about what was really going on here. You set up a dialogue between the persona and the reader at the end.

Maxwell: What happened was that I reached the end of the narrative, but there were a lot of questions that weren't answered. I felt that the novelist has a moral obligation not to leave the reader with unanswered questions. The problem is then how to answer the questions if the novel is already over. I had a dear friend who read the manuscript through the first part because I needed somebody to tell me when the French people were speaking as French people would. I knew how to have the characters speak bad French, but I wanted to be sure about the good French. He read the novel and had some objections to it. He didn't like the Americans very much and thought they were kind of silly. So he gave me an imaginary person to talk to; I answered some of his objections in this thing, but it also set up the idea of a dialogue.

I loved doing the epilogue. But when it got to the publisher, a man named Harold Strauss, who was then an editor at Knopf, objected to it and wanted to cut it off. I am always so tired when I finish a book that I'm oversusceptible to other people's ideas, and I didn't really know whether it was a good idea or a bad idea. Alfred Knopf was sitting in the room not saying anything, and I turned to him. He said, "Have it the way you want it." So I did. Now, if I were to pick up *The Chateau* and that epilogue wasn't there, I think I would shoot myself.

Interviewer: It is tiresome, isn't it, that every time you have a novel where you have Americans going to Europe and stumbling their way through things and only finding out later what was really going on, inevitably people compare it to Henry James.

Maxwell: With James of course they were high moral dilemmas, and in my case they were social dilemmas, really. Many years later we went to have dinner with the French family, and the deaf woman, who was by then in her nineties and lying on a chaise lounge in a Paris apartment, said sweetly, "You know you were very naughty to write that book. Because you didn't speak French, you didn't understand things." Behind me I heard a whisper from her son-in-law: "He got everything right." It was very gratifying. I suffered the torments of the damned about what it might do to them, since so much of it is taken directly from their lives. I refused to let the book be published, not only in France but in England because I thought English books would get across the channel so easily. I didn't want to hurt them. Eventually they got hold of a copy and read it, and I had a letter from one of them. She said, "It was very naughty of you. Could we please have a copy ourselves?" The last time I saw them, I said, "A long, long time has passed. Is it all right to publish the book in France?" I'd had many offers for it. They said, "We'll read it again." So they read it again and the answer came back, "No, not now. Not ever."

Part II

Interviewer: You've said you learned from E. B. White that the "I" should always be a real character in any piece that you've written. Have you ever had a sense in your writing life that you were flying in the face of current convention, or being old-fashioned, by adhering to that principle?

Maxwell: I never worried about being old-fashioned because the books I've continued to read all my life have been the Russians. I wanted to write about people, men and women. What's old-fashioned about men and women? They are just as they are. E. B. White taught me to use the "I" unselfconsciously. The thing about White is, he is essentially an egoist—not an egotist, but an egoist. He has to start from himself as the center of his observations. But that self is never tiresome, usually amusing, always likable, always acceptable. I remember when I was younger, trying to write stories in the first person, or even novels. They went on and on and on, and were so garrulous. I couldn't somehow rein them in because I hadn't discovered how to treat myself in a way that wasn't the total interior life. The answer is to treat oneself as an outside person, as a character, who therefore is manageable. And also not the center of the action and of attention, but somewhat on the side, visible and sometimes an actor, but only momentarily. To find a place for you that is very much like the place you must find in social life, where you are not tiresome, but agreeable socially. Give other people a chance to talk, too. When I could finally use the first person I was happy, but it was like venturing into cold water.

Interviewer: There's a strong streak in your work of the disparity between the inner self and the outer self. Are you saying that in using yourself as a narrator and a persona, that this is the sort of thing you're also doing fictionally to deal with the material?
Maxwell: We're all so many selves, a whole cast of characters. Now I'm one person, now I'm another. There's a committee, and somebody is in charge of the committee. That's the person that the outside world knows. But the interior life is more or less bedlam.

Interviewer: It sounds like in the writing process if you're going to insert yourself as the "I" of the piece, you're creating that same duet, or dialogue.
Maxwell: You have to create something that somebody would recognize as a person. But not the whole person in the sense that you get from Joyce, or Virginia Woolf.

Interviewer: You've spoken and written of having been in analysis. With respect to the work, you can certainly see in *So Long, See You Tomorrow* and *They Came Like Swallows* the aspects of Freudian psychology. Was this Freudian analysis that you went into?
Maxwell: Oh, yes. It was Theodor Reik, who had been a pupil of Freud. When he won a prize in Vienna he was living in an attic and Freud climbed up god knows how many flights of stairs to tell him. He was, I think, a very good analyst. He made me feel that he cared about me. I don't think I could have done anything with him if he hadn't. I think often analysts don't do that, or don't feel they ought to, perhaps. But he did. He had a strong sense of literature, and he was ambitious for me. I think he saved my life because I had a strong tendency toward self-destruction.

Interviewer: This is what drew you into analysis?
Maxwell: No, I don't suppose I would have gone to him or to anybody if some friend hadn't pushed me into it. But in my early thirties I was haunted by the image of a tree; you know what happens to trees when you cut the main stem, and they grow out quite large on the side but they don't grow

very tall. I felt that was happening to me, that my center had been cut out, and I couldn't assume my proper shape. I tend to think in metaphors rather than direct, abstract ideas.

Interviewer: What was the center that you felt had been cut out?
Maxwell: I didn't seem to be growing. I didn't have anybody to love, nobody to love me, and I had no wife, no child. I was just an incomplete person. I was only in analysis with Reik a short time. When I got married he said, "Now you're on your own. You can come back and talk if you want to, but you better live through this yourself." I did go back for a short time, but after that, not. The effect of the analytic hour was to find that I was focused on why things happened, not what happened. You can't write novels that are based only on why. You have to say this happened, and this happened, and then and then and then and then. It took a little while to escape from the preoccupation with motivation, back into straight human behavior. But in time it fell away and I forgot about it.

Interviewer: When you speak of turning yourself into a character, it seems to me that you do that with everything. You turn houses into characters, you turn furniture into characters, you turn the dog into a character. What part of that just arises organically from the vision and what part is something you have learned, in term of craft, about how to tell the story?
Maxwell: I was an extremely imaginative child. But I think what happened was that when I got into my thirties, I became preoccupied with myself too much, too exclusively. What Theodor Reik did was make myself less of a problem to me. Made me accept myself. Therefore, and because of the theories he was presenting me with, I suddenly found myself intensely interested, not in myself but in other people. That interest in other people is just by a kind of poetic transposition done to furniture, to houses, to dogs, to anything. I found that the world around me, the people around me, were so interesting. From that time on I was interested in myself but only as one of them, not as the center of the world.

Interviewer: It seems to me too that what you show in your work is that as a child you weren't a victim, you were a survivor. Have you been conscious of a survivor element, an existential element in your work?
Maxwell: Brendan Gill wrote a preface to an interview in the *Paris Review* with me, in which he said I was an odd combination of somebody who was highly sensitive and hard as nails. That is to say, as an editor, when I had to

say "This doesn't work," I was able to say it. I think that hardness was really acquired by surviving. And also because my belief in the perfect thing, the right thing, the right story, was so total that I didn't want to accept something that wasn't right. I *couldn't* accept something that I thought wasn't right.

Interviewer: You've brought up the word "love," and other people have too with respect to William Maxwell and the vision out of which he writes. Do you have a sense that in many ways you've been extraordinarily blessed? It's apparent that the woman your father married after your mother died was somebody you must have loved very much. She was very wise. She knew not to presume to replace the mother you had lost, but instead to be just who she was and what she was. It strikes me that this in fact was a great blessing for you.

Maxwell: I think also now that I'm such an old man, what delights me is the friendships with the children of my friends or with people of that age, people around forty. These new, affectionate, marvelous relationships that make my life like a blossoming tree.

Interviewer: From whence comes the comfort and the acceptance, in William Maxwell, of being able to hold two apparently contradictory emotions simultaneously: the anger at your father for having the nerve to remarry, to tear down or to move out of the old house, sell it. To then uproot you and move you to Chicago. And yet, as you put it very succinctly in one place that I'm trying to remember, you've said that simultaneously, even though you quarreled and had a conflict kind of relationship with your dad, at the same time there was no other mode that you could envision.

Maxwell: The only person I trusted so completely. These dualistics are the very essence of life, don't you think? Things are not simple. They shouldn't be made to appear so.

Interviewer: Speaking of double lives and other existences—in a letter to you, John O'Hara asked you how you were coming with your "double life." He was feeling sorry for himself about things that were going on—"And then I think of you, and this double life you lead, that you go home on off-hour trains and try to do your own work, and yet you're carrying this baggage with you of all of us gypsies, and all these writers, and all the manuscripts." Let's talk about the relationship between William Maxwell the writer and William Maxwell the editor. How did you balance that? What did you learn from your editing that you brought to your writing? Or did you try to keep them separate?

Maxwell: I tried to keep my writing life invisible to the people I was editing. I wanted them to think I was their editor and that was all. Of course it wasn't totally invisible, but on the other hand I was not so successful as a writer that it was a problem. During the second half of the forty years that I was an editor I had a fair number of writers whose work I loved, and I loved them as people, the relationship was very close. I was deeply involved in their work, as I was in my own. But when I went home I didn't think about them. I thought about my own work.

Interviewer: Did you ever worry about borrowing from writers whose manuscripts you'd read?

Maxwell: There was nobody who was at all like me as a writer. I'm sure that my sense of how to write well was tremendously sharpened by working with such writers. So it was not a problem, it was a great help. If I imitated I wasn't aware of it, and they certainly didn't imitate me. They were fully crystallized. On the days I had to work at the *New Yorker*, I always shaved with pleasure, thinking, "I'm about to take the train and go be an editor." Whereas, when I was going to be a writer I sometimes said, "It's not going very well. This novel is really a travel diary. I'm in trouble." I never worried about being an editor. I was easy about it, happy about it. I didn't have to worry about money. It wasn't a high salary, but it was enough to live on. That was wonderful.

Interviewer: And it got you out of yourself. You got to go out into the world.

Maxwell: Yes, I stopped being an introvert and became an extrovert three days a week. Since I am part extrovert and part introvert that was a very satisfactory arrangement. There is a book by a woman named Beatrice Hinkle, and the subject is "the subjective extrovert." I seem to answer to the description.

Interviewer: There's a letter from John Cheever to Allan Gurganus in which he says to Allan Gurganus, "Bill Maxwell is a very fastidious person." By that he meant you were a neat-nik type. He said, "Once he called and said he was coming to tea. Mary scrambled around, she cleaned the house, we got tea ready. And here came Mr. Maxwell; we were having tea; everything seemed to be full of decorum, and in came Harmon the cat with a dead goldfish in his mouth." He said, "That just sums up my relationship with the Maxwells in a nutshell." Is there any story you could tell that you think would sum up in a nutshell your relationship with the Cheevers?

Maxwell: Yes. He asked me to leave the house once. I don't remember the goldfish in the cat's mouth, and I rather think it didn't happen. John was a fantasist. I think it has the higher truth, but I don't think it literally happened. Once as my wife and I were dressing to go to a dinner party to the Cheevers' in the country—I'd had a good day's writing, and I was feeling happy—I said, "I'm just going to be myself tonight, my real self." So I was. I didn't censor my conversation. I said whatever I felt. There was a young man across the table from me who was talking about his father. I understood so well what he was saying. It was the kind of joke that really hides pain, and isn't a joke. Having a couple of drinks in me I leaned across the table and said, "Why don't you kill your father?" A few more remarks like that during the course of the evening, and suddenly John was standing in front of me—I was talking to one of the guests—and he said, "Will you go home now?" I was startled, but I realized he meant it. I got Emmy. It was dead winter, and snow on the ground, and we got our coats and left. I came out and I saw a faint glow on the car lights. I had left the ignition on, and the battery wouldn't turn over. I had to go back in the house and get John, and ask him to push us, which he did. Fortunately they lived at the crest of a hill. We started downhill and went home. Our relationship was rather cool for maybe about a year but I told somebody who I knew would repeat it to him, that I thought he was the best short-story writer in America. After that, things got better.

Interviewer: He says things got better with you after he changed the dedication of one of his novels from "To Bill Maxwell" to "To W.M." and that made you change your tune about the book.

Maxwell: He did dedicate the book with my initials but I didn't change my tune about the book. It wasn't a book I liked, and he knew that I didn't like it. At the end of his life—not the beginning—he was a quite unreliable witness.

Interviewer: His son makes that clear in the letters. He says, "My dad tells this, but I for the life of me don't think that ever really happened." There's another story that Cheever tells in his letters. I don't know if it's true or not. He says he gave a dinner party and greeted everybody without his clothes on.

Maxwell: No, that's not true. Wonderful story, but I don't think it is true.

Interviewer: In what sense did you view your editing, if at all, as a creative process?

Maxwell: It was as if we were in a boat together. They were doing the rowing and I was saying, "Look out for that snag." A very affectionate relationship, usually.

Interviewer: That's apparent from the letters I've read, from John O'Hara and from Cheever. One of the things that Cheever claims that he was always saying to you was, "You may have invented Salinger and Harold Brodkey but you didn't invent me."
Maxwell: It's not true. I didn't invent him, or Brodkey or Salinger, but it's not something he ever said to me.

Interviewer: What about Salinger? As I understand, you're one of the few people who really knows Salinger because of your editing relationship. Is this true?
Maxwell: The reason I still have any relationship with Salinger at all is that I've never talked about him. And so I'm not going to now. He doesn't like to be talked about.

Interviewer: Can you say this much? Has your relationship with Salinger been mostly in correspondence, with letters back and forth about the work?
Maxwell: Here is something I can tell you: Once a proofreader came in to me and said, "This sentence has to have a comma in it." It was just going to the printer and I couldn't reach Salinger. It seemed clear to me that it needed a comma, and I had faith in that particular proofreader, so I said, "All right." Salinger was very sad afterwards because he didn't want that comma. It wasn't necessary. That's what it was like editing Salinger, really. You couldn't safely put a comma into him, and I made a terrible mistake in agreeing to it.

Interviewer: You took a lot of heat from your writers at the *New Yorker* over their perceived fastidiousness about the *New Yorker*. John O'Hara's letters are full of that. And Cheever's, too. What's your assessment of the relationship of the writers with the *New Yorker* and those accusations that have been made, that writers felt that Ross and Shawn were trying to keep it too prudish?
Maxwell: Ross felt that the *New Yorker* was a family magazine and came into the house once a week, and you couldn't control who saw what was in it. There were children in the house, so you should avoid anything salacious. I think this also reflected his own kind of fastidiousness. I thought it was sometimes confining to the writer. Once John Cheever, in one of his sto-

ries—there is a description of a man who had been making love to his wife, and he's outdoors, walking across the lawn—wrote, "He walked across the lawn with love in his heart and lust in his trousers." I thought it was wonderful. Shawn thought it wouldn't do, and I argued—I seldom argued with Shawn, but I did the best arguing I could—and failed. It distressed me very much. But now, of course, think what's happened.

Interviewer: There were two things that came up in the letters of O'Hara—or the same thing came up in both the letters of O'Hara and of John Cheever. John O'Hara wrote at length about his distaste for Hemingway's *Death in the Afternoon*, of Hemingway's having adopted these two bullfighters, and that here he loved them but wanted to see them dead. What an awful thing he thought that was. Later, in a letter that Cheever wrote about you as his editor, he said, "He loves me, and would love to see me dead." He'd seen you as indecipherable, and it seemed to him—he said it *seemed* to him; I think that would imply that he realizes this isn't true—that you were a man who mistook power for love in your role as an editor.
Maxwell: You've been talking to me for something like four hours. What do you think?

Interviewer: I think that it says more about Cheever than it says about William Maxwell.
Maxwell: Could we leave it there?

Interviewer: It seems apparent in the letters of Cheever that there was a deep, deep friendship there between the two of you.
Maxwell: The problem was, Cheever was really a modernist, moving toward being a modernist, and at a certain point fantasy came into his stories. Usually those stories were rejected. At another point he abandoned the consistency of character. Characters in his stories did things which it was not in their character to do. He released them from this obligation to be consistent, recognizable characters. In doing that he was departing from Tolstoy and Turgenev and Chekhov. I couldn't go with him. I think that the surrealistic work that he did is perhaps the most admired by a great many people, so I don't feel I was right and he was wrong. It's just that I couldn't follow him there.

Interviewer: I was struck by the difference in the letters that Cheever wrote you and the letters that John O'Hara wrote. I got the sense from both that there was a deep friendship there on both sides—and yet John O'Hara's letters went, "Points 1, 2, 3, 4. About this comma here . . . okay. Now, this is why I want the characters addressed by their whole name instead of . . ." I thought it was fascinating, what he wrote you about the use of directives and asides, or "he saids" and "she saids" and characters' names, elements which have been touted as the *New Yorker* style, where they make you do things a certain way. He said, "Dammit, there's an aesthetic reason for this."

Maxwell: I remember that letter vividly. What I was objecting to was that every time a character spoke, O'Hara wanted always to use the character's name. "John Hopkins said, John Hopkins said, John Hopkins said." I thought it was in danger of becoming a mannerism. Couldn't he just alternate with a few "he saids"? And O'Hara said, "No, that's the way I do it." I think I was right, it was a mannerism. Editors always think they're right. But he thought I should just shut up about it. That wasn't the way he wanted to write. It's the only time I remember a disagreement of any kind between us.

Interviewer: I was struck by the distinct differences in those two writers, between John O'Hara and John Cheever, and how those differences were reflected in the nature of their correspondence with you. John O'Hara's is full of bills of sale: "If you want to get a good coat in London, here's where you go." John Cheever is talking about the cats and the dogs and trying to assure you that he's been treating this one cat all right, even though he doesn't like cats. And he talks to you about your children and about his children, and summer camp.

Maxwell: O'Hara had been a very difficult young man, especially when he was drunk. For example, Robert Benchley was the most good-natured man in the world, and O'Hara, for no reason whatsoever—they were in a bar somewhere—just hit him in the face. The next day he called up to apologize and Benchley said, "Oh, that's all right John, you're just a shit," forgiving him. I was aware that he had been Gibbs's writer; and Gibbs particularly admired him; he had been Gibbs's favorite writer. I inherited him, and he was half a generation older. I didn't try to push him around. I treated him with great respect, and I really had no difficulties ever. But I was aware that I was putting my head in the lion's mouth. In fact what really happened was that after his wife died—he'd loved his wife very much indeed, his second wife—and after she died he said the most beautiful thing about her. He said, "The only bad thing she ever did was die on me." After her death his doctor said to him, "If you want to see your daughter come of age you have to stop drinking." He never touched another drop. That's why I could safely put my head in the lion's mouth. If he had been drinking I would have lost my face sooner or later.

Interviewer: That's one thing I wondered about, too. How you managed all these personalities—people coming at you with their complaints about money, "aren't I due for a raise?" or "how dare you take this comma out!" You must have some kind of real skill with people.

Maxwell: I had two loves. One was literature and the other was them.

Edward Hirsch and William Maxwell

Edward Hirsch/1996

From *Doubletake*, 3 (Summer 1997), 20-29. Reprinted by permission of Edward Hirsch.

The thought of William Maxwell's eighty-eighth birthday filled me with giddy anticipation and joy—I wouldn't have missed the small lunch party in Westchester for anything. I was also eager to conduct an interview, which Bill insisted on calling a "conversation," focusing on the subject of old age. And so I took a flight to the East Coast, spent a night in a hotel in Gramercy Park slowly rereading *So Long, See You Tomorrow* for the seventh or eighth time (the lure of New York City could scarcely compare to the magnetism of this dreamy and austere American masterpiece), and then caught an early morning train from Manhattan to Croton-Harmon. I disembarked and there, as if by magic rather than arrangement, was Emmy Maxwell—remarkably beautiful at seventy-five—pulling up in the family car to meet me. We drove through a couple of picturesque villages, meandered off to admire a forceful local waterfall, and traveled down various country lanes before turning into the gravel driveway of the house on Baptist Church Road.

I had arrived at last, and there was my friend emerging from the house, disconcertingly thin and frail-looking, as always, but also reassuringly present. It has been the same ever since we first met: I look into Bill Maxwell's slightly sunken and wholly radiant face, I peer into those amazingly kind eyes, which look out at the world with such searching curiosity, such passionate attention, and suddenly I am swept away by happiness.

William Maxwell has published six novels, three collections of short fiction now brought together in the collected stories (*All the Days and Nights*), an autobiographical memoir, a collection of literary essays and reviews, and a book for children. I feel as if I have known him my entire adult life—maybe because I first stumbled upon his darkly wondrous coming-of-age novel, *The Folded Leaf*, as a freshman in college, and I've been reading him avidly

210

ever since. Long before I met him I had cried more than a few times reading about the death of his mother as it's described in the novels *They Came Like Swallows* and *So Long, See You Tomorrow*. (His narrative genealogy, *Ancestors*, confirmed that not much was made up in the account of his mother's death from influenza when he was ten years old.) Born in 1908, he had described his Midwestern childhood and adolescence so vividly that they were nearly as real to me as my own experience of growing up in Chicago in the 1950s. And so it's jarring to recall that when I first met William Maxwell he was already in his late seventies—an old man.

We came together over a shared admiration for the poet William Meredith. Meredith had suffered from a stroke some years before and so, under the auspices of the Academy of American Poets, a group of writers gathered in a theater to read his poems aloud. Maxwell was one of the last to recite. When he stood up at the podium I was startled by how fragile he looked. He had an intimate, slightly quavering voice, which also had something steely in it. He swayed a bit as he talked, and the years fell away from him. He was a rapturist. He said, "Listening to William Meredith's poems being read aloud, I felt as if I could die with happiness."

At the dinner afterward I made sure to sit with the Maxwells. Anyone could see that William Maxwell had the manner—the deeper qualities— that had allowed him to flourish for forty years at the *New Yorker*, where he edited and nurtured such writers as Frank O'Connor, Eudora Welty, J. D. Salinger, John Cheever, Mavis Gallant, John Updike, Shirley Hazzard, Larry Woiwode, and innumerable others, in the process becoming perhaps the most significant editor of short fiction in the history of American letters. He was modest and incisive; he had an unassuming urbanity mixed with an odd forthrightness. I had scarcely ever met anyone who seemed so emotionally available, so present. I recall that he spoke about Louise Bogan and Howard Moss, two poets he loved. "People die and they're gone," he said. "I'll never get used to it."

Even that first night I recognized that when William Maxwell talks about the past, about, say, growing up in Lincoln, Illinois, the experience is still completely alive in him. One can see it in his face. It's as if at any moment he can close his eyes and slip through a thin membrane of time. He doesn't need a *petite madeleine* to send him there. Maybe it's because there's a clear Before and After in his life, which was sundered by the death of his mother. Everything was fastened at a specific moment in time when his childhood was lost forever. That's when he discovered what he has called, in a resonant phrase, "the fragility of human happiness." I have an image of him as a scrawny ten-year-old pacing up and down the floor of an empty house night after night with his father, both of them in bewildered mourning, in numb grief, unable to comfort each other. His fate was sealed on those nights. There's a poignant moment in *So Long, See You Tomorrow* when the narrator is talking to his psychiatrist about his mother's death. He means to say "I couldn't stand it," but instead he blurts out, "I can't stand it," and then rushes out into the city in tears. In some sense, the maternal loss was so traumatic and intolerable for William Maxwell that his memory—supplemented by his imagination—set out to defy it.

It has always struck me as something of a miracle of character that someone who suffered such early sorrow later developed such a talent for friendship, for shared happiness. He elicits your childhood from you, and he gives freely of his own. I took it as a gift when he talked about growing up in a small town, about the way the houses set back calmly from the wide streets and the elm trees cast a pattern of light and shade on the pavement. That first night we met I remembered something he had written about Sylvia Townsend Warner's initial visit to the *New Yorker* in 1939. He said, "Her conversation was so enchanting that it made my head swim. I did not want to let her out of my sight. Ever." That's precisely how I felt about William Maxwell. I was magnetized by the quality of his affections.

Over the years we have said so much to each other that I cannot sort out all the occasions. Mostly I've visited the Maxwells in their apartment on the Upper East Side of Manhattan—what it feels like to be up there is acutely described in his signature story "Over by the River"—but I've also enjoyed coming out to their country place—a tiny prefab house that arrived in Westchester on a truck sometime in the early 1920s, and now stands on an acre and a half of land. Bill bought it for about five thousand dollars in the early 1940s before he was married. Over the years the Maxwells have done a few things to make it more comfortable. They enclosed the front porch and converted it into Bill's study, built a freestanding screened-in gazebo, and another freestanding studio for Emmy, who is an artist. Bill is mad for flowers, and as we drove up toward the house I could see the grounds covered with large patches of color. I carried my suitcase up to the house, settled into the guest room, and then went looking for Bill again, who had disappeared. "Oh, he's already in the study," Emmy said. "I think he's ready to work."

Sure enough, Bill was stationed at his desk—a simple sturdy piece of pearwood—in his small study crammed with papers, books, photographs, paintings, records—the accumulation of years. "I am slowly being crowded out by the objects," he told me, "but even more by the associations around the objects."

I noticed photographs of his two daughters, Brookie and Kate, a couple of Emmy's watercolors depicting places where they had lived, a postcard of a young man with one hand on his forehead, bent over a piece of paper, lost in thought. "I think it's a picture of the inner life," Bill said.

There was an oversize photograph of Colette, a photograph of the Wisconsin novelist Zona Gale—the first writer he ever met and a sort of literary fairy godmother to him ("She had one foot in the mystic camp," he once told me)—and another of Robert Fitzgerald, a friend he cherished almost above all others. "I knew he was something I needed, and that he didn't suffer fools gladly," Bill had explained about their initial meeting. "I loved him on first sight. He was so difficult, so intransigent, and so obviously a true poet." Over the decades Bill has effected his own eccentric way of conducting an interview. I had heard about the ritual many times before, and I was amused to be participating in it. It went like this. I'd lob a question aloud. Bill would take a moment, swivel around on his chair, grab a sheet of blank paper, and then start typing on his old Smith Corona 1200. He has a sort of pecking, rapid-fire method of typing. "All the thoughts are in the typewriter," he told me. I liked watching him work. He'd pause, type, stop, read what he had written, scowl, then start typing again, faster now, following the heartbeat of a thought, the development of an idea. When he was done he peeled off the page and handed it to me, searching my face while I read his answer. If I had a follow-up question he'd take the paper and insert it back into the typewriter. If I had a new question, he'd reel in a new sheet and start typing. I found it strangely effective—a way of mixing the intimacy of conversations with the precision of writing.

While Bill answered the questions I snooped around the bookshelves. I found a full set of Chekhov's stories—an obvious model—two shelves of works by Sylvia Townsend Warner, a couple of shelves of his own books in no particular order, a collection of Eudora Welty's photographs (preface by William Maxwell). There were no biographies, a genre he dislikes, but lots of collections of letters. I found full editions of the letters of Horace Walpole, William James, and Robert Louis Stevenson, about which he has written so well. And there was his own recently published epistolary exchanges with Frank O'Connor, *The Happiness of Getting It Down Right*.

While our interview was proceeding the preparations for the birthday party were also going into full swing. A friend of Emmy's arrived to help set things up. The gardener stopped by, someone dropped off the wine. The phone rang constantly. Some of the well-wishers wouldn't be put off, and so Bill was called off to the kitchen. He'd come right back and sit down at his desk. All morning there was a question of whether or not it would rain that day (certainly it wouldn't rain on Bill's birthday!) And where the luncheon should take place. It was finally decided to have the lunch in Emmy's air-conditioned studio rather than on the outdoor porch (a good thing, too, since it ended up pouring rain during most of the lunch). There was also the question of their friend Harriet's fish. Harriet had sent a salmon from Ireland and it still hadn't arrived. There was a flurry of international phone calls over a couple of hours until the fish was finally tracked down. It had been delayed in customs at Kennedy Airport. We never did get to eat it, though no doubt some lucky customs official had a very fresh lunch. Listening to the party taking shape all over the house, asking Bill questions and then watching his hands floating fluidly over the typewriter, I started to feel as if I were participating in a Chekhov story. What a splendid story it was! And what a delightful ending it had, too, when the guests started arriving for the party. What happiness we all felt in getting it down right, in celebrating the story of our American Chekhov.

Edward Hirsch

EH: What do you think about having another birthday?

WM: I've read in the last few days that there are or tend to be set periods in which old people are vulnerable—"bumps" the article said, and I am now eighty-eight, which is one of the bumps. Eighty-eight, ninety. So I think about things undone, left for Emmy to do if I should be so fortunate as to die in my sleep. But actually the days take their pattern and form from how much energy I have. Just when I think I have arthritis in my knees and will have to have new ones, it all goes away and my knees are an uncomplaining part of me. I said once to Joe Mitchell that the only part about dying that I minded was that when you are dead you can't read Tolstoy. But if I had really allowed myself to think about the immobility of the dead, the lack of consciousness, the not very slow physical deterioration or quick incineration, I doubt if I would dismiss it in a flip remark. I think while we are alive, the thing is to live, and never mind what happens after we aren't living.

EH: Do you have a strong sense of time passing?

WM: It isn't so much the passing of time—it is nothing so leisurely as that. It is more as if time were in the hands of a vaudeville magician, who makes it appear or disappear. One minute we are planning to do this interview after you get back from Prague, and I go get a drink of water, and there you are sitting in a chair in my study conducting the interview.

EH: Are you surprised to be the age you are?

WM: I am no longer surprised at being as old as I am because I went through two or three preliminary shocks that prepared me for it. They all occurred in front of the bathroom mirror while I was shaving. The first was "What am I doing attached to that old man?" The second, a few days later, was "But I don't want to leave the party!" There were others, but I have forgotten them. Now when I shave I am shaving the face I expect to shave. But somewhere, having a considerable influence on my feelings and behavior, the child survives, who expects (rather than intends) to live forever. The man says, not a good idea. But they don't argue about it.

EH: Does time strike you as mysterious?

WM: It isn't so much that time seems mysterious to me as that I wonder if it is necessary. Up to when I graduated from college I never wore a watch and usually managed to get to where I was supposed to be when I was supposed to be there. My father, who was concerned that I should be able to function in the real world and not be too caught up in the world of my imagination, said that he was going to give me a watch for a graduating present. I said, "I don't want a watch." He said, "You must have a watch. Otherwise you won't know what time it is." "I don't need a watch," I insisted. "When I want to know what time it is I look in a butcher shop window." He gave me a watch, and I have been time-ridden ever since. Less so now than when I was younger. I think what of all the things I ought to be doing, and try to do that, which turns out to be all there is time for.

EH: Do you miss the past?

WM: I don't miss the past because I am never separated from it. I have a huge set of memories which I carry around me like a packed suitcase, and then these last few years there are new ones, from my remote childhood. Or from my youth. I think how nice, and stick them in the suitcase. There was a time when I used to think that I would like to buy our old house on Ninth Street in Lincoln, and get back all the furniture my father sold or gave to the Salvation Army and restore the house to the way it was when my mother was alive. Which is what Pen Browning did after Elizabeth Barrett Browning died. It didn't work. I suppose because furniture can evoke but not be a person. Anyway, what cured me of this fantasy was the simple thought that Emmy wouldn't be happy living in Lincoln.

The house actually did come up for sale not long ago and I felt no pull to own it.

EH: Do you miss the people from the past?

WM: I think of the people in various stages of my past, few of whom are now alive. And there are friends I have lost contact with, and I sometimes wonder if they are dead or alive. But there are friends who are still alive, whom I do hear from, a postcard or a telephone call. I realize that if I brought my mother back to live she wouldn't like or be happy in the modern world. I think of my Uncle Doc, who loved children so and didn't have any, and I am grateful that I knew and was loved by him.

I think of Robert Fitzgerald and I think of the physical changes he went through while he was dying of cancer, and that his last remark as we were leaving him for the last time was "Aren't you going to kiss me?" So Emmy did. And I kissed his hand, not feeling sure he was talking to her or to me or both. But I AM UNRECONCILED TO HIS NOT BEING ALIVE.

There was a time when I was able to feel (even though I knew it was irrational) that they would all be waiting for me when I died—my mother, my Uncle Doc, my Aunts Edith and Annette. What that amounts to is that the child expected it, and the man humored him in this idea. There was a woman, one of several surrogate mothers, who lived on a farm in Wisconsin [Bonnie Oaks], where I went to work when I was eighteen, and which afterward became a second home to me. She was a very vital woman. She lived to be ninety-five or ninety-six, and told her daughter at the end of her life that she was tired, that she had lived long enough. This has been a great comfort to me. I think, people get tired, and have had enough. When I am tired I take a nap. Only it will be a longer one than the usual one.

EH: Do you have any regrets about the life you've led—or haven't led?

WM: No. I did things I shouldn't have but have been on the whole so fortunate that it would seem ungrateful to regret anything. But you haven't asked about my mind. It is beginning to fray. I notice it only when I am typing. And the word I write (this happened a minute ago) is "enough" when what I meant to type was "a nap." And I realize there is slippage in the upper story. Also, the energy that it requires to imagine a novel and then carry this idea through to the final page is simply not there anymore. When people ask me, "What are you writing?" even though I know they have asked the question merely out of politeness, I want to pick up something and throw it at them. Which must mean some resentment on my part at the diminishment of certain powers that old age inevitably means.

Sitting here, I suddenly remembered that I did have regrets at one point. I was haunted by two or three occasions when I behaved rather badly. They were thirty or forty years ago, but still bothered me. So I wrote a letter of apology to the people I have behaved badly to, and it turned out that none of them remembered it.

EH: You have always struck me as a model of kindness. Is kindness—or compassion—instinctual in you?

WM: About kindness. I have taken so much of my emotional "attitudes," if that is the right word, from my mother. When I was a very small child I was out riding with my father and mother one evening after supper and as they were going through the town, my father suddenly pulled on the reins and stopped the carriage. A little boy had darted into the street and been run over just ahead of us. He was about my age, and the son of a doctor, and he was carried into his father's office. My father and mother got out of the carriage and, taking me with them, went into the waiting room. My mother disappeared behind a glass wall and I could tell she was holding the boy and talking to him, saying "Now, now . . . now, now . . ." Using just the tone of voice she used when I was upset. But it sunk in that anyone in trouble had a claim on her feelings.

On another occasion we were at dinner and the phone rang, and when my mother came back from the telephone she said, "There has been a cyclone in Mattoon, and they want people to send food down to a freight car in the station." Whereupon she took all the food off the table, when we had barely started to eat, wrapped it in a cloth and gave it to my father who took it downtown, and I went to bed hungry.

Both my father and mother were aware of other people's troubles and when they could do anything about them, did. How much Sunday school enters into it I am not sure. Mainly, I guess, I can't stand to see somebody in a difficult situation and not be unmoved or not want to help them.

The little boy who was run over grew up and graduated from the Naval Academy at Annapolis.

EH: You seem to me wonderfully, even bravely frank. Is it true?

WM: "Bravely frank!" How can you say such a thing? I am truthful only once in a month of Sundays. And only when I am fairly sure the person can stand it. Mostly people can't, as Eliot said, bear very much reality. If I were to die and go to Heaven and if there were a Heaven, I would go around telling the truth all day long, never mind the angels and their harping.

EH: Do you think of experience—and people—as fragile?

WM: When I was a child and would tell my mother, "My feelings are hurt," I felt that they existed, my feelings, with the solidity of material objects. Because my older brother teased me and nobody could make him stop, I cried at least once a day until he went away to college, after which I didn't cry any more than people normally do. But I listened, in a manner of speaking, to my feelings and when it was sensible always tried to act on them.

In answer to your question, yes, I think people are fragile. That is to say, their emotional equilibrium can be upset in a way that can have serious consequences. And experience is fragile because you can fail to appreciate what you have and let it slip through your fingers. Or by insensitivity alter it.

But this is my unconscious assumption. I don't go around thinking about it. Before I was analyzed, I was terribly alone, and all I could think, or rather feel, was if only someone would love me and save me from being alone. But I was totally self-centered, without knowing it, and when this gave way I saw people all around me, saw what they were like, understood what they were going through, and without waiting for them to love me, loved them.

EH: Sometimes you speak about your books as if they were written by someone else. Do you really feel as if each of your books was something that had just happened to you, like a dream?

WM: I am not sure they *weren't* written by someone else:

When I am writing a novel or even a story it is as if I had entered a room and closed the door behind me. The concentration it takes to shape a story, to watch characters emerge and become in the round, to move sentences around a dozen times until they are locked into place usually involves a withdrawal from one's present and exterior life. Those farmers in *So Long, See You Tomorrow* I have come to feel I knew as intimately as I know you, only it isn't I but the novelist that knew them. The one who patiently waits for me to stop frittering away my life with small obligations and use my mind to some effect. Don't you and the poet live side by side and lie awake with insomnia in the same bed at night?

EH: Do you think of yourself as obsessive?

WM: I don't think of myself as being obsessive, but instead as being embarrassingly repetitive. I would have preferred not to be. The trouble was, is, that you get an idea for a story or a book, and if it has autobiographical aspects, you have to go into your life. And the life you go into is, alas, already familiar to a certain number of readers. This is not a problem that major writers have. Tolstoy, for example. Not many things have happened to me, but I have felt some of them deeply.

EH: Would it be accurate to say that as you have gotten older you have put more and more faith in what actually happened?

WM: The answer is yes, I have come to put more faith in what actually happened. I have come to feel that life is the Sheherazade. My first novel, which I have swept under the rug, was about a group of people on a Wisconsin farm. I wrote in a room on the third floor of a water tower, among the treetops. And I would come down to lunch and people would say something I had imagined some character in the novel saying. It was spooky.

With my second novel, *They Came Like Swallows*, there was a terrible struggle with form. I knew what I wanted, which was for the book to be like a stone thrown into a pond, creating a widening circle, and then a second stone thrown into the pond, creating a circle inside the circle, and a third doing the same. All that meant was that as the book progressed the point of view was each time of an older person. But I had hell's own time with the beginning. I wrote it seven times, and mainly, at the MacDowell Colony during the summer of 1935, I did it the eighth time and it stuck. The second part, I wrote during the following winter in Urbana, Illinois, living in the house of a friend, and in a room that looked out on a very uninteresting tin roof, so when my mind wandered it was immediately driven back to the novel. The third part I wrote there also, but in two weeks, much of the time walking the floor in tears that I would have to brush away in order to see the typewriter.

With *The Folded Leaf* half of the time I was inventing scenes and characters and half of the time following what really happened. When I reread the book now I have trouble deciding what is or isn't invented.

I think I wrote one more novel, and then in stories found I could use the first person without being long-winded or boring, and at the same time was dealing with experiences that were not improved by invention of any kind. But, of course, sometimes when you think you are following the actual truth, it turns out you were inventing.

EH: Do you think your sense of your mother's death—and your coming to terms with it—changed from book to book?

WM: I think it has changed. In *They Came Like Swallows* it was pretty much raw grief. In *The Folded Leaf* she is a shadowy figure in the background of Lymie Peters. I don't remember whether it is in the novel or not, but when, in actual life, I did cut my throat with the intention to die, it was also with the expectation that I would join my mother.

The woman in *Time Will Darken It* is not drawn from her, though she lived in my mother's house.

In *So Long, See You Tomorrow* I wasn't so much writing about her (although I did briefly) as her absence. But perhaps emotionally speaking there is no difference.

In *Ancestors* the chapter about the happiness of our family life was a kind of testifying. It was also like painting. As if years and habits and feelings could also be made visual. But it is done, I think, from a distance and with acceptance.

By the time I came to write the two stories about the black people, Billie Dyer and his sister who was my mother's housekeeper, I tried to abandon the child's viewpoint and see my mother as an adult would have. Allowing her to be less than perfect, but at the same time, with no withdrawal of love. More as if I had become Isherwood's camera and were photographing her in this or that moment.

But also, I wrote less about how she was, what she meant to me, and more about what she was and meant to other people.

While I was in analysis I wrote a full-length play which I told to Theodor Reik, lying on the couch. My mother arrived at a mysterious airport, having managed a return to life in this world. Only to find that my father had remarried and didn't need her. That I was on the point of marrying, and if she stayed I would be torn between my love for her and my love for the young woman I was about to marry. Feeling that there was no longer any place for her, that life had closed over and she was shut out, she returned to the airport. The curtain line was the "I" character saying to his fiancée, "Hold me!"

Whether you want to or mean to or not, in old age you find yourself thinking whatever is simply is and must be accepted. I suppose the child goes on grieving. The man—

EH: Do you like to reread your work? Do you have favorites among your books?

WM: If enough time has passed I enjoy reading things I have written. And am often surprised by things I didn't know I wrote. It used to be that I thought *The Folded Leaf* was the best. Now I think *So Long, See You Tomorrow* is. The hand is steady and confident. A great many sentences were in ten other places before I found where they belong and they were locked into place. And I hadn't yet started to turn into an old man.

The fact that it was written after I had stopped being an editor may have something to do with its seeming all of a piece. Until that time I had for two or three days a week to juggle my own writing with a concern for the work of others, which may have, unconsciously, amounted to some degree of attention withheld. I feel in this book that my mind was all there.

EH: Do you think it was the right thing to do, committing to a double life as a writer and editor?

WM: From the theoretical point of view, if I had tried to support myself and a family through writing, we would have had to go on relief, because of my slow, perfectionist habits and my usually not knowing what it was I was trying to write until I had written it. If I had had a trust fund, I perhaps might have written more or better books, but it might have insulated me from life. Emmy had an aunt who was married to the lawyer for the New York Central Railroad, and lived in Cold Spring Harbor in a house that was large, well-staffed, and pleasant, but when I was there I felt suffocated by luxury and comfort. And kept thinking if I lived here I couldn't write.

Actually, I loved being an editor, once I got to the point where I could do pretty much what I thought was right—under Shawn the fiction editors had a great deal of latitude, and it was deeply satisfying work. Also, my own life has been singularly uneventful. The few times when I tried to branch out, be adventurous, escape from the security I was born into, my efforts always miscarried. As if I was trying to do something inappropriate. I am happy when I think of the writers that I watched mature and do wonderful work, and feel it was a privilege to have been of service to those who had nothing to learn from me. And then I hold some book in my hands that I wrote at one time or another and am so glad I didn't get swallowed up in editing. The whole thing strikes me as most fortunate.

EH: Is there anything you miss about editing?
WM: No.

EH: It seems as if you have always been close to poets.

WM: Fitzgerald and Bogan had a profound effect on my life. When I first met Robert, I was a graduate student at Harvard and he was an undergraduate but very much better educated than I. I had just come from the University of Illinois where the admired poets were Frost and Millay and Elinor Wylie and Robinson. And partly as a result of my having tried to commit suicide and failed, I was lighthearted. Robert had lost his mother when he was even younger than I was when my mother died, and his father died just before I met him. In his view life was tragic. And when I tried to defend the plays of J. M. Barrie I drove him up the wall. He was also, through Dudley Fitts, made aware of the Modern movement. I struggled to understand *The Waste Land* and gave up Galsworthy and Barrie and Elinor Wylie and accepted the idea that literature, though not necessarily tragic, was serious business.

When I got older, and especially after I met Emmy, the friendship with Robert changed. I was less in awe of him and was simply happy to have a chance to be with him. He used to stop off for a night or two when he came from Italy to teach at Harvard, and when I opened the front door and saw him I would say, "Come in, come in, and take off your shoes, and I'll get the whiskey and put some Schubert on the record player." And then the three of us would sit in delight at the reunion.

Once when he was between marriages, he telephoned me and asked if he could come and stay with us for a time. I said yes, without asking Emmy. And he came and lived in what had been Brookie's room for three or four months, translating Virgil all day and at dinnertime joining us in the living room. He rested on the household with no more weight than a feather. There was so much affection among all concerned. For a longer while I had in my study a large box containing all his sacred objects, photographs, I don't know what, and it made me happy to think that he had trusted me with them. He was at the same time magisterial and then—no, not at the same time, alternately—magisterial and extremely funny. And one of the things he laughed at was himself. About practical matters he was sometimes something of a bumbler but the essential thing got done somehow.

At a time when I was working five days a week at the *New Yorker* and met Louise Bogan, I was becoming more and more absorbed by editing. She encouraged me to write, and so I went on doing it. Her standards were so strict that I felt her belief in me was a kind of guarantee that there was something there.

It is also true that in college I wrote poetry, of no consequence. And that I have trouble enjoying the work of any novelist (Trollope, for example) who doesn't have some degree of the poet in him.

The young poets I have come to love in my old age are just a gift from life.

EH: Are you surprised by how your life has turned out?

WM: Deeply surprised. I was not surprised by being chased home from school by coal miners' sons, but I expected things to go on that way and they haven't. I am, so far as I know, accepted for what I am. And the really surprising thing is that the adopted son of one of those miner's sons, who was a particularly talented tormentor, became a musicologist and got to know me through my work, and is now a friend. What life resembles sometimes, though fortunately not too often, is a jack-in-the-box.

Maxwell's Silver Typewriter

Economist/1999

From the *Economist* (London), June 26, 1999, vol. 351, no. 8125, 97.

"I wouldn't like to live in a world where nobody ever told stories." With this modest introduction, William Maxwell begins to talk about his art. With all six of his novels and a compendium of short stories recently reissued to astonishing acclaim in celebration of his ninetieth birthday, a more grandiloquent observation might be expected of this distinguished veteran of American letters and legendary editor from the golden age of the *New Yorker*. But the very idea of grandiloquence evaporates in the tranquility of Mr. Maxwell's presence.

From a small and comfortably cluttered study at the back of his New York apartment, with windows wide open and an electric fan compounding the noises from the street, he finds it easier to type out answers to questions than to make his gentle, warmly inflected voice heard over the din. The nostalgic sound of a typewriter clacking is strangely appropriate to the unhurried yet apposite answers which emanate, in his unmistakable cadence, from the typed page.

Mr. Maxwell came to writing with the same haphazard inevitability that characterizes his written style. While working for his PhD at the University of Illinois, intending to become a teacher, he was asked to help out with the book reviews that his landlady occasionally wrote for the *New York Herald-Tribune*. Among the projects that came their way was to prepare a forty-page consideration of the life of Thomas Coke, first Earl of Leicester (of Holkham) for a historian at Yale. They divided up the job and while she tackled eighteenth-century English agriculture, he tackled eighteenth-century English social life. Here he made the acquaintance of a "marvelous eccentric," Lady Mary Coke, who divorced her boorish husband, slept in a dresser drawer, and was convinced that the Empress Maria Theresa was trying to steal her servants. "I was beside myself with pleasure over this woman." Inspired, he sought material closer to home to write about.

If delight in the variety and unpredictability of human nature first prompted him to take up pen, the experience of inconsolable grief was the wellspring to which his art returned again and again. His mother's death from influenza when he was ten years old informs in one way or another all subsequent work. The scars of sorrow and remembered rapture bear witness in every tone of Mr. Maxwell's unique authorial voice. It is a voice full of humor, unflinchingly truthful and sharp, yet without a barb. On the contrary, the very acuteness of his scrutiny serves to drive any hint of sickly sentimentality from the compassion with which he imbues his characters, mankind, and life itself. "What you can't bear you find some way around. I couldn't bear to part with my mother so I took on aspects of her personality. She was affectionate and outgoing and enjoyed people. Though naturally introspective, I took on those traits. So she's not dead. She's sitting right here."

Content and commas

Thrown untrained into teaching freshman composition at the University of Illinois ("creative writing" being at that time an unheard-of course of study), Mr. Maxwell took along a book he liked and read from it. He was expected to fail a student for using commas incorrectly. Not wishing to discourage their promising but comma-defective efforts, he adopted the strategy of giving two grades, one for content and one for form. "Eventually they got the idea, God knows how, of when to use commas."

He thought it best not to mention his teaching past when he went to work for the *New Yorker*, but when Mrs. White, the fiction editor, read his letters to the authors of rejected manuscripts, she asked, "'Mr. Maxwell, did you ever teach school?' I confessed that I had, and she said firmly, 'It is not the duty of the editor to teach the writer how to write.' Looking back over my shoulder I find I don't agree with her. The thing is that it must be done so tactfully—the teaching has to be delicate, unnoticeable, and affectionate."

This approach made Mr. Maxwell the most sought-after fiction editor at the *New Yorker*, and he guided many young writers to literary maturity. "As a writer I don't very much enjoy being edited. As an editor I try to work so slightly on the manuscript that ten years later the writer would read his story and not be aware that anybody was involved but him. This involves listening and watching the writer's face for signs of dissatisfaction. Again, it is a simple matter of love."

Asked if such painstaking patience is not unusual in an editor, he replies, "I don't know." Which writers does he claim as literary successors? None. He trusts them to take care of themselves. What does he think of the latest trends in contemporary fiction? "I haven't been attentive. I am a very old man and it isn't about things that I know about or take an interest in—so long as fiction is truthful and accurate it will have value." There is nothing self-conscious or self-effacing about his modesty. It is natural, easy, and assured.

His own heroes are the great Russians: Turgenev, "a magician in what he can do with an ordinary day," and Tolstoy—"the horse's mouth full of snow at the end of 'Master and Man'—the ability to put death on the page. I wanted to get down on my knees to him. Awful man, not to know better what his real talents were."

Unbecoming dresses

"Harold Ross (a former editor of the *New Yorker*) once remarked, 'Talent does not care where it resides.' You can expect anything of artists—good and bad. They don't have to be decent. What I can't forgive is when they are not better than they are. Why Somerset Maugham is not a first-rate writer I find unforgiveable. Like someone wearing an unbecoming dress. The conclusions he derived from life were insufficient to the majesty of life—sounds rather preachy, doesn't it?"

That Mr. Maxwell found grandeur in his small home town does not strike him as improbable. When he was fourteen his family moved to Chicago and his childhood memories with their burden of joy and heartbreak were sealed over, a treasure chest intact, waiting to be rediscovered by the grown writer. Gossip being the principal recreation of small-town life there were storytellers in abundance. His first stories came to him through the inventive curiosity of an eavesdropping child. His artist's awareness told him that they were precious and fragile. Writing was the way to preserve them.

At first he consciously remolded and reordered the reality. He was as patient with his characters as he was with fledgling writers, waiting for them to show him the direction they must follow. As he became surer, his style became more direct. "I realized that life is so remarkable, so astonishing, you simply cannot improve on it—so full of meaning and possibility. Some moments are works of art in themselves."

In his last novel *So Long, See You Tomorrow*, the reader is clearly informed which parts happened and which are imagined. The facts are recorded and life breathed into them through loving detail. There is no need to call attention to their wider significance. The great plains on which the small town stands are never portentously conjured up. The reader senses their vast presence and shudders with awe.

How did the good folk of Lincoln react to finding themselves in published novels? Did he feel no compunction at feeding off their lives in his writing? "Oh, I am a scoundrel," laughs that voice that John Updike has called the wisest and kindest in American fiction, "and I don't care!"

Index

Chekhov, Anton, 46, 124, 139, 207; *The Cherry Orchard*, 17; *In the Ravine*, 185; influence on WM, xv, 213; *Ward No. 6*, 185; WM as American Chekhov, 214

Cherry Orchard, The (Chekhov), 17

Chicago, Illinois, 17, 71; Art Institute of Chicago, 112, 123, 143, 188; Michigan Avenue, 118; move to, 59, 117–18, 136, 143, 186, 226; rides the "El" with father, 91; Rogers Park neighborhood, 118; as setting in *The Folded Leaf*, 59, 97, 100; years at Nicholas Senn High School, 28, 43, 59, 64, 65, 112, 118, 143, 155

Chicago Tribune, xi, 91

Childhood, 85–87, 107, 164, 174, 183

Cocteau (Steegmuller), 179

Cocteau, Jean, 180

Cohen, Sol, 137

Coke, Thomas, of Holkham, 43, 167, 189, 224

Coleridge, Samuel Taylor, 144

Colette, 34, 123, 124, 135, 139, 173–74, 213

Conrad, Joseph, 72, 91, 106, 139, 143, 171

Constable, John, 132

Cooper, Douglas, 180

Copland, Aaron, xix

Cotton, William, 48–49

Counterfeiters, The (Gide), 123

"Country Husband, The" (Cheever), 52

Cowley, Malcolm, xviii, 13, 120

Craig, Gordon, 145

Crane, Stephen: influence on WM, xv, 93; "The Open Boat," 57, 93

Croton-Harmon, New York, and Harmon station, 123

cummings, e.e., 123

Dahlin, Robert, xiii

de la Mare, Walter, as literary influence, 123, 139, 167

Death, xxi, 194, 216, 226; of Grandfather Blinn, 174–75; of Margery Latimer, 20; life after death, 115, 133; of mother, xxiii, 39, 42, 59, 60, 61, 71–72, 77, 85, 86, 90, 94, 102, 155, 162, 164, 168, 169, 173, 187, 188, 211, 212, 216, 220, 222, 225; in tribute by Eudora Welty, xxi

Death in the Afternoon (Hemingway), 207

Death in Venice, 10

Degas, Edgar, 132

D'Epinay, Louise, 180

Deuel, Susan. *See* Shattuck, Susan Deuel

Die Fledermaus (Strauss), 120

Dineson, Isak, 139

Domestic Fiction, 118–19

Don Juan (Byron), 144

Dos Passos, John, 113, 123

Dostoevsky, Fyodor, 8; *The Brothers Karamazov*, 91

Doubletake, xiv

Dreiser, Theodore, *Sister Carrie*, 10

Duino Elegies (Rilke), 166

Dyer, Billie, 220. *See also* "Billie Dyer"

Dyer, Hattie, 197, 220

Edel, Leon, xix

Editing, xii–xiv, xx, 22, 23, 26–27, 37, 47, 49, 55, 56, 57–58, 69, 95–96, 109–10, 133–34, 136, 140, 151, 159–60, 161, 172, 175–76, 181, 186, 192, 202–4, 206, 208–9, 211, 221, 224–26. *See also* Maxwell, William K., Jr.; *New Yorker, The*

Egyptian sculpture, 56

Eliot, T. S., 3, 34, 108, 123, 139, 218; *Four Quartets*, 35, 41

Printed in the United States
by Baker & Taylor Publisher Services